María Martínez Sierra:
A Great Playwright Hidden in Plain Sight

Three Plays translated by
Helen and Harley Granville-Barker

María Martínez Sierra:
A Great Playwright Hidden in Plain Sight

The Kingdom of God
The Romantic Young Lady
Take Two from One

MARÍA MARTÍNEZ SIERRA

Plays translated by
HELEN *and* HARLEY GRANVILLE-BARKER

Edited by
COLIN CHAMBERS *and* RICHARD NELSON

methuen | drama
LONDON · NEW YORK · OXFORD · NEW DELHI · SYDNEY

METHUEN DRAMA
Bloomsbury Publishing Plc
50 Bedford Square, London, WC1B 3DP, UK
1385 Broadway, New York, NY 10018, USA
29 Earlsfort Terrace, Dublin 2, Ireland

BLOOMSBURY, METHUEN DRAMA and the Methuen Drama logo are trademarks
of Bloomsbury Publishing Plc

First published in Great Britain 2023

Copyright © Colin Chambers, Richard Nelson and contributors, 2023
Introduction © Patricia W. O'Connor, 2023
Take Two from One Translation © The Society of Authors as the Literary Representative
of the Estates of Helen and Harley Granville-Barker, 2023

The authors have asserted their right under the Copyright, Designs and Patents Act, 1988,
to be identified as authors of this work.

Cover design: Rebecca Heselton
Cover images: Top: Harley Granville-Barker © Hulton Archive/Getty Images.
Middle: María Martínez-Sierra © Archivo Manuel de Falla. Bottom: Helen Huntington,
from Add MS 71913/40, British Library. For information about the source of the photograph
of Helen Huntington, thanks to Simon Shepherd, author of *The Unknown Granville Barker* (2021),
Society for Theatre Research. Ripped paper: AVS-Images/ shutterstock and Flas100/ shutterstock.

All rights reserved. No part of this publication may be reproduced or transmitted in any form or
by any means, electronic or mechanical, including photocopying, recording, or any information storage or
retrieval system, without prior permission in writing from the publishers.

Bloomsbury Publishing Plc does not have any control over, or responsibility for, any third-party websites
referred to or in this book. All internet addresses given in this book were correct at the time of going to press.
The author and publisher regret any inconvenience caused if addresses have changed or sites have ceased to
exist, but can accept no responsibility for any such changes.

No rights in incidental music or songs contained in the work are hereby granted and performance rights for any
performance/presentation whatsoever must be obtained from the respective copyright owners.

All rights whatsoever in this play are strictly reserved and application for performance etc. should be made
before rehearsals to Bloomsbury Permissions Department, Bloomsbury Publishing Plc, 50 Bedford Square,
London, WC1B 3DP, UK. No performance may be given unless a licence has been obtained.

A catalogue record for this book is available from the British Library.

Library of Congress Cataloging-in-Publication Data
Names: Martínez Sierra, María, 1874–1974, author. | Granville-Barker, Helen, 1867-1950, editor. |
Granville-Barker, Harley, 1877–1946, editor. | Chambers, Colin, translator. | Nelson, Richard, 1950- translator. |
Martínez Sierra, María, 1874–1974. Reino de Dios. English. | Martínez Sierra, María, 1874–1974. Sueño de una
noche de agosto. English. | Martínez Sierra, María, 1874–1974. Triángulo. English.
Title: María Martínez Sierra : four plays from Spanish theatre's silver age / María Martínez Sierra ; plays
translated by Helen and Harley Granville Barker ; edited by Colin Chambers and Richard Nelson.
Description: London ; New York : Methuen Drama, 2022. | Identifiers: LCCN 2022012059 (print) |
LCCN 2022012060 (ebook) | ISBN 9781350300187 (hardback) | ISBN 9781350300170 (paperback) |
ISBN 9781350300194 (epub) | ISBN 9781350300200 (pdf)
Subjects: LCSH: Martínez Sierra, María, 1874–1974–Translations into English. | LCGFT: Drama.
Classification: LCC PQ6663.A75184 M37 2022 (print) | LCC PQ6663.A75184 (ebook) |
DDC 862/.64—dc23/eng/20220325
LC record available at https://lccn.loc.gov/2022012059
LC ebook record available at https://lccn.loc.gov/2022012060

ISBN: HB: 978-1-3503-0018-7
      PB: 978-1-3503-0017-0
      ePDF: 978-1-3503-0020-0
      eBook: 978-1-3503-0019-4

Typeset by RefineCatch Limited, Bungay, Suffolk

To find out more about our authors and books visit www.bloomsbury.com
and sign up for our newsletters.

Contents

Acknowledgements viii

1 María Martínez Sierra
Introduction: Hidden in Plain Sight: Spain's Most Successful Woman Dramatist by Patricia W. O'Connor 3
A Critical Appreciation of the Plays (1922) by H. Granville Barker 11
Selected Works by María Martínez Sierra 17

2 The Plays
The Kingdom of God 21
The Romantic Young Lady 95
Take Two from One 153

3 The Granville-Barkers
Postscript: Helen and Harley: Translating Together by Richard Nelson with Colin Chambers 227
Translations of Helen and Harley Granville-Barker 237

María Martínez Sierra was a dramatist, librettist, narrator, essayist, feminist, translator, screenwriter and politician. She was born María de la O Lejárraga in San Millán de la Cogolla, La Rioja, 28 December 1874. After marriage in 1900 to Gregorio Martínez Sierra (1881–1947), she adopted his name and started writing with him. As he became intensely involved in ventures such as publishing, editing and directing, he left the writing to María, who signed everything as Gregorio even after he left her in 1922. María translated works from several languages (e.g. Dante, Ibsen, Ionesco, Jonson, Maeterlinck, Miller, de Musset, Pirandello, Shakespeare, Shaw, Wilder and Williams), and her vast output includes librettos for operas, operettas, ballets (e.g. *The Three-Cornered Hat*) and other musical works. Her plays include *El reino de Dios* (*The Kingdom of God*, 1915), *Sueño de una noche de agosto* (*The Romantic Young Lady*, 1918), *Triángulo* (*Take Two from One*, 1929) – all translated by Helen and Harley Granville-Barker – and her daring tragedy *Sortilegio* (*Bewitched*, 1930), which was performed successfully all over Europe and South America but never in Spain. *Canción de cuna* (*The Cradle Song*, 1911), María's signature success which develops the story of an infant girl abandoned in a convent, has been seen in many translations and five film adaptations (including one by María).

She left Spain in the early 1920s and lived in France for a decade before returning to Spain and, in 1933, being elected Granada's Socialist representative to parliament. The Civil War forced her abroad again, living in exile in France and Buenos Aires, where she died on 28 June 1974. Although after Gregorio's death, she used her own name for publication, her role as author of about sixty plays along with other works attributed to Gregorio was not officially recognized until after her own death when, among her possessions, letters from Gregorio written on world tours surfaced to establish firmly her sole authorship. Her singular achievements and fascinating life have inspired contemporary novels and dramatic works.

Helen Granville-Barker (1867–1950) was a poet and novelist, and with her husband, Harley, a translator of Spanish and French plays. Her novels include *Ada*, *Living Mirrors*, *Come, Julia*, *Moon in Scorpio* and *Traitor Angel*. She is also the likely author of the anonymously published best-selling novel *Madame Solario*.

Harley Granville-Barker (1877–1946) was an actor, playwright, director, producer and theatre visionary. His plays include *The Voysey Inheritance*, *Waste*, *The Madras House* and *The Secret Life*. A key figure in the movement to transform British theatre, he was a champion of ensemble playing and the repertory system. He ran groundbreaking seasons at the Royal Court (1904–7) and his Shakespeare productions at the Savoy Theatre (1912 and 1914) were considered revolutionary. Following his marriage to Helen in 1918, he dedicated his life to writing; as well as translating with Helen and completing two full-length plays, he also wrote numerous essays, articles and reviews, a major book on the theatre, four others based on his lectures and his influential *Prefaces* to Shakespeare.

Colin Chambers, a former journalist and theatre critic, was Literary Manager of the Royal Shakespeare Company (1981–97), and since 2014 has been Emeritus Professor of Drama at Kingston University, UK. He is co-author with Richard Nelson of *Kenneth's*

First Play and *Tynan*, and he adapted with Steven Pimlott Molière's *The Learned Ladies*, selected and edited for performance *Three Farces* by John Maddison Morton and adapted David Pinski's *Treasure*. He edited *Peggy to Her Playwrights*, co-edited with Richard Nelson *Granville Barker on Theatre* and edited the *Continuum Companion to Twentieth Century Theatre*. He has written extensively on the theatre, including *Other Spaces: New Writing and the RSC*; *The Story of Unity Theatre*; *Peggy: the Life of Margaret Ramsay, Play Agent* (winner of the inaugural Theatre Book Prize); *Inside the Royal Shakespeare Company*; *Here We Stand: Politics, Performers and Performance – Paul Robeson, Isadora Duncan and Charlie Chaplin*; and *Black and Asian Theatre in Britain: A History*.

Richard Nelson is an Olivier and Tony Award-winning playwright and director. His plays include *The Apple Family: A Pandemic Trilogy* (three Zoom plays) as well as *The Michaels, What Happened?*; *The Michaels Abroad*; *Illyria*; *The Gabriels*; *The Apple Family Plays*; *Nikolai and The Others*; *Farewell to the Theatre*; *Conversations in Tusculum*; *Goodnight Children Everywhere* (Olivier Award, Best Play); *Two Shakespearean Actors* (Tony Award nomination, Best Play) and *Some Americans Abroad* (Olivier Award nomination, Best Comedy). His musicals include *James Joyce's The Dead* (with Shaun Davey, Tony Award Best Book of a Musical). His screenplays include *Hyde Park on Hudson* (Roger Michell, director). He directed *Uncle Vanya* in 2018 for the Hunter Theater Project. With Richard Pevear and Larissa Volokhonsky, he has co-translated plays by Chekhov, Gogol, Turgenev and Bulgakov. He is an Honorary Associate Artist of the Royal Shakespeare Company and recipient of the PEN/Laura Pels 'Master Playwright' Award. He co-edited with Colin Chambers *Granville Barker on Theatre*.

Acknowledgements

Thanks to Alda Blanco, Antonio Gonzalez Lejárraga at the Archivo María Lejárraga, Pat O'Connor and Anya Ward.

1 María Martínez Sierra

Introduction

HIDDEN IN PLAIN SIGHT: SPAIN'S MOST SUCCESSFUL WOMAN DRAMATIST

'Gregorio has a merchant's soul. Until now, he has exploited the talent of his wife, who writes his works.'[1]
Rufino Blanco-Fombona, literary historian

'Gregorio Martínez Sierra never wrote anything that circulates under his name, whether it be novel, poetry or theatre. That is something that . . . I know very well. . . . But the ones who knew it best were the actors who were always nervous: "The third act that doña María has to send isn't here, so rehearsals will be cancelled."'[2]
Xavi Ayén, writer and journalist

Recognition

When the Granville-Barkers published the first two translations contained in this collection in 1923, the author was presumed to be Gregorio Martínez Sierra. It is now known that María, Gregorio's wife, was often the sole author of the works that appeared under Gregorio's name, and this is the case with all three plays published here. Although María Martínez Sierra was in plain sight as a well-known feminist, she was not recognized as the author because, wanting all the credit to go to her husband, she did not sign the works. After her death in 1974 in Buenos Aires, a large steamer trunk was sent to her relatives in Madrid containing, among many other possessions, 144 letters from Gregorio, written on tour between 1915 and 1931, and during his years in Hollywood (1931–5). These proved definitively María's exclusive authorship of many, if not most, of the plays. In these letters, Gregorio acknowledges receipt of specific works, lauds them, and presses her to write him prologues, translations, lectures and even letters of sympathy.[3]

The Authors' Society of Spain credits the Gregorio Martínez Sierra name with approximately 200 works: plays, novels, short stories, essays, operas, operettas, poetry, translations and adaptations. Critics wondered how one man could produce so much; the answer, of course, is that two very gifted people with many different but compatible talents and interests were responsible. Gregorio was the businessman, journal editor and theatre director while María wrote works about the subjects that mattered most to her: freedom, love, the maternal instinct, women's rights and help for the less fortunate. These plays featured contemporary settings and tended to centre on strong women protagonists who resolved conflicts usually to produce a happy ending. María is the sole author of most of 'Gregorio's' works, a large number of which have been translated to other languages performed to critical acclaim in major theatres around the world. Without any doubt, she is Spain's most accomplished woman dramatist.

For María finally to be recognized as author of so many significant plays is important in historical and literary as well as in human terms, for few women have successfully written for the stage. Since the Greek poet Sappho wrote lyric verse in the sixth century BCE, there have been numerous women poets, novelists, short story writers and essayists whose works continue to be read, but plays by women are rarely revived. Spain has had female dramatists for centuries, but what Spaniard, besides specialists, could recall any of their names? Plays by women, staged and admired in their lifetimes, typically remain unperformed and forgotten afterwards. For example, plays by Ana Diosdado (1938–2015) are no longer performed, while those of Antonio Buero Vallejo (1916–2000) continue to be presented and admired.

Europe and North America have had women dramatists, but they too have largely been forgotten until efforts were made in the twentieth century to rectify the situation. In France, for example, an organized endeavour called *matrimoine* proposes to give belated recognition to French women playwrights and encourage revivals of their works in order to keep alive the values that women playwrights have long communicated through their theatre. Canada has started its own *matrimoine* with the additional goal of giving creative women their deserved place in online encyclopedias. A case in point is Wikipedia, with a mere 20 per cent of its pages devoted to women.

I hope that the plays in this collection will not only be read and enjoyed but that they will spark an interest in the many other works of Spain's most successful woman dramatist and will inspire the reading of other works by women in Spain and other countries.

María and Gregorio

María de la O Lejárraga García, better known as María Martínez Sierra, was born in San Millán de la Cogolla (La Rioja) on 28 December 1874. The first of seven children of Leandro Lejárraga, a doctor, and Natividad García, María lived in La Rioja until her father was transferred to Carabanchel, a town in the province of Madrid close to the capital. At five María discovered what was to become her life's passion when she saw a magic show for children in Madrid's Teatro Español.[4] Her favourite toy then became a cardboard theatre with painted walls and paper characters for whom she could create scenes and dialogues. Initially home-schooled by her mother, María learned world history and geography in both Castilian and French, and at sixteen began training to become a language teacher of French, English, German and Russian. At twenty, after having passed all exams, she took a teaching position in a working-class neighbourhood of Madrid, an experience that brought her face to face with poverty for the first time.

Gregorio, the eldest of nine children, was born 6 May 1881, and his family, like María's, was comfortably middle class. Six years younger than María, he had known her only as the older sister of a playmate. But at a village dance in 1897, María, already a teacher, and Gregorio, sixteen, sat together on the side lines, as neither cared to dance. Soon, their common interest in theatre would activate a multi-faceted relationship. They started writing together and, in the next three years, had four of their works published; three with Gregorio's name as sole author, and the fourth, *Cuentos breves*, with María's name, because these short stories were for children. When María's intellectual parents took little notice of her first book, she decided that they would never see her name on another. After she and Gregorio were married on 30 November 1900, María even shed the name 'Lejárraga' and adopted the surname of her husband.[5]

Initially María's teaching supported the couple as they wrote together. But as Gregorio became involved in publishing, editing literary journals and directing plays, María gave up teaching to take over the writing. [6] In fact, the only work known to have been written entirely by Gregorio, *La casa de la primavera* (*The House of Spring*, 1907), is a volume of poems in which María figures exclusively as muse for Gregorio's poetic expression of marital bliss. Ironically, it was about this time that Gregorio met Catalina Bárcena, the beautiful ingénue actress born in Cuba and reared in Spain, who would join his theatre company and, under his guidance, become Spain's leading actress in the years 1915–30.

Besides plays, María composed under Gregorio's name librettos for operas, operettas, ballets and other musical works with important composers including José María Usandizaga, who chose to base his first work with María on a story of hers from *Teatro de ensueño* (*Dream Theatre*, 1905), *Saltimbaquis* (*Tumblers*). The final product, *Las golondrinas* (*The Swallows*), performed in 1913, was successful, but Usandizaga was already fatally infected with tuberculosis, and their only subsequent collaboration, *La llama* (*The Flame*), was performed in 1918, three years after the composer's death.

María also wrote librettos for two of Joaquín Turina's operas, *Margot* (1914) and *El jardín de Oriente* (1924). In 1915 Turina had composed a musical portrait ('Retrato') of María that initiates his piano series entitled *Album de Viaje* (*My Trip Album*), with all parts dedicated to her. In the introductory portrait number, the modest but harmonious chords suggest María's attractively placid temperament, and a subsequent segment illustrates her greatly admired musical laughter via a series of gracefully dancing thirds.

María's libretto with Manuel de Falla, *El amor brujo* (1915, performed in English under various titles: *Love, the Magician*; *Spellbound Love*; *Wedded by Witchcraft*), was commissioned by the famous gypsy flamenco dancer Pastora Imperio and features distinctively Andalusian music. The libretto concerns Candela, a widow now attracted to her childhood sweetheart, but who continues to be haunted by her deceased husband's ghost who dances with her nightly. She tricks Lucía, a woman with whom her husband had had an affair, to come one evening, and when the ghost appears to dance, Candela allows Lucía to be taken away by her departed lover.

María and Falla also produced a version of Alarcón's popular novel *The Three-Cornered Hat* that was successfully produced in Madrid as *El corregidor y la molinera* (*The Judge and the Miller*) in 1917. When Serge Diaghilev, choreographer of the Ballet Russe, saw the production, he requested a ballet version. Now with the title of *Le Tricorne* (*The Three-Cornered Hat*), the work opened in London in 1919 with sets and costumes by Pablo Picasso.[7]

While María worked with and became close friends with musicians, Gregorio was on tour in Spain with Catalina Bárcena. On his return, Gregorio, never hesitant to promote his own name, launched his theatre group as the Gregorio Martínez Sierra Company with Catalina as star at the Eslava Theatre, conveniently located just off the Puerta del Sol in the centre of Madrid.[8]

Along with the considerable financial and artistic success of the Martínez Sierra name came personal pain for María. As Gregorio became more and more openly involved with Catalina, María kept the anguish she felt to herself, and provided the outward appearance, at least, of marital harmony. Catalina, on the other hand, was

María's opposite. Although demure and captivating on stage, off stage she could be loud, rude and childish. She was vocal about her jealousy of María, and wanted Gregorio to leave her. In 1922, when Catalina gave birth to Gregorio's child (Catalinita), she demanded that he live with her or she would no longer perform with his company. Gregorio now found himself in a terrible predicament: he needed both the writer and the actress for the success that was so important to him. Knowing both women well, Gregorio acquiesced to Catalina's demands, and María, never openly critical of him, simply left for France and established residence near Nice. There, incredibly, she continued to write works for Gregorio to perform and publish as his.[9]

Gregorio may have thought it prudent to leave Madrid as well, for in 1924, he took his company to Barcelona and performed for a year at the Novedades Theatre before leaving in 1925 on a five-year performance tour of Europe, the United States and South America. With Gregorio far away, María wrote feminist essays, supported socialist causes and composed plays reflective of the more liberal attitudes of her French surroundings, but she continued to reconstruct her own life and values in her theatre, although now by using more experimental techniques. She mailed these plays to Gregorio, and his company performed them on tour.

In 1930, several of María's dramatist friends left for Hollywood to assist in the preparation of films in Spanish. At first, Gregorio refused to support this audacious rival, but eventually he recognized that motion pictures could be an important source of income and accepted an offer from Metro-Goldwyn-Mayer and later with Fox Studios. In 1931, Gregorio sold movie rights to *Mamá* (1912), evocative of *A Doll's House* (1879), which María, an admirer of Ibsen, had written, and in 1933 Paramount filmed a major production of her signature play *The Cradle Song* (*Canción de cuna*). Back in Spain, María became Granada's socialist candidate for parliament, won the election and represented that region's interests until the eruption of the Spanish Civil War in 1936.

After spending several lucrative years in Hollywood, Gregorio returned to Spain in 1935 to contribute to Spain's emerging film industry with several plans, one of which was to create another movie version of *The Cradle Song* with Catalina as star. But filming was delayed, and the outbreak of the Spanish Civil War ended that project. When an Argentine film company offered to produce *The Cradle Song*, Gregorio and Catalina embarked for Buenos Aires, where they remained until September of 1947, when, ill with abdominal cancer, Gregorio returned to Spain, where he died two weeks later. María, who was living in exile in France at the time, heard the news via a British radio broadcast and composed a tribute, written, as she says in her first words, 'with love and pain', yet another proof of María's enduring devotion for Gregorio and her incredibly forgiving nature.[10]

She then moved to Buenos Aires, but getting work there was difficult; not only was she not recognized as an author, but Gregorio had spread the word that she had died in order to present Catalina as his wife. To make matters even worse, the rights to all the plays that María had written, and whose royalties were morally hers, were legally Gregorio's, and he had left everything to Catalina. At seventy-four, therefore, María had to support herself. Instead of going into a rage, she simply faced reality and considered her options. Her favoured solutions included writing, translating, contributing to newspapers, magazines and radio, and to give lectures. She also planned to publish the complete works of Gregorio under his sole name with her Introduction, but because of Catalina's fanatical objections the publishing house cancelled this project.

In Argentina, María produced two semi-autobiographies: *Una mujer por caminos de España* (*A Woman along Spanish Roads*, 1952), about her political activities during the Republic, and *Gregorio y yo, Medio siglo de colaboración* (*Gregorio and I, Half a Century of Collaboration*, 1953), but without revealing her absolutely essential role in the success of the works published under her husband's name.

On 28 June 1974, when María was six months from being 100 years old, she died, taking to her grave details of all that she had written under Gregorio's name, and why she had protected him by keeping the secret so long. The mystery of her decision has challenged and inspired several important women writers to delve into her life via novels and plays for answers.[11]

The plays

The Kingdom of God

In 1909, during a trip to Italy, María read a newspaper story about an infant girl abandoned in a convent and wondered if this might serve as subject for a play. Finding the baby and showing the reactions of the nuns who want to keep her could account for the first act, and a second act would show how that child, now a young woman, felt as she was about to leave her 'mothers' to marry. *Canción de cuna* (*The Cradle Song*) was the hit of the 1911 season, won the prestigious Royal Academy award, has had numerous translations and performances in Spain as well as abroad and has enjoyed five movie adaptations in four countries: Spain, Mexico, United States, Argentina. When the play opened, many wondered how Gregorio could know so much about convent life. But the real writer did; María's sister, with whom she was very close, was a nun, and parts of *The Kingdom of God*, a work that also touches on the spiritual life, were written in her sister's abbey.

The Kingdom of God (*El reino de Dios*), María's favourite play, premiered in 1915. The title is symbolic of the celestial happiness on earth that the protagonist, Sister Gracia, hopes to create for the world's needy. It enjoyed considerable success in Spain as well as abroad.

In the first act, Sister Gracia, just nineteen and whose vows are annual rather than perpetual, serves in an old people's home surrounded by the ill and helpless who have no other place to go. The second act takes place ten years later, and Sister Gracia is serving in a maternity home for unwed mothers. While there, a doctor falls in love with her and begs her to leave this life to serve humanity by his side. For this quintessential protagonist, charity is not enough; she refuses to allow herself the luxury of worldly love for she wants to give her life as an offering to the unfortunate. In the third act, Sister Gracia, now seventy, serves in an orphanage. A child who has grown up there becomes a bullfighter and returns to offer his 'mother', Sister Gracia, the gift of the bloody ear of a bull. When the children at the orphanage complain about the food, she reminds them that some people have no food at all or even a roof over their heads, and that they must remedy the misery of the world with their good works, for only in this way can they help to create the kingdom of God on earth.

The Romantic Young Lady

One of María's gently feminist and very successful plays, *The Romantic Young Lady* (*Sueño de una noche de agosto*) premiered in 1918. The protagonist Rosario, twenty-three, who lives with her grandmother and three brothers, very much favours equality of the sexes and would like to work, but her conservative brothers think she should marry and live a traditional woman's life. One night when the brothers are out and she is reading a sentimental novel by her favourite author, a hat sails through the window. When a man appears to retrieve it, he notices the book she is reading and claims to know the author, who, by coincidence, is looking for a secretary, so he writes her a note of introduction. When Rosario suggests that he should now leave by the window, he tells her that because the concierge of the building across the street is standing outside, he will see him leave and that her reputation will be compromised. Although Rosario agrees, she believes that both reputations should be compromised, for rights and obligations should be equal. When voices announce the return of the brothers, the stranger has no choice but to disappear through the window.

When Rosario applies for the secretarial position, she sees that the author she had admired is really the stranger with the hat, but she is disillusioned on witnessing a scene between him and an immodestly dressed chorus girl with whom he seemed to be involved. In spite of his pleas that she become his secretary, the disappointed Rosario refuses. When she leaves, the author sits down to write a novel he will entitle *The Romantic Young Lady*.[12]

In the third act, while Rosario and the grandmother are saying the rosary to pass the time, a hat again sails through the window. When the servant throws the statue of a dog at the source and it hits the author on the head, he is brought into the house for care and bandaging. After a short conversation in which he proposes marriage to Rosario, the grandmother serves them hot chocolate before conveniently falling asleep to allow them to resolve their problems. If they ever marry, Rosario demands not only equal rights with him but that he make certain modifications in his literature, suggesting that the two will collaborate on his novels. As Juan Aguilera Sastre observes of María's theatre: 'The collaboration of spouses is presented as the ideal of happiness and stability in marriage.'[13]

Take Two from One

When Gregorio's theatre company returned to Spain in 1930 to perform the four new plays María had written in France, critics noticed a new seriousness as well as innovation in the works attributed to Gregorio as the characters explore the meaning of reality and of life itself.[14] Continued, however, are the painful triangles in which romantic love, rarely rational, is seen as a form of black magic,

Take Two from One (*Triángulo*, 1929) uses symbolic names and the triangular structure of the love conflict, but in this play the problems of the male protagonist are central. Faustino, a handsome attorney husband, and his goddess-like bride, Diana, are on a honeymoon cruise when one of the passengers develops a crush on Faustino. Because she admires a ring of Diana's that Faustino had worn as a child, Diana allows her to try it on. Then a fire breaks out, and passengers immediately board the lifeboats to abandon ship. We later learn that Diana's boat overturned and what was presumed to be her body was found at sea.

In the second act, Faustino, married again, has been happy for a year with Diana's opposite: kindly, serene, smart Marcela (who shares the first three letters of her name with María as well as her characteristics).[10] The conflict begins when Diana suddenly reappears. The living Diana was rescued at sea and sold to a primitive tribe in Africa, whose aboriginal peoples worshipped her as their idol. Eventually, a plane downed in the jungle allows her to escape back to Europe.

The solution to this predicament is more complicated than in other plays, for the resolution is not simply Faustino's personal preference but rather involves both religious and legal regulations and precedents. Which of the wives is legitimate? Who is the sinner? The women compete in their own ways for their husband, and Faustino continues to love both. In the third act, as tension builds, Faustino, true to his Faustian name, adds a philosophical dimension to his character as he steps off the stage from one truth into another. When the two women try to follow him, they find themselves trapped in their literary reality. When the stage lights begin to fade, Faustino assures them that he, like other non-entities, will fade as well but that they may meet again the following day, referring to another reality: the next performance of this play.

Patricia W. O'Connor

Patricia W. O'Connor is Professor Emerita at the University of Cincinnati, and renowned expert on María Martínez Sierra; her books include *Gregorio y María Martínez Sierra: Cronica De Una Colaboracion* (1987) and *Mito y realidad de una dramaturga espanola: María Martínez Sierra* (2003).

Notes

1 Juan Aguilera Sastre, 'María Lejárraga y el teatro', *Homenaje del Ateneo Riojano a María de la O Lejárraga* (Logroño: Ateneo Riojano, 1994), 51–61.
2 Xavi Ayén, 'Esposa y negra en la vida', *La Vanguardia,* 17 November (2000), 50.
3 These letters are published in *Mito y realidad de una dramaturga* (*Myth and Reality of a Woman Dramatist*) (Logroño: Instituto de Estudios Riojanos, 2003).
4 Antonina Rodrigo, *María Lejárraga: una mujer en la sombra* (Madrid: Ediciones Vosa, 1994), 27.
5 Without the 'de' (of) in front of the husband's surname, as is traditional in Spain.
6 Her writing included translations from several languages, e.g. of Dante, Ibsen, Ionesco, Jonson, Maeterlinck, Miller, de Musset, Pirandello, Shakespeare, Shaw, Wilder and Williams.
7 For abundant and fascinating information regarding María's work with musicians, see articles by Joseph R. Jones: 'Lejárraga as Librettist and Lyricist: The State of the Question', *Estreno* 29, no. 1 (spring 2003), 18–22, and 'María Lejárraga de (sic.) Martínez Sierra (1874–1974), libretista y letrista', *Berceo,* 147 (2004), 55–95.
8 At Teatro Eslava, Gregorio performed plays attributed to him as well as works by other established or new authors, including, in 1920, Lorca's first play, *El maleficio de la mariposa* (*The Butterfly's Curse*).
9 After the separation, defenders of Gregorio as exclusive author of the works observed that the author's plays continued their regular and successful performances and therefore felt

their position had been vindicated, for a feminist would never continue to write for a husband who had left her for another woman, as this one did. Truth can be stranger than fiction.
10 A copy of this two-page tribute, 'In Memoriam', is in the Archives of the University of Cincinnati's Blegen Library.
11 A few contemporary and published novels and plays that probe the enigmas of María's life include: *Llevaré tu nombre* (2002), a novel by Laura Hynes; *Firmado Lejárraga* (2019), a play by Vanessa Montfort; *Luz ajena* (2020), a novel by Isabel Lizárraga; *La mujer sin nombre* (2020), a novel by Vanessa Montfort.
12 This play would later be made into a film in Hollywood (1932) starring Catalina Bárcena, but because Catalina was forty-two at the time, the film adaptation by José López Rubio and Paul Pérez is entitled 'A Romantic Widow' while following the general plot of the play.
13 *Take Two from One: A Farce in Three Acts*, trans. Helen and Harley Granville-Barker (London: Sidgwick & Jackson, 1931), 60.
14 The four plays María wrote in this period include *Sortilegio* (*Spellbound*, 1930), the text of which was contained in the steamer trunk that arrived after her death. Her most daring play and only tragedy, it concerns a homosexual who has helped waste his family's fortune and feels compelled to marry for money a woman who irrationally adores him, but he can never give her the love she needs. It was successfully performed in Buenos Aires but was much too daring for any theatre in Spain at the time and would have been forbidden by censors in the Franco years (1939–75).

A Critical Appreciation of the Plays

This was first published in 1922 in Plays of G. Martinez Sierra (*New York: E. P. Dutton & Co.*). *The volume contains* The Cradle Song, The Lover, Love Magic, Poor John *and* Madame Pepita. *All were translated by John Garrett Underhill, who also contributed a Foreword, which at the end mentions María as an important collaborator of Gregorio's. The critical appreciation was reprinted in 1929 as an introduction in* The Kingdom of God and Other Plays (*New York: E. P. Dutton & Co.*). *As well as the title play, this volume contains* The Two Shepherds, Wife to a Famous Man *and* The Romantic Young Lady, *all translated by the Granville-Barkers.*

While there may be much to say, there is really very little to explain about the plays of Martínez Sierra, for they have in the first place the supreme dramatic virtue of explaining themselves. They are not (those at least now under review) strikingly novel in technique. They certainly carry no abstruse philosophical message. But they are notable, the present writer holds, for simple excellence as plays, for the directness with which they set out to – and the fine economy with which they do – achieve their purpose. And what better, in this sort, can be said? Take, for instance, *The Cradle Song*. Sierra has the idea – the charming, unrecondite idea – of a foundling baby thrust upon the mercies of a convent of nuns, who bring her up, spend upon her all they can recover of their suppressed motherly instincts, give her to a young man in marriage, and so back to the world. Mark his means to this effect. The foundling, a varied chorus of nuns – among them one who is emotionally the play's protagonist, an old doctor (the child must acquire a legal parent) and the young bridegroom. No intrigue, no thesis, no rhetorical enlargements; two acts because his theme needs two, and no convention-satisfying third, which it does not need. The whole result is a story perfectly told for the sake of its innate humour and feeling, a picture filled and rounded. And – not that this affects the matter – it is interesting to note that with the Spanish public this play, conceding little or nothing to what is usually understood to be the popular demand in such things, was yet a great success – interesting from the point of view of public and theatre manager. The playwright at this juncture stands aside; his work is done, he bows with one emphasis or another to success or failure, advising himself merely of the future. But the *elements* of success – this is the important conclusion if it may be drawn – are probably pretty constant, though its incidentals may vary from country to country and year to year; and it might pay theatre managers to keep a tame crowd-psychologist or so to analyse them. Then all the English-speaking public – that part of it at least which has developed some taste and judgement – would not always be left asking, as they read translated, instead of hearing in their native tongue, plays like *The Cradle Song*, why – in the name of 'What the public wants' – they should be fobbed off, time after time, with entertainments which, with every well-tried appearance of being entertaining, do not *entertain*. To return, however, to Sierra, less occupied as a playwright with theatrical economics even than with an obtruding philosophy, though as a theatre manager – a second and successful occupation that has unluckily been thrusting aside his playwriting lately – his opinion on this point would be worth having.

The Two Shepherds may be coupled with *The Cradle Song*. It has the same simplicity of scheme, the same directness of approach. It is perhaps the more remarkable in that its action swings upon a stark fidelity of vision. And here is the chief of Sierra's dramatic (distinct for the moment from 'theatrical') virtues; he paints faithfully the thing he *sees*. Once he has his outline clear and true he may sentimentalise a little in filling in the detail; it is a venial fault. We could forgive, if need were, even more affectionate weakness on his creator's part for snuffy, frowsy, garlic-smelling old Don Antonio with his frayed cassock and his battered image of the Virgin, pummelling (as he says) his ill-conditioned village flock into righteousness, dragging them up to God by the scruffs of their dirty necks. Again Sierra needs his two acts and no more, seventy minutes, perhaps, of playing time, but in that space he shows us a dozen characters, individual and alive, and a picture of a Spanish village so consistent that, experience apart, we know it to be true. Mr Sam Weller remarked that if instead of eyes he had been gifted with a pair of double hextra million magnifying glasses he might have been able to see through two brick walls and a door, but having only eyes his vision was limited. Sam, though not given to literature was a bit of a genius, apt, as his creator was, at seeing the realities of cockneydom through things even more opaque to most sights than walls and doors. It is the one gift worth having. Sierra translates for us his Spanish village in terms, no doubt, of his own happy, humorous, ironic temperament. But he has seen it first without illusion, seen it naked, seen it true and, thanks to him, so can we – and have our fun into the bargain.

Lirio entre espinas ('Lily among Thorns') and *El enamorado* ('The Lover'), one-act plays, sound dominantly the note of irony, the one in its elaborately developed situation, the other in its treatment of the character of the Lover himself. The chancing of the timid little nun into the house of ill-fame, the circumstance by which her healing touch at a sudden sick-bed brings the inmates like good little children fetching and carrying at her call, disposes of the rowdy patrons in a sulky silence – all that is ironic and amusing enough; and (a carping critic might continue) we have had that sort of thing before (Maupassant!) and many another playwright could make as much effect with it! But mark again, the clarity of vision. Sierra has seen each single figure and has informed it with a life of its own before he started the mere making use of it for his group. Even the rather fantastically unpleasant little figure of the half-witted child (it reminds one, dependent for knowledge of Spain chiefly on books and pictures, of a Velázquez dwarf) has a pitiful little individual place – and a purpose. For – and this is what every clever dramatist fired with a good idea would not give us – one is struck with the fine humanity of Sierra's treatment of his theme. No condescension either! He writes about the nun and the fallen women and the gay young blackguards, their visitors, alike without vulgar astonishment, unselfconsciously, with a perfect courtesy of mind. He writes as a gentleman should.

The saliency of 'The Lover', as a study of the entirely absurd gentleman who spends his life, regardless of his personal affairs, in rapt and unregarded worship of the Queen, is technically the sureness of the touch – it is drawn in spare outline so that one false stroke might be fatal – and above and beyond that the fearlessly comic treatment of the subject. No spice of ridicule is spared. The fellow has even a foolish-sounding name; he ran a margarine factory before he ruined himself trapesing over the world after his Dulcinea (*aliter visum*); cruellest stroke of all, he has to confess that as he watches in the palace grounds through winter nights for the Queen to come out at dawn to feed her pigeons, he has, lest he perish with cold, to seek the comfortable cage, the friendly society of the orang-outang. He has a ridiculous collection of souvenirs, for which he has refused some Englishman's offer of a good round sum (Englishman = eccentric, c.f., of course, the Danish gravedigger's 'They are all mad there.' How odd – an Englishman writes – that this should be still the typical European joke about us!); he refuses the costly ring the Queen offers him – for after all, while her courtiers stood by helpless with etiquette, this preposterous being did really save her life. He asks to be allowed to kiss her hand. Is he, then, to turn heroic after all? No! for his final request is a free pass over the State railways that he may continue his foolish, useless trapesing as before.

Surely that is good art. And, with the courageous consistency, note the final effect. The fellow wins us, we take off our hats to him; the Queen is stirred to a passing emotion she never felt before. 'She feels' (it is also a warning to the actress of the part not to tumble into sentiment) 'that for the first time in her life she has really been loved.' Sierra is not Cervantes' countryman for nothing; and, quoting that great name, we need enlarge the general argument no further. But glancing at the purely dramatic value of irony it is perhaps worth while to consider for a moment the peculiar difficulty of its use in the theatre. This resides, of course, mainly in the natural constitution of the actor himself. It is not, as some contemptuous critics of the art would say, an objection to being made ridiculous (though let us admit that one may now and then meet that in the self-conscious or over-popular actor), so much as a far more reasonable desire that his audience should, from the beginning, have no doubt of his intentions, should be sure that, however big a fool he is making of himself, he is doing it deliberately with his eyes open. There is nothing the actor hates more than to be at cross-purposes with his audience. Hence the practical difficulty for a dramatist of the gradual disclosure of an ironic purpose, but the necessity of a ruthless consistency, by which the end shall justify both the beginning and the means. And we rule out of course any concluding claptrap of a sudden direct sentimental appeal for sympathy. 'The Lover' is a simple admirable example of what an ironic play should be. For it is by the sustaining of the irony that our proper sympathy is won. The actor can round off his performance, the play's last scheme come full circle. Still something more than technique is involved. If Sierra did not love his man well enough to want to tell the truth about him and love him the better for truth being told, the silly fool could not touch the Queen's imagination and ours as he does. It is respect for poor humanity that counts. Sierra has that.

El Reino de Dios ('The Kingdom of God') is in some ways the most considerable of Sierra's work. He devises for himself a larger canvas than usual and, if for nothing else, the play would be remarkable for the number, variety, fidelity, vitality of the sketched characters with which it is so economically filled. He demands great assistance from his actors, no doubt, but he sets them no problems of psychology, no modelling, so to speak, is asked of them, they have but to colour in 'on the flat' the firm outlines of his drawing. And for more immediate effect he places them against a background which is in itself dramatic, which in itself and in its changes, develops the action and purpose of the play. The action itself is unconventional more or less – though there is little in the shape of transgression against the unities which has not been tried in the post-Ibsen period of European drama by one dramatic experimentor or another. We mark Sierra yet once more as the accomplished man of the theatre by the ease and certainty with which he transgresses. He sacrifices everything to his purpose and contrives to sacrifice nothing. The play has, as its main thread, the story of a girl – in her girlhood, her middle and old age – who gives up her share in the things of this world to ensure, rather than seek, such a portion as she may snatch in this life of the kingdom of God. She joins a sisterhood. We find her in her girlhood ministering in an asylum for old men, foolish, tiresome and – if a stray peseta opens the door of an inn to them – drunken old men. Womanhood brings her to a home where the children of fallen women come into the world, a sadder beginning of life than was the preceding picture – so pitifully comic – of life's end. She refuses release from it in marriage (the vows of her order are not final) to a worthy doctor who worships her, with the flashing phrase 'And you dare to talk to me of love . . . *here!*' Old age finds her the Mother of an orphanage, with one of God's adopted returing in laurelled triumph as a bull fighter to lay his trophy – his first bull's ear – at her feet (How one envies a Spanish dramatist that scene, but with an admiring envy for Sierra's quite perfect treatment of it!) and as a crown and eding to the play we have her passionate plea with a young revolutionary in embryo (Spain has no immediate copyright in these at least) to abjure violence, to seek his kingdom of God in pity and in love. A very stirring play; and it is instructive to the student of drama to note the use made of the material, the means by which Sierra appeals – and most legitimately – to our emotions. He is not concerned (as an English dramatist choosing such a theme today would almost certainly be) with the growth or wane of the woman's religious belief, nor yet – but for that one flash already recorded – with her mental reaction to the social conditions she faces, not even with developing her 'character'; in fact, it is part of his theme that she does not bother, as certain of our self-conscious philanthropists do, with any such self-righteous thing – so why should he? He relies upon making as clear in his picture to us, as in the reality it was clear to her, the human needs and their claim upon us of disreputable age, sordid sins of the flesh, and of childhood, that will bate no claim, and should not, since upon it all the claims of the world must fall. And that he does so in terms which not the simplest soul in his audience can mistake, nor the most sophisticated deny, is, it may be claimed, an achievement – complete of its kind – in the reality of art.

La mujer del héroe ('Wife to a Famous Man') makes far fewer pretensions. It is a sound playable play, little more, interesting to us mainly for the peep that it takes into working-class Madrid. The dramatist, in fact, frankly tells us in a spoken epilogue that it is a passing tribute to the virtues of the Spanish woman of the people as you may walk down any street in any city to find her – as you might find her, *bien entendu*, had you Sierra's power to see and show beauty, pathos, humour in this laundry, and in the kindly, rough-tongued, honest-minded woman earning her family's living there; as good fun and as great a beauty, so felt and seen, as some of us go seeking in remoter places. He selects the rest of his material a trifle carelessly, perhaps; he has used some of it before. But it is an admirable notion, this, of a national hero made in a moment out of the winner of an air-race (this was in the days before the war); a common fellow, reckless and stout of nerve, but with a head which, though he can keep it in the air, is only made to be turned on earth; not too much of a hero to have lived on the laundry, rapidly too spoilt to live contentedly in it.

Sierra might have added in his epilogue almost as legitimately that the play is tribute in the shape of opportunity to the actress upon whom the chief burden is to fall. But this again might be remarked of all his work (though surely it should not call for particular remark in any dramatist!) how grateful his plays are to the actor. It comes of course partly from the extreme simplicity of his method and from his never trying to force into a play more matter than it will easily hold. He seems incapable of writing anything ineffective, though now and then he may yield to the too obvious effect. That is a venial fault – in the actor's eyes at least. And Sierra, one may judge from this, does genuinely like, admire and understand the art of acting.

It is a taste that every dramatist should have. It may sound superfluous to say so, but of late years there seems to have developed in certain dramatists a distrust, even a positive dislike, of acting, an unreasoning, if sometimes excusable anger with the actor himself and all his works. Now this reflects quite inevitably upon their own work and its result is to be seen in a stiff unyieldingness, a drabness and dryness, a self-sufficiency, as if to say, 'You actors are my megaphone merely. Please don't presume.' Upon such a perverse misunderstanding of what the free and full collaboration between actor and dramatist should be, the drama can never flourish. The trouble springs partly, one fears, from the quite uncalled-for acclaim of the modern dramatist as 'a literary man'. He bows, a bit snobbishly, to the intended compliment and then from literature's present pontifical height is apt to begin to look down on the motley theatre. In a short time, if he's not careful, he'll soon be writing plays fitter for the study than the stage. There is no good play of which that can be said. There are good plays enough that need better acting than our present theatre with its stupid system and its artistically uneducated public, by whose favour it must live, can be expected to supply. But no progress is possible in the art as a whole unless all concerned – dramatists, actors, yes, and public too – such a selection from the mob as can form a conscious third – move forward together. In England we are still far from that happy state of things. The theatre is commercially prosperous, artistically at cross-purposes. Dramatists may complain of their actors, but actors are bitterer about managements, and managements alternately curse at and despise the public – save, of course, during the runs of luck that most of them, gambling long and good-temperedly enough, may look for. Spain no doubt has her theatrical troubles too; we are not here concerned with them. But it is at least a sign of artistic good health to find such plays as Sierra's among its living drama, apt above all things for acting, and for such acting as, one is sure, is bread and meat to the appetite of the audience, wholesome and familiar fare that they know the good and the bad of.

If one comments no further it is not for lack of material. The author's works, his plays alone (there are novels and poems besides. He is forty. What is the secret of this amazing fecundity of the Spaniard?) would take a page or more only to list.

Plays like *Madame Pepita*, *Mamá*, *Sueño de una noche de agosto* (played in English as 'The Romantic Young Lady') and the little fantasy *Hechizo de amor* ('Love Magic') are of a content to which we are more accustomed in the French and English-spoken drama of today. There are yet others, less usual in form and content too, but these will find their way to translation some day and may then more appropriately be dealt with. This must suffice now, an inadequate introduction, perhaps, to a playwright whose adequacy is, in any case, beyond question.

H. Granville Barker

Selected Works by María Martínez Sierra

Gregorio Martínez Sierra is credited with more than 200 titles, including plays, novels, short stories, operettas, essays, poetry and translations. It has now been determined that the vast majority of these were written by María Martínez Sierra. (Titles of works published in English appear in brackets.)

Cuentos breves (children's short stories, in María's name, 1899)
Teatro de ensueño (dialogues, including *Pastoral* [*Idyll*], 1905)
Tú eres la paz (novel, *Ana María*, 1906)
Juventud, divino tesoro (1908)
Hechizo de amor (*Love Magic*, 1908)
La sombra del padre (1909)
El ama de la casa (1910)
Primavera en otoño (*Spring in Autumn*, 1911)
Canción de cuna (*The Cradle Song*, 1911)
El palacio triste (1911)
La suerte de Isabelita (1911)
Lirio entre espinas (*Lily among Thorns*, 1911)
El Pobrecito Juan (*Poor John*, 1912)
Madame Pepita (1912)
Las golondrinas (libretto, 1913)
El enamorado (*The Lover*, 1913)
Mamá (1913)
Sólo para mujeres (1913)
Madrigal (1913)
Los Pastores (*The Two Shepherds*, 1913)
La tirana (1913)
Margot (libretto, 1914)
La mujer del héroe (*Wife to a Famous Man*, 1914)
La pasión (1914)
El amor brujo (several English titles, libretto, 1915)
Amanecer (1915)
El reino de Dios (*The Kingdom of God*, 1915)
Cartas a las mujeres de España (essays, 1916)
Navidad (*Holy Night*, 1916)
Para hacerse amar locamente (1917)
La adultere penitente (1917)
Esperanza nuestra (1917)
Sueño de una noche de agosto (*The Romantic Young Lady*, 1918)
Rosina es frágil (1918)
El Sombrero de tres picos (*The Three-Cornered Hat*, libretto, 1919)
Cada uno y su vida (1919)
El Corazon ciegó (1919)
Vida y dulzura (1920)

Don Juan de España (1921)
El ideal (1921)
Torre de marfil (1924)
Mujer (1925)
Seamos felices (*Let Us Be Happy*, 1929)
Triángulo (*Take Two from One*, credited to Gregorio and María, 1929)
La hora del diablo (1930)
Sortilegio (manuscript credits Gregorio and María, 1930)
Obras completas (complete works, 1920–30, 14 vols)
La mujer Española ante la republica (published lecture, in María's name, 1931)
Cartas a las mujeres de América (essays, 1941)
Una mujer por caminos de España (autobiographical writing, in María's name, 1952)
Gregorio y yo (memoir, in María's name, 1953)
Viajes de una gota de agua (plays for children, in María's name, 1954)
Fiesta en el Olimpo (collection of late works, in María's name, 1960)

2 The Plays

The Kingdom of God
(El Reino de Dios)

A Play in Three Acts

Teatro de Novedades, Barcelona (1915)
Abbey Theatre, Dublin (1924)
Strand Theatre, London (1927)
Ethel Barrymore Theatre, New York (1928)

Abbey Theatre, Dublin (3 November 1924) cast included:

Sister Gracia	Eileen Crowe
Don Lorenzo	Tom Moran
Sister Juliana	Eileeen O'Kelly
Lulu	Lilian Roberts
María Isabela	Maeve McMurrough
Juan de Dios	Arthur Shields
Margarita	Sara Allgood
Vicente	P. J. Carolan
Candelas	Maureen Delany
Paquita	Norma Joyce

Director: Michael J. Dolan

Strand Theatre, London (26 October 1927) cast included:

Sister Gracia	Gillian Scaife
Don Lorenzo	Lancelot Hilton
Sister Juliana	Peggy Rae
Lulu	Natalie Moya
María Isabela	Dorothy Massingham
Juan de Dios	Harold Young
Margarita	Kathleen O'Regan
Vicente	Ronald Kerr
Candelas	Ivy Des Voeux
Paquita	Joan Hill

Director: Anmer Hall

Ethel Barrymore Theatre, New York (20 December 1928) cast included:

Sister Gracia	Ethel Barrymore
Don Lorenzo	George Alison
Sister Juliana	Phyllis Blake
Lulu	Susan Blake
María Isabela	Lenore Chippendale
Juan de Dios	Elisha Cook, Jr.
Margarita	Madeline Delmar
Vincente	Marcel Dill
Candelas	Ernestine Gaines
Quica	Georgia Harvey

Producer: Lee Shubert
Director: E. M. Blyth

Characters

First Act	*Second Act*	*Third Act*
Sister Gracia	**Sister Gracia**	**Sister Gracia**
Sister Juliana	**Margarita**	**Sister Dionisia**
Sister Manuela	**Candelas**	**Engracia**
María Isabel	**Quica**	**The Innocent**
Lulu	**Cecilia**	**Paquita**
Don Lorenzo	**Dumb Girl**	**Lorenza**
Trajano	**Sister Cristina**	**Morenito**
Gabriel	**Sister Feliciana**	**Felipe**
Liborio	**Enrique**	**Juan de Dios**
Two Old Men		**Vicente**
		Policarpo
		Several Children

The first act takes place in an asylum for poor old men; the second in a maternity home; the third in an orphanage.

In the first act **Sister Gracia** *is nineteen, in the second twenty-nine, and in the third act she is seventy.*

It should be noted that **Sister Gracia** *is not a nun. She belongs to the order of St Vincent de Paul, which is dedicated to the care of the sick and the teaching of children. The Sisters take their vows year by year, and they may renew them or not as they wish.*

Act One

The garden of a ducal palace that has been converted to a home for poverty-stricken old men. The garden itself is still both stately and charming. We are in a part of it that is walled with clipped hedges of box and myrtle; upon the left is a bower of cypress; in the half distance a screen of plane trees and chestnuts. In the middle is a fountain surrounded by beds of flowers. And in the arbour and behind the fountain are marble benches of classic design. Upon the right stands the ci-devant palace which is reached by marble steps across a terrace that is of marble too. Upon this terrace open the long windows of the rooms which were once the salons, but are now the dormitories and living-rooms of the present inmates. Below the terrace a little service door shows the way into the lower regions of the house.

It is autumn. The leaves of the plane trees and chestnuts have already turned red and gold. Over the terrace balustrade is twined a flaming creeper. In the flower beds are dahlias and chrysanthemums, and upon the rose trees a few last roses cling. Dead leaves drift upon the walks and steps where the autumn wind has blown them.

It is the afternoon of a clear bright October day in Castile. The sun soon begins to set; the sky is lit by flaming colours which fade after a little to a pallor that is brightened, then, by the evening star.

Gabriel, *one of the old pensioners, is sitting on a bench cracking pine nuts with a stone. He is a very thin old man, shrunk within his blue uniform. But he is as sharp as a needle and as lively as a lizard; and his eyes are always expressionlessly ablink. He eats the pine kernels with all the pleasure of second childhood.*

Trajano, *a still older inmate, is walking backwards and forwards evidently somewhat out of temper. He has a fine, rather apostolic, head; he limps a little from rheumatism.*

Another **Old Man**, *passing at the back, salutes them both.*

Old Man   Good afternoon, gentlemen.

Gabriel   Same to you.

The **Old Man** *passes on.*

Gabriel   And a beautiful afternoon it is. Good to sit and warm one's bones in such an October sun.

He gives a little shrill laugh. **Trajano**, *for all that he was spoken to, makes no pause in his walking and gives no answer but a grunt.* **Gabriel** *goes on cracking his nuts and, as* **Trajano** *passes him, holds one out, ready peeled.*

Gabriel   Have one?

Trajano *looks him up and down with quite an Olympic disdain.*

Trajano   What is that, pray?

Gabriel   A pine nut.

Trajano (*contemptuously*) A pine nut!

For all his contempt, however, he takes – not the one offered him, but a whole handful that are lying there cracked, and munches them as he talks.

Trajano And how did you come by these, may I ask?

Gabriel Sister Josefita gave them to me.

Trajano The cook! Oh indeed . . . filched them out of our tomorrow's dessert, did she?

Gabriel No, she did not. These are not asylum pine nuts. They are some that were specially given to the Sisters by the Warden . . . God bless him. (*He politely lifts his hat.*)

Trajano (*with ill-concealed envy*) I say, I say . . . is that a new hat you've got?

Gabriel (*with mischievous satisfaction*) Yes indeed . . . it's a new hat. I had it dealt out to me this morning.

Trajano Sister Martina gave it to you, did she?

Gabriel (*delighted that* **Trajano** *is losing his temper*) Yes, Señor . . . Sister Martina.

Trajano That's flat favouritism! There are hats about much worse than your hat was.

Gabriel *smiles even more maliciously, and* **Trajano** *begins to walk up and down again, grumbling to himself.*

Trajano But as long as you can get round the Sisters . . .! Pull . . . that's all it is . . . pull! (*Suddenly stopping in front of* **Gabriel**.) Look here now . . . how do you work it . . . every Sister in the place ready to black your boots for you?

Gabriel (*still highly delighted*) The Sisters do treat me better than I deserve, no doubt . . . because, I should say, they are ladies who know how to value good breeding. And . . . though I say it that shouldn't . . . I have breeding!

Trajano You're a snob . . . that's what you are.

Gabriel Well, I'd sooner be a snob than an anarchist!

Trajano Are you referring to me?

Gabriel If the cap fits you can wear it.

Trajano *again looks him up and down with supreme disdain, and then resumes his pacing, while* **Gabriel** *goes back to cracking his nuts.*

Gabriel Not walking out this afternoon?

Trajano Are you addressing me?

Gabriel (*urbanely*) Yes . . . if I may so far presume.

Trajano (*relaxing a little*) No, Señor . . . I am not going out.

Gabriel   For a very good reason, I'm sure.

Trajano   I have no wish to go out.

Gabriel *laughs slyly.*

Trajano   And what the devil are you grinning at?

Gabriel   Oh . . . I'm staying in just for the same reason.

Trajano *interrogates him with a haughty stare.*

Gabriel   For where can a man go to without a penny in his pocket?

Trajano   Thank you . . . I have all the money I need. And enough to take you with me . . . if I wanted to. Look here!

He takes out his pocket-book, and out of the pocket-book a folded piece of paper, and with great care he produces a silver coin. **Gabriel** *darts up and gazes at the money as if a miracle had just been performed.*

Gabriel   A peseta!

Trajano (*folding it away again as if he feared it might evaporate*)   Yes, Señor . . . and earned by honest toil . . . not by licking people's boots, mark you . . . like some I know.

Gabriel   Licking people's . . .! Do you mean that for me?

Trajano   Aha, my friend . . . if the cap fits you can wear it.

This time **Gabriel** *sits down in a sulk,* **Trajano**, *cheered by his little revenge, starts his pacing again and flourishes out his words like a very Cyrano.*

Trajano   A peseta . . . Yes, Señor Gabriel, (*He pronounces the name with utter contempt.*) yes, indeed . . . a peseta. The Warden gave it me . . . God bless him (*and he takes off his hat in ironic imitation*) for mending a lock for him. I've no need to lower myself to praying to the Saints when I don't believe in them . . . so that the Sisters shall run after me and spoil me. Trajano Fernandez's conscience is not to be bought with a handful of pine nuts. (*Then follows a solemn pause till he says.*) And if I do not walk out this afternoon . . . and it remains to be seen whether I do walk out or not . . . I have not the remotest intention of first asking leave from any lady-bishop alive.

Gabriel   Lady-bishop! My good man . . . when you want to speak of Sister Manuela can't you call her by her proper name as every other well-mannered person does?

He rises, very fussed. But **Trajano** *only laughs.*

Gabriel   Don't laugh . . . don't laugh, please. It makes me very angry.

Trajano   I didn't confer the title on her! The chaplain calls her that . . . and the Warden . . . God bless him. And so do the parish priest and the doctor and all the other sisters. And quite right too . . . for a more dictatorial woman was never born.

Gabriel   And so she should be. What else is she the Superior for?

Trajano But as for yours truly he takes no orders from any Sister of Mercy. Don't the rules lay it down that we have a right to walk out on a Sunday afternoon? Do they or don't they? Well if they do . . . it'll take a ton of pine nuts to make me go asking leave from a lot of petticoats . . . as if I was a schoolboy. Thank you . . . I left school some time ago.

Gabriel (*between his teeth*) Where they didn't teach you manners anyhow!

He begins to pick up the nutshells that **Trajano** *has scattered and puts them with his own into a blue-and-white-checked pocket-handkerchief.*

Trajano What's that you're doing?

Gabriel Picking up the nutshells you threw about. You know well enough that Sister Manuela doesn't like to see rubbish lying around.

Trajano (*grumbling*) There again! Tidy up! I'm fed up with being told to tidy up. Don't throw nutshells about! Don't spit! Wipe your boots before entering a room . . . so that the lady-bishop can show off her nice waxed floors to the visitors. Wash your face once a day . . . and your hands twice a day at least . . . and your feet every Saturday, rain or fine! And as if that weren't enough . . . take a bath every two months! Am I a man or a frog? Water . . . water . . . water! Give me wine. Yes, indeed . . . a glass of wine for dinner . . . that's what we need . . . as I keep on saying. What an idea to put a place like this in the charge of Sisters of Charity! Women do not understand men. Am I right or not?

Gabriel (*sighing in spite of himself*) Well . . . about the water about the water . . . amd about the wine . . . why, yes, I think you are.

At this moment a little burst of women's laughter is heard; and **Sister Gracia** *and* **Sister Juliana** *come along the path at the back carrying between them – and hardly able to carry – an immense basket of potatoes. They are laughing because, as the basket is so full, some of the potatoes keep rolling out on to the ground.* **Sister Gracia** *is a girl of nineteen, pretty, fragile and very gay.* **Sister Juliana** *is about the same age, but commonplace to look at, her face high-coloured. She talks rather affectedly and self-consciously, trying to appear refined.*

Sister Gracia There go some more good potatoes. Ooh . . . this basket's heavier than a mortal sin.

She lets go the handle, but as **Sister Juliana** *keeps hold of hers quantities of potatoes roll out as the basket tips.*

Sister Gracia (*still laughing*) Now we've done it!

Sister Juliana Aie . . .! Sister . . . Sister . . . don't laugh like that. Some one might hear you.

Gabriel *rushes forward to help pick up the potatoes.*

Sister Gracia Thank you, Gabriel.

Gabriel Don't mention it, Señorita.

Sister Gracia Señorita! Why ever must you call me that?

Gabriel Oh, Señorita, I beg your pardon . . . Sister Gracia I meant to say. But I'm so used to think of you as . . . you see. And though you do wear the habit now, I can never forget that you're the Marquis's granddaughter . . . rest his soul.

Sister Gracia I'm nobody's granddaughter here, Gabriel. I'm a Sister of Charity . . . and that's all you need to remember. (*Then to* **Trajano** *who stands by majestically indifferent.*) And you might help too . . . mightn't you?

Sister Juliana He help us! He's an atheist. He'd like to see us all killed and eaten.

Trajano I am not an atheist . . . I want no one killed and eaten. I am a Radical and a Freethinker.

Gabriel (*maliciously*) And a Freemason.

Trajano (*rounding on him*) Yes . . . and a Freemason . . . and proud to be one.

Sister Juliana (*crossing herself in terror*) Ave Maria . . . hold your tongue . . . hold your tongue.

Trajano *turns very oratorical and solemn. He is glad to have shocked her, as he dislikes her extremely.*

Trajano And of the Scottish Rite . . . as is the German Emperor . . . and the King of England . . . and King Victor Emmanuel . . . who in 1870 made Rome the capital of Italy.

Sister Gracia (*rallying him affectionately*) Quite so . . . most suitable company for you, I'm sure.

Trajano (*gallantly*) And I was in your father's company too.

Sister Juliana Holy Virgin!

Trajano (*rounding on her*) Yes, Señora . . . in the company of Lorenzo Benevidez . . . an honoured tribune of the people . . . and a spiritual heir of that great republic that said to the black slave, 'Arise, be free . . . you also are a man.'

Sister Gracia (*a little sadly*) Quite so, quite so . . . that'll do.

Trajano But what is there to sigh about in that? Your father and those like him . . . though indeed there aren't many like him . . . are the only hope of Spain. And thanks to them there shall one day be no more social injustice. But rich and poor will feast together . . .

Sister Juliana And there'll be lots of wine on the table.

Trajano (*turning on her viperously*) A little more than we get here . . . yes, let's hope so. (*Then to* **Sister Gracia** *again.*) No more privileged classes . . . no aristocrats . . . no convents.

He begins to get excited, and **Sister Gracia**, *to quiet him, says pleasantly and gaily.*

Sister Gracia Well, I daresay not . . . but you needn't choke over it. And if you'll pick up some of these potatoes God will reward you for that.

Trajano (*as he stoops with some difficulty*) I pick up these potatoes for your father's daughter. But . . . (*The blood is rushing to his head.*) for all that, a day will come . . . a day will come . . .

Sister Gracia When you and your King of England will cut off our heads . . . we're quite aware of that. Yes, you'll cut off our heads and then we shall go straight to heaven . . . and be very glad to get there. And once we're there we shall pray to God for you and get you to glory in spite of yourselves. And with that beard and bald head of yours they may even mistake you for St Peter . . . who knows! (*Then as she takes the potatoes.*) Many thanks.

Trajano (*wheezing and coughing*) The . . . Social . . . Revolution . . . will come . . .

He sinks on a bench, half choking with asthma. **Sister Gracia** *goes to him and wipes the sweat from his forehead.*

Sister Gracia Come now . . . here's a Marquis's granddaughter wiping your forehead for you. How much further can your Social Revolution take you?

Sister Juliana *and* **Gabriel** *are putting the last potatoes in the basket. She looks up suddenly and then says.*

Sister Juliana Sister Manuela!

Trajano (*trying to struggle to his feet and like a scared schoolboy*) The lady-bishop!

Sister Gracia *rests her hand on his shoulder to quiet him as* **Sister Manuela** *comes majestically down the marble steps. She is a woman of fifty, energetic, a little harsh of speech but good at heart. She wears spectacles.*

Sister Manuela (*to the two girls*) What are you doing here?

Sister Juliana Picking up the potatoes . . . the basket upset.

Sister Manuela Couldn't the gardener have carried it for you?

Sister Gracia Well . . . it's Sunday you see . . . and he was in such a hurry to get down to the village. There's a dance on and his sweetheart was waiting for him. So we told him . . . begging your pardon . . . that we could manage it ourselves quite well.

Sister Manuela Well . . . don't let it happen again. You know that I don't like the Sisters to carry such heavy loads. We all have our appointed tasks . . . and God keeps us from failing in those.

Sister Gracia Yes, Reverend Mother.

Sister Manuela (*to the two old men*) You two can carry it to the kitchen. A little exercise won't do you any harm.

Trajano *and* **Gabriel** *lay hold of the basket, and* **Sister Manuela** *is passing on when* **Sister Gracia** *detains her by saying*:

Sister Gracia Reverend Mother.

Sister Manuela   What is it?

Sister Gracia   May I ask a favour? Will you give Trajano leave to go into town? This is the day for it.

Sister Manuela   Why doesn't he ask me himself?

Sister Gracia (*glancing at* **Trajano** *out of the corner of her eye*)   He doesn't like to.

Sister Manuela (*assuming a tone of great severity*)   Because . . . I suppose . . . the last time he went he came home drunk.

Trajano (*feebly protesting*)   Not drunk, Señora . . . no, not really drunk.

Sister Manuela   As drunk as an owl. Have you forgotten, pray, that you tried to proclaim a Spanish Republic in the middle of supper?

Sister Gracia   But he won't get drunk today. I'll answer for him. (*To* **Trajano**.) That's so, isn't it? If you may go out you won't touch one drop . . . now will you?

Trajano *gestures his promise by kissing his crossed fingers, and with mock solemnity she copies him.*

Sister Gracia   There . . . the daughter of the tribune of the people has gone bail for you.

Sister Manuela   Well . . . I haven't much confidence in him. However, he can go out if he likes. What I do not like, though, is his going alone.

Gabriel (*quickly*)   If the Reverend Mother would graciously permit me I should be most happy to accompany him.

Trajano (*only half to himself*)   Parasite!

Sister Manuela (*looking at* **Gabriel**)   And I haven't much faith in him either. However . . . be off, both of you. You must be back before dark . . . remember that. (*She looks* **Trajano** *up and down and he trembles under her eye.*) And perhaps you'd oblige me by making yourself look a little respectable before you go. You're a disgrace to the institution. (**Trajano** *surveys himself, puzzled and confused.*) How long since you washed your beard? There are wild beasts in that jungle I expect. My fault! I should have made you shave like the rest.

Trajano (*much offended*)   Let me assure you, Señora, that this venerable beard has never harboured . . .

Sister Manuela   You put it in the basin next time and soap it well. And now . . . take that away (*the potato basket*) at once.

Trajano *and* **Gabriel** *go out carrying the basket between them,* **Trajano** *saying between his teeth* . . .

Trajano   Before they made her a lady-bishop she must have been Grand Inquisitor of Spain . . . !

Sister Gracia   Thank you, oh, thank you, Reverend Mother . . . and God reward you.

Sister Manuela   He'll come back as he always does . . . and you'll be to blame. Well, that'll teach you not to be so soft-hearted. (**Sister Gracia** *looks abashed at this.*) Cheer up . . . there are visitors coming for you.

Sister Gracia   For me?

Sister Manuela   Your family telephoned they'd be here this afternoon . . . and quite soon. You can receive them in the garden here, if you like.

Sister Gracia   Yes . . . thank you, Reverend Mother.

Sister Manuela *now passes on and away.* **Sister Gracia** *sits on one of the benches, and after a moment sighs pensively.*

Sister Gracia   . . . coming to see me!

Sister Juliana (*rather officiously*)   Well, aren't you glad?

Sister Gracia   Oh yes . . . of course . . . I shall be glad to see them . . . very glad. Though Mother will give me a bad ten minutes as usual. She can't make up her mind to my being here. (*Then with an almost childish vexation.*) Well, no more can anyone else for that matter. No one will believe that I have a vocation. Good heavens . . . why ever shouldn't I have! I know I'm not a saint. But . . . (*Very simply.*) God makes his choice from among us as he thinks best, after all. Besides we needn't wait for God to call us, need we? If we call to him, he'll answer . . . even though in ourselves we're of no account. That is so, don't you think? (*She gets up from the bench and passes her hands across her face as if to brush away the shadow of melancholy.*) Well, well . . . we can all feel certain of ourselves if we want to . . . and if we don't, so much the worse for us.

Sister Juliana (*looking at her as if hypnotised*)   Of course . . .

Sister Gracia   Why are you looking at me like that? (*She looks down as if something might be wrong with her dress.*)

Sister Juliana   What a wonderful complexion you have! (*She goes up to* **Sister Gracia** *and takes her hand.*) What do Society ladies use to get themselves a skin like that?

Sister Gracia (*drawing her hand away*)   Soap and water . . . just what we have here.

Sister Juliana   Nothing else?

Sister Gracia (*a little amused at the other's passionate curiosity*)   Well . . . it was all I was ever given.

Sister Juliana (*still more eagerly*)   I say . . . was your grandfather a Marquis?

Sister Gracia   Yes, he was.

Sister Juliana   And your father's a most important person in Parliament?

Sister Gracia   Well, yes . . . he's one of the people who make most noise there.

Sister Juliana   I say . . . (*Whenever she uses this phrase she half chokes with eagerness.*) Did you ever see the King?

Sister Gracia   Yes . . . often.

Sister Juliana   Close to?

Sister Gracia   Quite close. About a fortnight before I came here on probation I was dancing with him.

Sister Juliana (*her eyes starting from her head*)   Dancing with him!

Sister Gracia (*quite simply*)   Yes . . . at a fête some San Sebastian ladies gave for the shipwrecked seamen.

Sister Juliana *is torn between her fear of discussing something she thinks sinful and her desire to know it at all hazards.*

Sister Juliana   Was it . . . fun?

Sister Gracia   For the King?

Sister Juliana   For you.

Sister Gracia   For me! Oh . . . when I hear the hand organ that stops outside the gate every morning . . . if you only knew how hard it is to stop myself taking a turn round the room with the nearest chair!

Sister Juliana (*professionally scandalised*)   Mother of God . . . don't say that. (*But after a moment, more curious than ever.*) And at the . . . at that ball . . . did you wear a dress with a train to it?

Sister Gracia   No . . . they're not in fashion.

Sister Juliana (*with such an effort; as if she were hauling a bucket out of a well*)   But . . . your dress was cut low, wasn't it?

Sister Gracia   Just a little . . . down to here . . . that's all.

Sister Juliana (*crossing herself*)   Blessed Jesus . . . weren't you ashamed? I say . . . did you put rouge on?

Sister Gracia   Why on earth should I?

Sister Juliana (*lowering her eyes hypocritically*)   They say all Society ladies do.

Sister Gracia   Well, if they think they look too pale I daresay they do.

Sister Juliana   I say . . . and have you ever been to a theatre?

Sister Gracia   Well, of course.

Sister Juliana   Yes, of course . . . when you were in the world you did as they all do. (*Then she asks, very fearfully, so monstrous does it seem.*) And you've read novels?

Sister Gracia (*a little impatient at last*)   Well . . . haven't you?

Sister Juliana (*scandalised*)   I? Why, you know I was an orphan and brought up in a convent . . . so I never had a chance. (*Then, her conscience pricking her for the lie.*) That's to say . . . once, a long time ago, I did read one. Another girl brought it in, hidden in her dress and lent it us. (*Prudishly, but still with a little pleasure remaining.*) Blessed Jesus . . . I wish I could forget about it. 'Claudine's Adventures in Paris' it was called.

Sister Gracia *goes off into peals of laughter, much to the other's annoyance.*

Sister Juliana   What are you laughing at? Have you never read that?

Sister Gracia   The girls I was brought up amongst didn't read books of that sort.

She laughs still, and **Sister Juliana** *gets up most offended.*

Sister Juliana   Sister . . . you upset me exceedingly by laughing like that.

And she goes towards the house with much dignity.

Sister Gracia   Oh, don't be angry . . . please. I didn't mean to offend you . . . Sister Juliana . . . listen!

But **Sister Juliana** *has vanished.* **Sister Gracia** *is on the point of following her, when she meets* **Trajano** *and* **Gabriel** *coming out arm in arm.*

Gabriel (*very gallant*)   Any commissions to execute in town for the most beautiful of Sisters?

Sister Gracia   Nothing, thank you. Have a good time and don't waste your money.

Gabriel (*with an insinuating laugh*)   No affair of mine! Señor Trajano is the capitalist today.

Trajano *is in a very bad humour because of the company that has been forced on him.*

Trajano   I shall spend my money if I want to . . . but I shall spend it on myself!

Gabriel (*magnanimously*)   Man alive . . . who wants your money?

The bell at the front gate is heard ringing.

Gabriel   Some one at the gate. Visitors.

Don Lorenzo's *voice is heard saying,* 'Don't trouble yourself, Sister, please. We know the way.'

Sister Gracia (*with suppressed joy*)   Father!

Don Lorenzo, María Isabel *and* **Lulu** *come along the path.* **Sister Gracia** *unrestrainedly throws her arms round her father's neck, and then kisses her mother and sister.*

Sister Gracia   Father . . . Father, how good to see you! Dear Mother! Lulu!

Trajano   Lorenzo Benevidez . . . friend of the People. (*He goes up and takes off his hat in fine style.*) I salute the Tribune.

Trajano, *having accomplished this, goes his way with great dignity.* **Lorenzo** *is a little surprised, but most amiably returns the salute.*

Lorenzo   Good afternoon.

Sister Gracia (*to her mother*)   How warm you look. (*Then to* **Lulu**.) So do you. Sit down . . . it's shady here.

María Isabel (*as she sits, fanning herself*)   Oh, my dear child . . . the heat . . . and the dust! And the road . . . seven times at least I thought the car had broken in two. It shows how much we must want to see you . . . when we take such a terrible journey.

Sister Gracia   But if you've a saint in the family you must expect to make these hard pilgrimages. But it's so good to see you.

María Isabel   Oh . . . much you care whether we come or not.

Sister Gracia   Don't say that, Mother, please.

María Isabel   Mother! Don't call me Mother. Call me Mamma as you did at home.

Sister Gracia   Yes, Mamma, I will.

She is sitting by her mother, gentle, affectionate.

María Isabel   Oh . . . your hands! What makes your fingers like that?

Sister Gracia   Peeling potatoes.

María Isabel   You have been peeling potatoes!

Sister Gracia   Why, of course. You see, when it's my week in the kitchen . . .

María Isabel   No, please . . . I don't want to hear about it.

Trajano *has departed, but* **Gabriel** *lingers, surveying the group; and now he approaches* **María Isabel**, *with great elegance of deportment.*

Gabriel   Will you allow me to wish you a good afternoon, Señorita María Isabel?

María Isabel (*blankly*)   Good afternoon.

Sister Gracia   Don't you recognise him? It's Gabriel.

Gabriel   Gabriel, Señorita . . . valet to the late Marquis . . . now in glory, and God rest his soul! Doesn't the Señorita remember me? I'm not so young as I was, of course, and . . . (*He looks himself up and down with a little laugh.*) the livery here isn't quite so fine as the Marquis's . . . now in glory. Not that I want to grumble . . . no indeed, one might be much worse off.

While **Gabriel** *stands talking to* **María Isabel**, **Sister Gracia** *goes to her father who is pacing up and down, silently slips her hand in his and walks with him, as if she were a little girl. He is moved by this, holds her hand very tight, looks down at her tenderly. But he is silent too.*

María Isabel   Yes, indeed you might. You have a palace to live in, and a garden that a millionaire might envy you. What things are coming to, I don't know. An almshouse! Think of all the money that was spent on this place . . . the famous parties they gave here, when I was a girl . . . everybody used to talk about them.

Gabriel Yes . . . even from the pulpit. The Duke of Torre Blanca's palace . . . these high places of our Modern Babylon . . . that's what his Grace the Archbishop said.

María Isabel If these trees could speak!

Gabriel (*chuckling*) They'd have some pretty stories to tell! Look here, Señorita . . . this arbour used to be called the Bower of Venus. And it had a statue in it which his Grace the Duke had brought from Italy . . . a very female statue . . . the Señorita will understand me. And now, you see, the Sisters have put the blessed Saint Cayetano there instead . . . our mediator in heaven. (*He chuckles again.*) But the ghosts that come walking back here must give him some very queer nights of it. Oh, but all the best gentlemen of Madrid used to come here . . .

María Isabel And the worst women!

Gabriel Well . . . God created the one lot to balance the other, I suppose. And a fine lot they were, I tell you . . . worth staring at. They made the house what it was . . . and what it is. (*He grows confidential and important.*) For when his Grace the Duke went and died . . . his Grace, now in glory . . . probably . . . oh, they say they're not very hard on you up there when it has only been petticoats . . . when his Grace the Duke died here . . . for it was here he came back to die after trapesing all over the world . . . he'd hardly drawn his last breath when his two latest lady friends . . . one was fair and one was dark, and a pretty picture they made, I can tell you . . . they started to fill all the baskets and trunks in the place with whatever they could lay their hands on . . . clothes, pictures, mirrors, books, china . . . why, they took the very quilt off the poor gentleman's bed, a satin quilt it was, as thick as that, and embroidered in colours with history-pictures two hundred years old! They didn't let the grass grow under their feet . . . the baggages. Why, it was like the day of judgment. And I saw it. For I'd been sent to enquire after the sick man by the Marquis . . . now in glory . . . and he was just at his last gasp when I got here . . . and there was the undertaker driving up at one door and the wagon full of things . . . piled high with them . . . driving off from the other. If they left the walls standing it was only that they shouldn't dirty their pretty hands with the bricks and mortar.

Sister Gracia (*from her father's side*) Gabriel . . . you'll lose Trajano.

Gabriel Quite right, Señorita . . . and I won't trouble the Señorita María Isabel any longer . . . and I hope she'll forgive me having taken the liberty. . . .

María Isabel Not at all . . . I'm glad to see that you're so happy here.

Sister Gracia (*quietly to her father – more a gesture than a sentence*) Give him something.

Gabriel A very good afternoon to you, Don Lorenzo.

Lorenzo God be with you.

He gives him a coin. **Gabriel** *protests as he takes it.*

Gabriel No, no . . . I couldn't think of it . . . I really couldn't. There's nothing that we want here . . . thank you, thank you! (*He glances furtively at the coin, and is overwhelmed.*) Two pesetas . . . oh, a thousand thanks!

Sister Gracia   Run along now . . . run along.

Gabriel *disappears, contemplating the coin and murmuring ecstatically, 'Two pesetas!'* **María Isabel** *remains seated on the bench, musing over what she has just heard.* **Lulu** *gets up and goes to peep through the foliage into the arbour.* **Sister Gracia** *still holds her father's hand.*

Sister Gracia   How silent you are, Father. Talk to me a little.

Lorenzo   What about?

Sister Gracia   About yourself. What are you busy at now?

Lorenzo   The usual things. I'm rather pressed with . . . lots of things to think about . . . and getting to feel rather old.

Sister Gracia   Old . . . you! Since when, pray?

Lorenzo   Ever since a certain little witch gave up coming into my study and untidying my papers for me. (*His voice turns a little husky, but he keeps it firm.*) There's a vacant place there, young lady.

Sister Gracia   Ah . . . don't say that to me . . . don't say that.

Lorenzo (*smiling again*)   There, there, never mind! When I'm quite decrepit I'll petition the authorities to admit me here . . . and then you will look after me, won't you?

She doesn't answer; just kisses his hand. There are tears in his eyes.

Lorenzo   As long as you're content . . . that's all that matters.

Sister Gracia   I am, Father . . . indeed I am.

Lorenzo   Truly?

She lifts her face like a child, so that he may see she is not lying, and he looks her in the eyes.

Sister Gracia   Yes, look at me . . . truly, truly. And more than content today . . . because you've come to see me.

Without answering he rests his hand affectionately on her shoulder. **María Isabel** *surveys her husband and her daughter with a mixture of envy and commiseration.* **Lulu**, *who has gone into the arbour, now gives a sudden cry, and rushes out again. They all turn to her.*

María Isabel   What is it . . . what has happened?

Lulu   There . . . in the arbour . . . a man . . . or an animal . . . I don't know. But with eyes all burning . . . and it growled.

Sister Gracia   Don't be frightened. (*She goes and looks into the arbour.*) Oh, poor thing . . . it's Liborio. (*She calls gently.*) Come here. What are you doing in the arbour? Come out now . . . come out.

She pulls out a decrepit, pitiful, huddled up, trembling old man, and draws him to a bench, talking the while.

Sister Gracia This is the unluckiest of them all, poor fellow. He's . . . not quite right (*She taps her forehead.*) . . . but he's harmless.

María Isabel *surveys the old thing with horror, and* **Lulu** *with disgust,* **Lorenzo** *with some interest.*

Sister Gracia (*speaking as to a child*) Look . . . you've frightened this lady. There now . . . take off your hat to her.

Liborio Liborio . . . not take off his hat . . . nobody loves him here . . . this not his country.

Sister Gracia Yes it is . . . oh yes, it is.

Liborio (*getting a little excited*) No . . . oh no . . . not his country. His country lost . . . Cuba was lost. (*To* **Lorenzo**.) That true, Señor? . . . yes . . . Cuba lost. (*Very mournfully.*) Liborio born in Cuba . . . no Cuba . . . so can't go back . . . no doubt of that . . . is there, Señor? (*Then a strange tone comes into his voice.*) No . . . not lost . . . the sea swallowed Cuba. But where's the sea . . . there's no sea either . . . no sea here. Only roads . . . roads . . . and Liborio walks . . . walks . . . walks. Oh, where is the sea? No sea . . . no sea. But policemen . . . and they beat you . . . and it's so cold . . . it's always cold here (*He is almost crying.*) . . . Liborio's cold.

Sister Gracia (*putting her arm round his shoulders as if really to warm him*) No, no, you're not cold . . . that's all imagination. There . . . sit down now . . . and don't shake so. (*Then, over her shoulder, to her father.*) Give me a cigar.

Lorenzo *takes out a cigar.*

Sister Gracia Look, Liborio . . . just look what this gentleman is giving us.

Liborio (*his eye kindling a little*) A cigar . . . a cigar!

Sister Gracia (*as pleased as he*) Yes, a cigar . . . and look at the band on it . . . that says it's from your country . . . from Cuba.

Liborio What – what then . . . Cuba not lost?

Sister Gracia Why no . . . how can it be lost? Now off with you and light it . . . and see how warm the smoke will make you.

Liborio (*like a child*) Yes . . . yes.

Sister Gracia And then go to the kitchen . . . and tell Sister Juliana that I said she was to give you a cup of hot coffee.

Liborio Coffee!

Sister Gracia Yes . . . black coffee . . . as black as you are. Come along . . . I'll take you as far as the door, so that you shan't lose yourself. (*To her family.*) I'll be back in a minute. Come along.

She takes the old man out through the little doorway that leads to the kitchens.

María Isabel   What a horrible man . . . he must have the palsy . . . it gives one the creeps to look at him.

Lulu   And he smelt! How can she go near him!

María Isabel   The girl's stark mad. Lorenzo, we must get her away from here at all costs.

Sister Gracia *comes back and goes straight to her father. She is still full of her care for the poor creature.*

Sister Gracia   Look here, Father . . . you're going to send me some cheap cigars . . . some of those confiscated smuggled ones they sell off . . . and you're to keep all the bands from your Havanas, so that I can put them on the others . . . and then the poor thing can imagine. . . .

María Isabel (*suddenly breaking out*)   What your father will do if he has one ounce of common sense . . . for you haven't . . . is to take you home with him this very minute.

Sister Gracia (*startled and grieved*)   Mother!

María Isabel   My dear child . . . this has been a very pretty whim . . . but it has lasted long enough. Three months in a hospital dressing people's sores and laying them out when they were dead. Six months a probationer . . . making yourself look such a fright with that thing on your head. And now here . . . among these disgusting old men . . . why, they may be lepers! No . . . no more of it . . . Home you come with us this very minute.

Sister Gracia (*her eyes cast down . . . but her voice firm*)   No . . . I can't do that, Mother.

María Isabel   Why can't you, pray?

Sister Gracia   I have taken a vow.

María Isabel   Oh yes . . . for a year.

Sister Gracia   In my heart . . . I took it for all my life.

María Isabel   Don't talk nonsense.

Sister Gracia   It's not nonsense, Mother.

María Isabel   It is ridiculous affectation. You're a spoiled child . . . you've always been given your own way. And now you want to play at being a nun . . . just as you used to play sweethearts.

Sister Gracia   Mother!

María Isabel   But please remember, my dear, that you're not of age yet. Your father can have something to say to this.

Sister Gracia   Father gave his consent.

María Isabel   He did not . . . and you know that perfectly well. He let you go and said nothing about it . . . which is not the same thing at all. You took very good care to leave the house when he wasn't there. And why? Because you were afraid he'd stop you.

Sister Gracia   That wasn't the reason.

María Isabel   Wasn't it? Then perhaps it was because you hadn't the courage to say goodbye to him. Well . . . answer me.

Sister Gracia   Yes, that was why.

María Isabel   Oh, you never found it very hard to get round people. (*Then to her husband.*) Well, here's your spoilt baby . . . Papa's darling . . . always in his pocket . . . crying if her dear father left home without saying goodbye to her . . . couldn't go to sleep at night unless he came in to kiss her . . . was to grow up to be the comfort of his old age. Well, here you have it . . . the comfort and happiness she promised you. And because she calls her conduct by a fine-sounding name . . .

Sister Gracia   But, Mother, I've done nothing wrong.

María Isabel (*with a final fling of sorrowful wrath*)   And this is what children are given us for!

Lorenzo (*quietly intervening*)   María Isabel . . . children are not an idle gift.

María Isabel   What do you mean?

Lorenzo   I mean that they are not our own just to do as we like with.

María Isabel   So like a man! Easy to see that you don't suffer to bring them into the world.

Lorenzo (*gravely*)   We sweat blood though, sometimes, to keep them alive in it. But we owe them more than that. Did we so deliberately plan to bring them into the world? They are ours through our frailty.

María Isabel   Frailty!

Lorenzo   What else? And if they are the fruit of our happiness what right have we to deny them their own . . . unless they seek it in evil ways?

María Isabel   And you believe she'll find happiness here?

Lorenzo   She has made herself believe so. What then can I say?

Sister Gracia   But I haven't *made* myself believe it, Father . . . I haven't indeed.

María Isabel   Petted and brought up in luxury as she has been!

Lorenzo   You were brought up in just such luxury. You were rich and came of a great family and you were nineteen as she is now. Every sort of pleasure was yours for the asking, and life promised you very many of them. Then you met me . . . a good for nothing, a firebrand . . . so your family told you. And certainly I was a nobody. But you gave up everything to endure privations and persecutions and suffering by my side. Isabel, have you forgotten the courage with which you faced it all . . . just for the sake of the love that we so believed in? Our first child was born in an attic . . . that's twenty-five years ago. Have you forgotten? I've not forgotten my debt to you. (*He kisses her hand.*) Ah, my dear . . . don't give your own nature the lie when you see it again in your daugher.

María Isabel What I did, I did because I loved you. That was very different.

Sister Gracia Mother . . . I do this for love.

María Isabel (*recovering her ill-temper*) Love . . . who for? God! D'you imagine you're Saint Teresa?

Sister Gracia No, Mother . . . I don't imagine any such thing. I know that I'm nobody. But then you don't need to be anybody here . . . for we're all nobodies together. Here, you see, we gather in people that the world has no more use for . . . no one loves them or wants them . . . they've nowhere to go . . . the poor, the sick, the homeless. Well, then, one needs to be a nobody to be of any use to them . . . it's so much better to be a nobody . . . for the less you count in the world yourself . . . the closer you come to them.

María Isabel You need not live among poor people in order to help them.

Sister Gracia Oh yes, Mother . . . oh yes, you must.

María Isabel Not at all. You can be charitable . . . you can give alms.

Sister Gracia (*quite carried away now*) Give alms! No . . . no . . . oh, no! Where's the good in giving away a little of what you have too much of . . . and keeping the rest . . . and not caring . . . spending money amusing oneself . . . while they have so much to endure . . . and you do nothing for them, nothing at all. Because giving alms is nothing . . . oh, I don't mean one shouldn't give alms. But no . . . (*To her father.*) oh, isn't this true . . . for you've said so a thousand times . . . that one must give one's life, one's whole life . . . to the last breath and the last drop of blood, if one wants to atone for the wickedness of the world. For misery is wickedness and want is a crime . . . because God gave his world to us all alike . . . and our daily bread. And if his children starve and are homeless . . . that's a crime, yes, a crime. And the man who keeps more than he needs robs the man who's in need. Turn away your eyes when your brother is dying . . . and you're an accomplice in his death. Oh, Father, Father . . . when I've heard you speak . . . if only I could have been a man, a man like you . . . to speak like that so that people must hear me . . . and plead the cause of the oppressed, stand up for them, make laws that will help them! But of course I'm only an ignorant girl. What can I do? I might stand and shout for ever, and no one would listen. I'm no use. I'm nobody. I've nothing to give but my happiness . . . so I want to give that, you see, to those that have none.

Lorenzo My dear . . . my dear . . .

Sister Gracia Because no one seems to think of giving that. Food, oh yes . . . but happiness! Why, if it's only to amuse them a little . . . to joke with them . . . and then to make believe, so that just for a little they *may* believe that there's still something left for them to hope for . . . that they still count for something in the world . . . that they're human beings still. That's what matters, isn't it, Father?

Lorenzo   Yes, you're right. That's to say. . . . Ah yes, my dear . . . believing as you do you are right to be doing what you do.

María Isabel   And you say that, do you . . . when you believe in nothing at all.

Lorenzo   I may not . . . but then she does.

María Isabel (*to* **Sister Gracia**)   You show great consideration . . . for everybody but us.

Sister Gracia   But you don't need me.

María Isabel   And to think that when you were so high . . . how I cried and cried when they said you might die of diphtheria . . . and I took a vow to wear a penitent's dress for a year . . . and I cut off all my hair that your father was so fond of . . . and now . . . this is what happens. (*She begins to cry.*) One never does know what one is really asking God to grant.

Sister Gracia (*putting her arms round her mother, but smiling in spite of herself*)   Oh, Mamma, don't say that . . . just because I'm still alive.

Lulu, *when this discussion began, had moved away to a further bench and begun to read a letter she took from her bag. She puts it away now, and rejoins the group.*

Lulu   Well . . . is the storm over? (*To* **Sister Gracia**.) Oh, my dear . . . mothers are very hard things to understand, aren't they? She's angry with you because you want to be a nun . . . and just as angry with me because I want to get married. (*Then with juvenile superiority.*) The fact is, I suppose, that if older people couldn't amuse themselves by upsetting themselves about nothing, they'd be bored to death . . . poor things!

María Isabel   What's that you say?

Lulu (*with her soubrettish air*)   Oh . . . each time of life has its own sort of trouble. Young people are desperate because old people won't let them have their own way, and the old people are furious because the young ones won't do what they think right. So nobody's content.

María Isabel   What has come over these girls . . . (*To her husband.*) And you listen to this so calmly. . . .

Lulu   Papa always listens calmly when one's in the right.

Lorenzo   But even if you're in the right you could put it more prettily.

Sister Manuela *comes back along the path.*

Sister Gracia   The Superior, Mother.

Sister Manuela   Good afternoon.

She looks at everybody and can tell well enough what has been going on. One should note that Sisters of Charity in Spain do not shake hands with men, though they may embrace their fathers and mothers.

Lorenzo Good afternoon, Señora.

María Isabel Good afternoon.

She rises, still a little disturbed. **Lulu** *salutes* **Sister Manuela** *who acknowledges it. The sun has now set and it begins to grow dark.*

Sister Gracia My mother . . . my father . . . my sister.

Sister Manuela So pleased. Well . . . at last you have made up your minds to come. Sister Gracia must be delighted . . . she has been longing to see you. So have we. She has been with us five weeks now . . . and though you're so near you've not been to visit her . . .

María Isabel (*a little aggressively*) You can understand, I think, that it isn't very pleasant for a father and mother to come only to make up their minds to their daughter burying herself alive in such a depressing place as this.

Sister Gracia Mamma!

Sister Manuela (*with a touch of irony*) Oh, it isn't so bad. We have our small share of the pleasures of life too. Blue sky . . . fresh air . . . sunshine . . . and if you listen you can hear the birds singing quite contentedly before going to bed.

Lulu It is a beautiful garden.

Sister Manuela Do you think so? Would you like, perhaps, to follow your sister's example . . . and come to us too?

María Isabel No, no . . . for heaven's sake! One crack-brain in the family is enough. Our only hope is that this one will recover her senses and come home again.

Sister Manuela Well . . . she always can, of course. Our order takes no perpetual vows. Our sainted founder thought well to account for the weakness of human will. If any one of us finds her chain too heavy she can break it whenever she likes.

Lorenzo (*smiling*) Yes . . . it's an ideal union, no doubt. A heavenly marriage . . . with divorce at the discretion of one of the parties.

Sister Manuela (*taking this quite well*) Oh really, really! But if you knew how very seldom anyone wants to leave us. . . .

Lorenzo Why, of course . . . easy divorce makes marriage lasting.

Sister Manuela Ah . . . don't talk like that, please. But do sit down.

María Isabel No, thank you . . . we must be going. And I'm sure you've lots to do . . . both of you.

Sister Manuela As it's Sunday the dinner bell won't ring till half past five. And Sister Gracia's on duty . . . so she has to wait in the garden till all the old men that have been out for their walk are safely back again. You can quite well keep her company here if you like.

María Isabel No . . . no, thank you . . . we really must go.

Act One   43

Sister Manuela   Well, come this way. We'll go through the greenhouse and I'll ask them to pick you a bunch of flowers. Sister Gracia always tells us how fond her mother is of flowers. So am I. That's a worldly failing I brought here with me twenty years ago . . . unconquered still.

The **Mother Superior** *goes on with* **Lorenzo** *and* **María Isabel**. **Sister Gracia** *and* **Lulu** *follow them. Just as they disappear* **Sister Juliana** *can be seen at the little kitchen door looking after them curiously. She has a kitchen apron over her habit, a knife and a loaf in her hands, for she is slicing the bread for supper.*

Sister Juliana   Oh . . . how pretty they look. And what hats!

She sighs and goes back to the kitchen. The dusk is deepening now. After a moment three old men pass along on their way in. The first, leaning heavily on his stick, does not stop. The second pauses at each bench he comes to, and sits down, wiping it first very carefully with his handkerchief. The third stops at every other step, gesticulating, talking to himself as if he were addressing someone else. First he argues, hotly, wrathfully. Then he looks at his supposed adversary with pitying condescension and assents ironically to what the fellow has been saying, as if he were humouring a madman. Finally he takes off his hat and bows, as if to let him pass. And then when the phantom has turned his back, he laughs, shrugs, watches him disappear and then goes on his own way with the greatest complacency. Then a Sister of Charity passes with some flowers in her hand. And then **Liborio** *comes from the kitchens, with his cigar still in his hand, and singing in great content . . .*

Liborio   Far off I see the Cuban mountains . . .

The bell calling the Sisters to their refectory begins to ring.

Liborio   Bell! Sisters now going to supper. Sunday! Chicken! Chicken and ham! Let them have chicken and let them have ham. Good women . . . give me coffee . . . and tobacco. (*He kisses the cigar.*) Aha . . . brown darling . . . brown darling . . . I kiss you because you were born . . . so happy . . . over there.

He goes on his way. The horn of a motor car is heard; and then **Sister Gracia** *comes back looking anxiously about.*

Sister Gracia   Oh . . . it's nearly dark . . . and those two are not back. (*Calling.*) Trajano! Gabriel!

Trajano's *voice is now heard, for he is singing at the top of it. After a moment he appears. He is a little drunk and in high good fellowship with* **Gabriel**, *who is very cheery and a little drunk too, and has his arm protectingly round* **Trajano**'s *shoulder.*

Trajano (*trolling it out*)

   Democracy's bright sword shall shine,
   Its dauntless trumpet blow;
   The blood of noble and of priest . . .

Sister Gracia   What's that you're singing?

Trajano The throne shall be the first to fall,
  The church the last to end . . .

Gabriel That's right! Hurrah for the Republic! Glory be to the Goddess of Liberty!

Sister Gracia Oh, Trajano! Oh, Gabriel . . .

Trajano That wildest beast of all no more
  The Nation's heart shall rend!

Sister Gracia Well, this time you've surpassed yourself, Trajano! This is how you keep your word to a lady! Drunk again!

Trajano (*with the utmost dignity*) I . . . drunk! Well . . . let me see now, let me see. Are you drunk, Trajano? Speak the truth, now. Yes, Señor Trajano Fernandez is undoubtedly drunk. But he is a free citizen . . . so what has anyone to say to that? And what has the lady-bishop to say to that? Bring her here . . . fetch her right out here . . . the lady-bishop, so that I can drink her health in the name of the most worshipful Republic.

Gabriel In the name of her royal highness the Republic . . .

He laughs foolishly and then pretends to open a carriage door and to bow the lady out.

Will your royal highness the Republic be pleased to step in? If your royal highness will be good enough to give me your card, I will immediately acquaint the Warden . . . whom God preserve.

Trajano I drink to the lady-bishop! Can't you see that I'm drinking to the lady-bishop?

Sister Gracia Oh . . . for God's sake, Trajano . . .

Trajano (*solemnly*) For whose sake? Will you please to remember that my god is not the god of Sinai? No, indeed! (*Then to* **Gabriel**.) Is there a brotherhood of man, or is there not?

Gabriel Brotherhood-a-man? Please to step in, Señor Brotherhood-a-man. If your excellency would be kind enough . . .

Trajano Is there a brotherhood of man or is there not?

Sister Gracia Yes, by all means . . . only do be quiet or I shall get so scolded.

Trajano Oh no . . . I'll not have that. If they attempt to scold you I shall raise an insurrection . . . I say that I will raise an insurrection.

Sister Gracia Yes, yes . . . but quietly.

Trajano I will raise that insurrection because I wish to raise that insurrection . . .

Sister Gracia What you'd better do now at once is to go and put your head under the pump and see if cold water won't sober you. Then no one need find out the state you came back in.

She takes him firmly by the arm and tries to get him away.

Trajano Water . . . cold water! Never! Death rather than submission to tyranny.

Sister Gracia (*trying not to laugh*) Oh dear, oh dear!

Liborio *comes back. He is crying.* **Gabriel** *greets him ceremoniously.*

Gabriel Will your grace the duke kindly step in? If your grace will be kind enough to hand me your card . . .

Sister Gracia Now what's happened to you?

Trajano *looks at* **Liborio** *curiously and slowly goes up to him.*

Liborio Liborio cold . . . Liborio's cold.

Sister Gracia Cold . . . on a beautiful evening like this? Why . . . didn't you smoke the cigar I gave you?

Liborio Liborio not smoke . . . they beat him . . . they steal cigar.

Sister Gracia Stole the cigar . . . who did?

Trajano The government stole it, Señora . . . this damned tax-gathering government stole it. (*To* **Liborio**.) Now, don't you put up with it . . . you rise in rebellion.

Sister Gracia (*to* **Trajano**) Now you be quiet. (*To* **Liborio**.) Who stole it?

Liborio White man . . . Spanish man . . . down in orchard.

Sister Gracia In the orchard! Was it the gardener? The brute! There, don't cry . . . I'll make it all right.

Liborio So Liborio no smoke it . . . Liborio no smoke it.

Sister Gracia But you shall. Tomorrow I'll give you a cigar as big as . . . that.

The three old men are round **Sister Gracia** *looking at her attentively.* **Liborio** *is sitting on a bench and she holds his hand.*

Liborio No tobacco here . . . no tobacco here.

Sister Gracia Never mind then . . . we'll go to your country to find some.

Liborio No, no . . . not my country. Cuba lost . . . Cuba lost.

Sister Gracia Yes, I know it was. But now it has been found again.

Liborio Where?

Sister Gracia *looks round at a loss. Then, with an inspiration, she points to the evening star that is just visible in the sky.*

Sister Gracia There . . . look . . . look at it.

Liborio Where?

Sister Gracia There . . . up there . . . the star. Don't you see how beautiful it is . . . all alone . . . as it used to be on your flag. Look how it shines. There . . . there's your country.

Liborio   The star . . . the star! That Cuba?

Sister Gracia   Yes . . . didn't I tell you it had been found again? So now shall we go there . . . you and I together?

Trajano   And I?

Gabriel   And I?

Sister Gracia   Yes, all four of us. We'll sail away in a boat . . .

Liborio   No sea left now. . . .

Sister Gracia   But what do we want with the sea? We'll sail our boat through the air . . . tonight when the moon rises. So come along now.

Trajano   Yes indeed . . . 'tenshun . . . quick march!

   Democracy's bright sword shall shine
   Its dauntless trumpet . . .

Gabriel *sees* **Sister Manuela** *at one of the windows and whispers in terror.*

Gabriel   The lady-bishop!

Trajano   What?

He is as dumbfounded, and looks round wondering what to do or say. Then a happy thought strikes him and he breaks gently into a different song.

Trajano   Oh . . . bleeding heart of Mary,
   Our succour and . . .

Sister Manuela (*from the window*)   Who's that singing?

The old men now hold their breath in anguish.

Sister Gracia   It's Trajano. He's here with me, Reverend Mother.

Sister Manuela   Is any one missing?

Sister Gracia   No, Reverend Mother . . . they're all back now.

Sister Manuela   Bring them in then, or they'll take cold in this night air.

Sister Gracia   Yes, Reverend Mother.

Sister Manuela *disappears, and the old men breathe again.*

Sister Gracia   Come along now . . . come along.

She goes first with **Liborio**. *The two others follow her.* **Trajano** *singing in a whisper and hushing* **Gabriel**, *apparently under the impression that it is he.*

Trajano

   Democracy's bright sword shall shine . . .
Sh! . . .
   Its dauntless trumpet . . .
Sh! Sh! . . .

Gabriel   The most serene lady-bishop is served.

Sister Gracia   Come along now . . . quietly.

Liborio   The star . . . the star . . . Cuba not lost . . .

Trajano   The blood of nobles and of priests . . .
Sh ! . . .
      Unceasingly shall flow . . .
      The throne shall be . . .
Sh!. . .Sh!. . .

They go out by the little kitchen door. It is now quite dark.

Curtain.

Act Two

A large patio which serves as a place of recreation for the inmates of a maternity home (for women who have 'come to grief'), which has been established in some old noble mansion in the north of Castile.

The patio has thus something of the cloister about it, with its covered corridor, high gallery and great doors that open to the rooms which are now the eating and sleeping rooms of the institution.

The centre of the patio was once a garden, no doubt; now it is nothing but a jungle of uncared-for shrubs, lilies, celandine, hawthorn and a tree or two, a walnut, a chestnut tree. On one side there is a well with its bucket and wheel and a stone trough that serves for a washing place. It is springtime, and some of the shrubs are in flower. On their branches, though, hang sets of babies' clothing, aprons and handkerchiefs.

Candelas, **Cecilia** *and the* **Dumb Girl** *are in the patio.* **Candelas** *is a swarthy young woman, with a bit of the devil about her. She has fine black-green eyes, and looks serpentlike when she moves about. She is poorly dressed, in a calico skirt which has been much turned, a blouse and a knitted handkerchief crossed over her breast and tied at the back. Her voice is harsh. She has put a flower in her hair. Her sleeves are turned up over her brown arms while she washes some handkerchiefs in the trough. And she sings . . .*

Candelas   Aie!

> I asked a sick man the complaint
> Of which he was to die;
> 'Of loving you . . . of loving you,'
> The sick man made reply.

Cecilia *wearily lets fall the stocking she is knitting.*

Cecilia   Aie!

Candelas   And what's the matter with you?

Cecilia   Nothing, I know that song.

Candelas   Well . . . singing scares away your troubles.

Cecilia   That depends on what they are.

Candelas (*mockingly*)   Oh, Holy Mother . . . depends on what they are, does it? What *are* your troubles, I should like to know? You fell in love and you had a baby. Well . . . what else are women for? Then he deserted you and they took you in here out of charity . . . and your character's gone . . . but that had gone a bit earlier, hadn't it? What you've got to do, my girl, is to make the best of a bad job . . . there's no help for it now, anyway. Besides . . . things happen because they're meant to . . . and you make them no better by crying about them. The day that your mother bore you your steps in this world were all counted . . . from your first to your last one.

She goes on with her washing . . . vigorously.

Cecilia (*half to herself*)   Oh . . . if I'd known how it was all going to end . . .

Candelas   Yes, my girl . . . it's all been settled beforehand, every bit of it . . . and you've only to wait for it to come to pass. And nothing happens to anyone that hasn't happened sometime to someone else. I tell you this world's like a road with a lot of inns along it . . . and if you're not cheated in one of them, why, you will be in another . . . and whichever one of them it is, someone's always been cheated there before you. But I know . . . once you're all dressed up and ready to start you think you know everything . . . and nobody can advise you!

She keeps at her washing more furiously than ever and begins her song again. **Sister Cristina**, *a Sister of Charity, aged about forty-five, comes into the patio. She is the head of the home, and is a sympathetic, well-bred woman, with an unaffected motherly dignity about her. But she thinks of the women under her charge as lost souls, for all that she pities them, as a woman may who knows what life is.*

The great door by which she enters the patio has written over it in black letters the word 'Lactantia'. She unlocks and locks it again with the large key which is hung with the rosary at her belt. She crosses the patio slowly, taking in everything at a glance, picking up a little child's cap that has fallen from one of the branches and replacing it. She comes up to the group of women. **Candelas**, *when she sees her, leaves her washing and dries her hands on her apron.* **Cecilia** *picks up her stocking again. The* **Dumb Girl** *does not move.*

Cecilia (*as she rises*)   Here's the Superior.

Sister Cristina *goes to the* **Dumb Girl** *and, putting a hand on her head, says kindly:*

Sister Cristina   Good mornmg, my child . . . getting some fresh air . . . you're feeling stronger today.

The **Dumb Glrl** *presses the baby she has in her arms to her breast and makes a queer unintelligible but rather frightened sound.*

Sister Cristina   Why, I'm not going to take him away from you! Don't hold him so tight . . . you'll smother him. Yes, he's your very own . . . don't be afraid. But let me look at him. What a beautiful boy. (*Then she turns to* **Cecilia**.) And what about yours?

Cecilia (*hanging her head*)   He's asleep.

Cecilia's *baby is in a basket turned cradle close beside her. As she goes to take it out* **Sister Cristina** *bends over and says:*

Sister Cristina   Why, he must be nearly suffocated with all those clothes on him. Here, give him to me. Why, you don't even know how to dress a child. Little angel! So . . . let the air get to his head . . . then he may grow up with a few more brains than his mother has. Here . . . take him now.

She takes the heavy shawl from the child's head and after tidying him gives him back to **Cecilia**, *who immediately puts him back in the basket again.*

Sister Cristina   What . . . back in his basket again! Don't you feel like walking him up and down a little . . . or making some clothes for him . . . or even washing his face? What have you been doing all the morning . . . lying here like a log!

Cecilia   I've been crying . . .

Sister Cristina   Crying! It's too late for that now . . .

Candelas   That's just what I tell her.

Sister Cristina   Ah . . . and I've something to say to you too.

Candelas   Yes, please, Señora . . .

Sister Cristina   Yes, please, Señora! . . . but it goes in at one ear and out at the other.

Candelas   Oh no, Señora. Have I done something wrong? Honour bright . . I never meant to.

Sister Cristina   Never meant to glue your face to the dormitory window-grating and begin shouting at the top of your voice to those men, whoever they were, passing along the road?

Candelas   Muleteers they were . . . and they came from my village.

Sister Cristina   Indeed! You're very anxious to let your village know that you're in a place like this.

Candelas   Well, it's no disgrace.

Sister Cristina   Oh, not the least in the world, of course.

Candelas (*passionately*)   Why, this isn't a prison, is it? The police didn't bring me here for stealing or murder or doing any harm to anyone. I came because I chose to . . . and because I was unlucky enough to go loving a man far better than he deserved. And as I wasn't born a duchess or an Infanta of Spain myself I couldn't get my baby born into gold swaddling clothes, could I?

Sister Cristina   Very well . . . don't get excited about it.

She is going on her way. But **Candelas** *stops her.*

Candelas   Sister Cristina!

Sister Cristina   What is it?

Candelas   When are you going to let me go?

Sister Cristina   You know well enough . . . in another four months' time.

Candelas (*sullenly*)   I've been here two already.

Sister Cristina   Quite so . . . you have been here two, and there are four to come. That makes the six you have to stay.

Candelas (*protesting*)   Have to!

Sister Cristina (*quietly and gravely*)   Yes . . . have to, young lady. The institution receives you, cares for you, doctors you, gives you all that you need. And in return you have to stay here and nurse a child. You were told that when you came.

Candelas But mine's dead.

Sister Cristina And therefore you nurse someone else's . . . a poor little foundling. You have no child, and he has no mother, and our charity brings you together. But aren't you glad to be doing a good deed?

Candelas (*passionately*) Devils . . . heartless she devils . . . to leave a baby on your doorstep like a dog. Mother of God . . . if mine had lived wouldn't I have walked out of here with my head high . . . and him in my arms.

Cecilia That'd have been a fine sight, I'm sure!

Candelas (*in a fury*) A fine sight, would it? Well, I'd come here over again, so I would, if I could have him alive. Oh, let me go, Sister Cristina, do! Let me get away from here . . . for the love of God, let me. Look, I'll take the one I'm nursing now away with me, and treat it like my own . . . I will.

Sister Cristina And next week you'd leave it on the doorstep here and be off and up to your tricks again as gay and as careless as you please. No, my girl, no . . . I'm an old hand now and know you, all of you . . . much better than I could wish. Here you stay your four short months . . . for they'll be the only ones you'll live as God meant you to. . . . (*She turns.*) What's this?

Sister Feliciana, *a much older woman, comes through one of the doors, unlocking and locking it again with her key. She brings with her* **Quica**, *a woman from some Castilian village, ugly, dirty and unkempt. She is holding a black shawl up to her mouth, and has a cotton handkerchief roughly tied round her head.*

Sister Feliciana Here we have quite an unexpected guest to entertain! (*Then to* **Quica**, *who is hanging back in pretended shame.*) Come here, woman, and don't go on like that. You ought to be used to it by this time.

Quica Good afternoon, Sister Cristina.

Sister Cristina (*recognising her*) You . . . Quica . . . you!

Sister Feliciana (*sarcastically*) Yes, Señora . . . and in all her glory! And it's so long since we last had the pleasure of her company, isn't it?

Sister Cristina (*very angry*) But . . . here again . . . for the fourth time! And not a year since you left us!

Quica (*her head down but smiling ingratiatingly*) Well . . . I can't see that we're to blame . . . for the poor little brats being so anxious to come into the world. We don't want 'em . . . you may take it from me.

Sister Cristina Hold your tongue! Have you no shame?

Quica Well . . . anyone can make a mistake, I suppose.

Sister Cristina One mistake . . . yea. But three! And at your age too! You ought to know better.

Sister Feliciana (*with brutal sarcasm*)   And with that face . . . and got up as you are . . . a sight for sore eyes, I must say!

Quica   Well, you'd have to be precious ugly not to find someone that'd look at you.

Sister Feliciana *departs.*

Sister Cristina   Has the doctor seen you yet?

Quica   Yes, Sister. Sister Feliciana has got the form filled out.

Sister Cristina   Well, then . . . go and wash your face and tidy your hair. You don't earn enough by your wicked life, I see, to buy a brush and comb.

Quica *approaches* **Sister Cristina**, *wheedlingly, stoops and tries to kiss the crucifix that hangs from her rosary.*

Quica   Sister Cristina . . .

Sister Cristina   You know the way. No . . . I don't want to have anything to do with you.

Quica   Oh, don't be angry with me, Sister Cristina. It's me that's got to suffer after all.

Sister Cristina   Yes, my girl, that's true . . . and it seems as if you were all so anxious to get to hell that you didn't mind what you went through to make your way there. (*Then to* **Candelas** *as she walks away.*) And don't you stay here washing till the day of judgment. No one has asked you to. And if you catch cold we shall only have to take care of you.

Candelas   I want to earn the bread that I eat here . . . that's why I do it.

Sister Cristina (*smiling*)   You're very scrupulous all of a sudden.

Candelas   Well, we've all got our pride!

Sister Cristina   There . . . don't be touchy. Our duty here is to befriend you whether you deserve it or not. (*Then to* **Cecilia**.) Look after that child now, addlepate. Goodness, woman . . . no one would think it was your own!

She crosses the patio and goes out, locking the door behind her.

Candelas   Look there now . . . bolts and bars so that you shan't run away. Mother of God . . . if I could fly . . . I'd be a carrion crow!

Cecilia   She never sees you without scolding at you.

Quica (*who has dropped her false shame and now seems rather pleased with herself*)   Yes, and she can scold . . . because she knows what she's scolding about. Before she put that dress on she was a woman the same as any of us . . . and she knows the world . . . not like the others . . . shocked at every mortal thing. (*Confidentially to* **Candelas**.) She was a widow, she was . . . and they say that she loved her man more than the apple of her eye . . . so did he her . . . and when he died she turned herself into a nun just so that she shouldn't love anyone else ever again . . . and she wasn't more than twenty-five!

Candelas (*passionately*) Well, she was right . . . for when you've lost your own man, the world's a deal too full of the rest of them.

Quica Oh, it all depends. Is this your first time here?

Candelas First and last . . . I take my oath.

Quica (*cheerfully*) But it's not so bad. To start with it doesn't cost you a cent . . . and you've a good doctor . . . and then there are the Sisters . . . and though they do think you the lowest of the low they look after you for dear charity's sake as if you were a queen. Why as soon as you're put to bed they kill a chicken for you . . . they do indeed. You get soup and your glass of sherry and chocolate and sponge cakes . . . and you've nothing to do for months but nurse a baby. And if you care to stay another six and nurse another they'll pay you four dollars a month for it. What more could you ask for? I've nursed seven already . . . counting my own and other people's. I've lived four years and six months for nothing . . . and I've had about a thousand pesetas out of them.

Candelas Well . . . I wouldn't come back for a million pesetas. I'd sooner die in the gutter like a dog . . . starve and freeze there . . . and be free. Why . . . here am I chained up for six months . . . and he with all the world to himself to do as he likes in . . . and forget me . . . if he gets a chance.

Quica Needn't ask who he is, I suppose?

Candelas No, Señora . . . he was the father of my son.

Quica Well, I shouldn't worry. If you do find he's forgotten you . . . you can find someone else to remember you quick enough. There are men in the world and to spare.

Candelas There's only one for me.

Quica Perhaps you're right . . . and they're all alike anyway! (*Then to* **Cecilia**.) That's so, isn't it?

Cecilia I've never known but one . . . and he was a cur. That's his baby. (*She points to the basket.*) . . . because it *is* his . . . though his devil of a mother does say it isn't. There it is in a basket and wrapped up in a few old rags like a kitten . . . and he riding in his carriage. Five dollars he gave me when the old lady threw me out of the house. Five dollars! And him with stacks of money. (*She started speaking quietly enough, but now her voice has risen with excitement.*) Just think what I was when I went into service there . . . and then where I was when left it! And then on the top of it all she had the face to say to me . . . the old swine . . . that I'd gone and seduced her son . . . because he wasn't of age! I know now what the old devil was up to. Wasn't of age! What about me? I wasn't eighteen. And I know what I ought to have done instead of coming here like a fool . . . made a scandal and put the two of them in gaol . . . yes, him and his mother both. For she knew well enough what was going on . . . and as long as there wasn't a baby coming she was quite pleased for the boy to be getting his fun at home . . . for then he didn't want to get married . . . for when he gets married he gets half all their money, and that doesn't suit her at all. Curse him . . . and his mother

... and his child ... and me too for a fool to trust what he said to me ... when he wanted to get his way. Said he was the master so he was ... and all that he had he'd give me. It didn't cost him much, when his mother threw me out of the house to get out of that little promise. Think of it ... think. Five dollars! Five dollars for life ... and me with a baby on my back. And if I leave it behind me here I'm a bad mother. And if I take it I'm marked down a bad lot wherever I turn.

Quica   Why don't you send it to its grandmamma by parcel post?

Candelas (*muttering gloomily to herself*)   Oh ... if mine had lived ...

Cecilia (*bitterly*)   Five dollars!

Quica   Yes ... if it was money you were after you did make a good bargain, didn't you!

Cecilia   And some women get motor-cars ...

Quica (*with confident philosophy*)   Ah ... you're too young for that yet. Nobody gets anything out of it the first time ... except (*She points to the baby in the basket.*) just what you've got out of it. Well, I'd better be off to my ward or Sister Cristina will be after me.

As she turns to go she literally tumbles over the **Dumb Girl**, *who, with her queer cry of alarm, clasps her baby tight to protect it.* **Quica** *herself is startled for the moment.*

Quica   Saints in heaven! Sorry ... I didn't see you. But whatever do you mean by sitting listening there ... as if you hadn't a mouth to open?

The **Dumb Girl** *glowers at her suspiciously.*

Candelas   She *is* dumb.

Quica (*with cheerful cynicism*)   Dumb is she! And they say that it's getting into talk with men is the ruin of you. Didn't make much odds to her! But there ... when it's God's will you've only got to nod your head. (*She turns again to the dumb girl reinforcing what she says with much gesture.*) What ... was he a handsome fellow, eh? ... baby's father?

Candelas   Don't waste your time ... she doesn't know a thing you're saying. You can make signs and write things to her in Spanish and French and everything else ... there's nothing they haven't tried. One of the Sisters that's been in a deaf and dumb school asked her and asked her who she was and where she came from and such like ... and she didn't even wink. The Warden says she's an idiot. But the doctor says she isn't ... and that it's a mystery ... and she must come from some country ... I forget where ... but it's a long way away and the sun shines there in the middle of the night.

Quica (*a little uneasily*)   But however did she get here?

Candelas   Nobody knows. One fine morning about two months back they opened the street door and found her lying flat on the ground in a faint ... half starved she was and nearly dead with the cold. So they brought her in and the baby was born before she ever came to ... and there she was at death's door for three weeks and longer. And now here she is . . . always staring at the baby as if she couldn't make out wherever it came from. And if you go near her she starts to howl like a perfect wolf for fear you're going to steal it from her.

Quica, *looking curiously at the child, almost by instinct takes a couple of steps towards the* **Dumb Girl** *who gives her queer cry of alarm.*

Candelas   There . . . I told you so!

Quica   All right . . . don't get scared, my girl. Nobody wants to steal another mouth to feed.

But the **Dumb Girl** *still looks at them all with intense suspicion.*

Candelas (*enviously*)   And the little brat's so pretty, what's more . . . got a skin like milk and hair on its head that's the colour of corn . . . just like its mother's. Mine had fair hair too . . . though where he got it from I don't know . . . for I'm pretty dark . . . well, you should see his father!

Suddenly she draws her arm roughly across her eyes and then goes back to the trough, plunging her hands in the water. And, sharply and defiantly, as if she meant to stop herself crying, she begins to sing again.

Candelas   Aie . . .

> Girl of the Mountains,
> You made too free
> When to ruin yourself
> You ruined me.

Sister Gracia *comes into the patio followed by two women carrying a large basket of rough-dried clothes. She points to the linen on the bushes.*

Sister Gracia   Gather up all that too, and take it to be ironed. It must be ready by this afternoon.

The women collect the linen in silence and go out again carrying their basket with them. **Sister Gracia** *is now twenty-nine. She is pale and evidently tired and overstrained, though she does her best to hide this by her smiles. When the women have gone she turns towards the* **Dumb Girl** *and her companions, but on the way to them she stops, gives a little sigh and murmurs, 'Oh, Blessed Jesus.' Then she leans against one of the pillars and closes her eyes. She is half fainting.* **Candelas** *sees and goes up to her anxiously.*

Candelas   D'you feel ill? Oh . . . what's the matter?

Sister Gracia (*pulling herself together*)   Nothing, thank you . . . nothing at all. Don't be frightened.

Candelas (*to* **Cecilia**)   Here . . . you! Go and fetch her a chair, can't you. D'you want some water?

Cecilia *goes out and doesn't return.* **Quica** *takes the* **Dumb Girl**'s *chair – she has risen too – and brings it to* **Sister Gracia**.

56   The Kingdom of God

Candelas   Sit down now.

Sister Gracia (*only anxious to get away from them*)   No, there's nothing the matter indeed. Please take no notice.

Candelas   Now, do sit down . . . won't you?

Sister Gracia   Oh . . . very well then.

She sits down and as soon as **Candelas** *sees her safely in the chair, she dashes out to the right.*

Quica   But whatever is the matter, Sister Gracia?

Sister Gracia (*recognising her amazedly*)   You here again?

Quica (*complacently*)   Yes, Señora.

Sister Gracia   And didn't you promise when you went away that you'd never so much as look at a man again?

Quica   Well, there it is . . . you can't be sensible all the time!

Sister Gracia (*with a sigh*)   God's will be done!

The **Dumb Girl** *now comes slowly to* **Sister Gracia** *and kneeling puts her baby in her lap, leaves it there and remains looking at her and smiling.*

Quica   There . . . see what a present the dumb woman's brought you.

Sister Gracia (*smiling*)   Thank you . . . thank you . . .

Quica (*to the* **Dumb Girl**)   So you're not afraid of her!

The **Dumb Girl** *looks from one to the other and smiles again at* **Sister Gracia**. **Candelas** *comes back, followed by* **Enrique**. *She is carrying a glass of water.*

Candelas   Look at her now . . . with the child on her lap! Isn't she beautiful? She's like the Blessed Virgin of Carmen. (*Then she goes down to* **Sister Gracia**, *very pleased with herself.*) Here's the doctor.

The doctor, **Enrique**, *is a man of about thirty-five, pleasant, quite good looking. He is dressed in a plain dark suit.* **Sister Gracia** *jumps up on seeing him.*

Sister Gracia   Oh, good heavens! (*Then to* **Candelas**.) But . . . what nonsense! Whoever told you to . . . ?

Candelas   Take what the saints provide, I say. What's the good of the doctor being here if we're not to call him when you're ill?

Sister Gracia (*giving the* **Dumb Girl** *back her child*)   Here.

Enrique (*anxiously*)   But . . . were you really taken ill?

Sister Gracia   No, Señor, of course not . . . it was nothing but this girl's foolishness.

Candelas (*a little slyly*)   And I tell you she was, Don Enrique. She leaned against that pillar . . . so. And she shut her eyes . . . so. And she went as white as a sheet, and if I hadn't got to her she'd have fallen flat on the ground.

Enrique Well . . . now let's see. What was the matter?

Sister Gracia Nothing, nothing . . . take no notice. I spent the whole morning in the laundry where it's half dark . . . so when I came out into the patio the light dazzled me and made me dizzy . . . that was all. But this silly girl (**Candelas**) is always making a fuss.

Candelas I'm sure I meant well.

Enrique You really don't need me at all?

Sister Gracia No really. Of course, if I do . . .! I'm so sorry you've been disturbed.

Enrique That's nothing. If you do want me, I'm in the convalescent ward. Goodbye.

He goes out without looking back. But he caresses the **Dumb Girl**'s *baby in passing and she looks at him smilingly too.*

Quica He's a handsome man.

Candelas And what a way with him . . . hasn't he, Sister Gracia?

Sister Gracia You know all about such things, I'm sure.

Candelas You're not cross with me, are you?

Sister Gracia Yes, I am. Fancy going and worrying the doctor over a thing like that.

Candelas Well, what else is he for? Besides, as it was you, he was only too glad to come (*To* **Quica**.) wasn't he?

Quica Trust him. He's got eyes in his head.

Candelas That he has . . . for I've seen him once a day going on for two months now . . . and I know he's got eyes in his head. He'll pass near a particular person and be knocked all of a heap, poor thing! Oh, everyone's noticed that. (*Then she looks at* **Sister Gracia** *and says coaxingly.*) You've an angel's face . . . that's a fact.

Sister Gracia What *are* you both talking about?

Quica *bursts into laughter.*

Sister Gracia And what are you laughing at, pray?

Quica Oh . . . nothing at all, Señora. Don't be angry . . . I meant no harm.

Candelas But what I say is that coifs can't hide faces . . . and in woman's face is man's perdition.

Quica Yes . . . and a woman's in a man's. . . .

Candelas And if she looks all pale and sad and seems just to be crying out for someone to take care of her . . .

The two are talking to each other, but with glances at **Sister Gracia**, *who says very severely:*

Sister Gracia   Will you please be quiet?

Candelas   We didn't mean you . . . for you're a saint . . . everyone knows that . . . but it's the very reason why I hate to see you here.

Sister Gracia   Do you indeed!

Candelas   I tell you, Sister . . . you don't know what you're missing.

Quica   You don't . . . she's right . . . you don't.

Sister Gracia (*turning away*)   You're talking nonsense.

Candelas   Would I be a woman . . . and young and pretty . . . and be shut up here washing other women's babies' faces . . . when I might be having my own? Yes, Señora . . . it's her own babies . . . and their father's, the man she could love and who'd be mad about her . . . that's what a woman wants . . . so I tell you.

Sister Gracia   You've nothing more to do here, have you, either of you? So be off now, to the refectory, it's nearly dinner time.

Candelas (*to herself, to* **Quica**, *to the things she collects to carry off with her*)   Holy Mother . . . you don't know whether she's more beautiful to look at when she's angry or when she's pleased. Eyes like that . . . in a place like this . . . where no one has a chance look at them. . . . (*Then she sings again.*)

> Oh, quickly drop your lids
> To keep me in your eyes,
> For there I've seen myself
> At last . . . in Paradise.

Sister Gracia (*irritably*)   Be quiet . . . be quiet. You have a voice like a watchman's rattle.

Candelas   Have I? It was my voice though that first brought him running after me . . . for all that he has gone and left me now! Oh, Holy Mother! . . .

> I have a grief, a grief
> Which if I longer bear . . .

Sister Gracia   Really, you seem to have taken leave of your senses today. And haven't I told you to be off to the refectory? It's time our private patient took her walk.

Quica   Oho . . . have we got a private patient here?

Candelas   Very private . . . for though she's done just what we all have, she can't possibly come and breathe the same air that we do . . . oh dear no!

Quica   Well . . . people of position must do something to keep it up. We've no shame at anytime, have we! Nor have they before things go wrong . . . but they have after . . . and that's always something. (*She laughs impudently at her own wit.*)

Sister Gracia   Are you both going . . . or are you not?

Quica Yes, Señora... this very minute...

As she is turning to go she comes against the basket cradle.

Well... just look what that girl's done... left her baby here!

Sister Gracia Take it with you then.

Candelas Yes, Señora... Aie... don't look at me as if I'd committed a crime!

Sister Gracia Oh, be off... be off!

Candelas Holy Mother....

> I have a grief, a grief
> Which if I longer bear
> A coffin and a grave
> For me they can prepare.

The song dies away. Left alone, **Sister Gracia** *leans a moment against the stone trough to rest. Her face is drawn and sad, but after a little she smiles to herself and then goes to a door that has not been opened yet, opens it, disappears and then comes back with* **Margarita**, *saying.*

Sister Gracia You can come out now.

Margarita There's no one here?

Sister Gracia No one at all. They've all gone to dinner.

Margarita *is a delicately pretty girl of twenty. Her plain dark dress and the large silk scarf of blue and black that she wears stamp her as belonging to the middle classes. The settled look on her face speaks of a medley of shame and anger, and her voice is sometimes sad and sometimes sharp with a sort of despair. She comes in not lifting her eyes, sinks into the first chair she finds and murmurs half-articulately.*

Margarita Mother of God...

Sister Gracia *goes to her and speaks very gently, very kindly.*

Sister Gracia Now, my child... you mustn't torment yourself any more. Look what a wonderful day it is. Aren't you glad of this sunshine after all the cold and rain?

Margarita, *her eyes on the ground, makes no reply.* **Sister Gracia** *goes to one of the blossoming trees and breaks off a little branch which she throws lightly into the girl's lap. Still no movement, no reply. Then* **Sister Gracia** *puts a hand to her forehead and lifts the sunk head.*

Sister Gracia Lift that head now. What do you want with your eyes always fixed on the ground? Look up at the sky. God is there, and he'll comfort you.

Margarita (*stubbornly*) God won't look at me.

Sister Gracia (*still kind, but a little more sternly*) Won't he? Is your sin too great ... or do you think his mercy is too small?

Margarita   God is merciful to you, isn't he, when your heart is softened. Mine has only been broken.

Sister Gracia   No, don't say that . . . you mustn't say that.

Margarita *hides her face in her hands and begins to cry.*

Sister Gracia   Now don't cry . . . you know how it upsets you . . . it's very dangerous. . . .

Margarita   Oh . . . I'm not going to die . . . no fear of that. You never do die when you want to.

Sister Gracia (*smiling*)   Hush now . . . or Death may hear . . . and come for you.

Margarita   I wish it would . . . Oh, I wish it would. If I could just die and forget . . . yes, die here . . . in this infamous place . . . and then no one would ever hear of me again! If I could be buried here and forgotten . . . with my shame and my wrongs. . . .

Sister Gracia (*a firm hand on her shoulder*)   And with your child too?

Margarita (*fixedly*)   Yes . . . my child too.

Sister Gracia (*horror-struck*)   Blessed Jesus! (*But she rallies her kind smile again.*) How sorry you'll be that you said that, once he's born and you hold him in your arms.

Margarita   My punishment.

Sister Gracia   No, no, no . . . a son can never be his mother's punishment.

Margarita   Not when he is her dishonour?

Sister Gracia   The child's no dishonour . . . only the sin is that.

Margarita   It's the same thing.

Sister Gracia   It is not. When God sends you a child he offers you pardon for your sin.

Margarita   Pardon . . .

Sister Gracia   Why yes. Would you have left sinning if the child had not come to convince you that you were sinning? God puts redemption in your arms. Don't miss the chance of it. Oh, think what it can mean to you to live and suffer for your child . . . and to teach him to be good. God in his mercy is calling to you . . . and you must answer . . . you must not turn away. Oh yes . . . cry if you want to because you repent . . . but not because you're in despair. And in a little while now an angel will come to dry your tears.

But **Margarita** *makes no answer, her eyes still stubbornly upon the ground. Defeated,* **Sister Gracia** *gives a sad little shrug to her shoulders and looks up.*

Sister Gracia   Oh dear God . . .!

Then she moves away, and taking her knitting from her pocket works as she stands there. After a moment, **Margarita** *says in a hard voice:*

Margarita   He'll have no father. He'll have no mother.

Sister Gracia   No mother, did you say? Did you say that? D'you mean you're thinking that you'll turn your back on him and leave him here . . . as these poor wretched women leave their children?

She has dropped her work and is so vehement, so shaken with indignation, that **Margarita** *gets up, a little frightened.*

Sister Gracia   Oh no, no I . . . You can't mean that . . . you couldn't do such an infamous thing. To give up your child altogether . . . oh, think . . . think! No, you couldn't do it . . . you couldn't. Promise me that you'll take him with you . . . and give him your name . . . and the love that he has a right to. Promise me.

Margarita   I can't.

Sister Gracia   Why not?

Margarita   My father knows nothing about it. We've told him that I've a vocation for the Sisterhood and he thinks that I'm here on probation. If he knew, he'd die of the shame of it.

Sister Gracia   And your mother . . . ?

Margarita   I've no mother. I've a step-mother.

Sister Gracia   She knows?

Margarita   Yes, she knows. She has helped me deceive my father and hide here. Not that she cares much for me! But at least she's a woman . . . and understands.

Sister Gracia   A woman, is she . . . and understands? Understands what? Has she never had children . . . ?

At this moment **Sister Feliciana** *comes across the back of the patio carrying some letters. On seeing her* **Margarita** *begins to tremble with excitement and runs to her crying.*

Margarita   Sister Feliciana . . . is that the post . . . is there anything for me?

Sister Feliciana   I'm sure I don't know. The Superior will give it you soon enough if there is.

She is going her way, but **Margarita** *desperately catches at her habit.*

Margarita   Oh, for the love of God, let me see them. I won't ask you for the letter . . . I won't indeed. I only want to know. Oh . . . please . . . won't you? Oh . . . I'll go on my knees . . .

Sister Feliciana   But . . . !

While **Margarita** *kneels and clings to her, she questions* **Sister Gracia** *with a look, which says, 'Is this girl mad?'*

Sister Gracia   Let her look.

Margarita, *when she gets the letters, runs through them with feverish anxiety and passes from hope to despondency and to despair.*

Margarita   No . . . yes? No . . . no . . . no! Nothing . . . oh, my God . . . nothing!

Sister Feliciana   Well . . . God's will be done, you know.

She philosophically packs the letters together again and departs. But **Margarita** *is left like a mad creature.*

Margarita   Nothing . . . nothing . . . nothing!

Sister Gracia   My child, my child . . . keep calm.

Marcarita   Not one word! I'm not worth even a word from him . . . and I've brought myself to this for him. He knows where I am . . . he knows . . . oh, he knows!

Sister Gracia (*to say something*)   He'll write tomorrow.

Margarita   He won't. I shall die here . . . alone. For he doesn't love me . . . he never did. I was the one . . . I . . . oh, God help me!

She breaks down again, sobbing helplessly. **Sister Gracia** *goes to her and says gently.*

Sister Gracia   There, there now . . . don't think of that anymore.

Suddenly **Margarita** *stops crying and looks fixedly in front of her.*

Margarita   He's wicked and heartless . . . everybody says that. Yes . . . wicked! No . . . no, he's not. It's only that he doesn't love me. And I didn't know how to make him love me. But there were those that did. Well . . . what more could I do? I gave myself to him, body and soul . . . and even that wasn't enough. For he was false to me. Oh, those women that took him away from me! And when I cried, all he said was . . . 'But if you really loved me.' (*She echoes distractedly.*) 'If you really loved me! If you really loved me!'

She has ranged through tears and anger to the climax of an almost hysterical scream. And now she gets up and goes up to **Sister Gracia**.

Margarita   You don't know what it is to be jealous.

Sister Gracia   I never want to know.

Margarita   It's hell. It's like being burnt alive. It's like having one's heart torn out. 'If you really loved me.' *Ay de mi . . . ay de mi*! As if I didn't . . . better than anyone else would.

Sister Gracia (*very moved*)   Yes . . . yes. Keep quiet now.

Margarita   For haven't I risked salvation . . . look what I've brought on myself just to please him. And I cried . . . I prayed God I might die . . . and it meant nothing to him. But there was one day . . . yes, just one . . . when he did love me. And I tell you, I'd lose my soul and see him lose his, to have that day over again!

Sister Gracia   Don't blaspheme!

Margarita Oh, I tell lies about it all . . . I do nothing but lie. For I'm not sorry for the sin and the shame of it . . . I'm not. If he wants me, what do I care about honour or dishonour . . . he's my life . . . I've no other.

Sister Gracia Be quiet . . . be quiet, I tell you. Are you mad . . . or do you want to lose your last hope of salvation?

Margarita *loses all self-control whatever. She clings hysterically to* **Sister Gracia** *and kneels to her without in the least knowing who she is.*

Margarita Where is he? For the love of God where is he? Tell me where he is so that I can go to him . . . barefoot . . . on my knees. . . .

Sister Gracia Let me go.

Margarita Carlos . . Carlos! We're here . . . both of us . . . your child . . . and I'm here. Carlos . . . love . . . life . . . Carlos . . .

She falls to the ground in a violent fit of hysterics. **Sister Gracia** *is really alarmed, and calls out.*

Sister Gracia Help . . . help!

Enrique *comes in by one door, and by the other* **Sister Feliciana**.

Enrique What is it . . . what has happened?

Sister Feliciana Who was that calling . . . ah!

She goes to succour **Margarita**, *while* **Sister Gracia**, *very distressed, hardly knowing what she is saying, crying indeed like a child, just manages to get out.*

Sister Gracia This woman . . . this woman . . .!

Enrique There now . . . don't be frightened . . . it's nothing.

He lifts up **Margarita**, *who grows quieter, little by little, sighing out 'Ay . . . ay,' and gradually getting some control over herself. He takes the glass of water that has been left by the trough and gives it to* **Sister Feliciana** *saying:*

Enrique Sprinkle a few drops in her face. Keep quiet, girl, keep quiet. Hysterics are over, I think. Now get on your feet.

Sister Feliciana *helps her up.*

Enrique That's right. Now take care you don't begin again . . . d'you understand?

Though he talks to **Margarita** *he is looking rather anxiously at* **Sister Gracia**, *who is leaning against one of the pillars still crying though she tries to control herself.*

Margarita Yes . . . I will . . .

Enrique (*taking a little bottle from his pocket*) Take a sniff of this. And now you're all right . . . wasn't anything serious, was it? (*To* **Sister Feliciana**.) Now . . . take her to her room . . . give her a little orange flower water . . . shut out the sun, and keep her quiet.

Sister Feliciana   Come along then . . . don't cry any more.

She takes **Margarita** *away and* **Sister Gracia**, *hardly herself even yet, is instinctively following them, when* **Enrique**, *gently authoritative, stops her.*

Enrique   Where are you going?

Sister Gracia   I . . . I was going with them.

Enrique   No.

Sister Gracia   Why not?

Enrique   Because it's quite possible that in a moment she'll have another attack . . . and you may have one too if you're there.

Sister Gracia   I?

Enrique   Yes . . . these nervous crises are very contagious things . . . Besides you're thoroughly upset . . . you're shaking all over. Sit down.

Sister Gracia   But. . . .

Enrique   Sit down, please. Doctor's orders.

Sister Gracia *sits down and after a moment tries to speak. But she is still so upset that she hardly knows what she is saying.*

Sister Gracia   Blessed Jesus . . . that poor girl . . . she seemed possessed . . .

Enrique   Don't talk . . . rest. Close your eyes a moment.

She obeys him. He then begins to walk up and down, but going no nearer to her. After a moment she says.

Sister Gracia   Can I open them now?

Enrique   Are you quite yourself again?

Sister Gracia   Yes, I am.

Enrique   Quite?

Sister Gracia   Quite. Don't be afraid . . . I've never had hysterics yet.

She gets up as if to go. Then he moves a step nearer.

Enrique   Sister Gracia. (*Struck by his tone she looks at him curiously.*) How old are you?

Sister Gracia   Oh . . . really, I hardly remember. Twenty-nine, I ought to be, I think, on my next birthday. Yes . . . that's it. Ten years I've been professed . . . and I was eighteen.

Enrique   You've been here since you were eighteen?

Sister Gracia   Oh no . . . I've only been here four years and a half. I started in an asylum for old men. Oh, poor old things . . . if you knew how miserable it made me to leave them . . . really it was almost worse than leaving my own home. They were so fond of me . . . and I was of them. Hard luck they'd all had! And they were so old . . . and I was such a child. They used to pretend . . . some of them . . . that I was their granddaughter . . . and sometimes I'd find myself thinking of them as if they were my dolls. Such fun we used to have together!

Enrique There's not much fun to be had here.

Sister Gracia I think that all the sorrow in the world is to be found here. These women . . . I don't know whether it makes me more wretched to have them suffer so . . . or for them to think nothing of it at all. And the babies . . . the ones that are born here . . . and those that they bring here . . . outcasts every one . . . with people only thinking how best they can be rid of them . . . as if they were something unclean and shameful altogether. And . . . oh, my God . . . a month ago, while you were away . . . one night when I was on duty, someone put a dead child into the basket at the gate. That is . . . it hadn't died – its throat was cut. I shall never forget it. With big blue wide open eyes that seemed to be asking . . . But why . . . but why?

Enrique This can't go on, you know, Sister Gracia.

Sister Gracia What do you mean?

Enrique You can't stay on here.

Sister Gracia Where?

Enrique Surrounded by this misery and pain . . . misery of the body and of the spirit too. For you're right . . . the whole world's unhappiness is centred here . . . we're at the very heart of its corruption. Vice or cowardice it may be . . . degeneracy, self-will . . . but over it all, despair. For what have they to look forward to . . . any of them?

Sister Gracia I know, I know . . . there's nothing . . . and that's what is so horrible. My poor old men now . . . who cared what became of them? But it was so easy to take them out of themselves . . . why, if I'd promised them the moon to play with, they'd have felt quite sure of getting it . . . because I'd promised. But these wretched souls . . . what visions can one give to them? Some of them are callous, and some only wish they were dead, and some just want to be revenged. But there's not one . . . not one that even *wants* to rise above it all. And, if they did . . . what could we promise them? They leave here . . . and what is waiting for them? More misery . . . more hunger . . . more vice . . . more shame. Do you know, I think sometimes . . . oh, not very often, but sometimes I can't help thinking . . . that if one of these women would only lift up her head, take her child in her arms, and outface what the world calls her dishonour . . . why, God at least would forgive her. For he always does forgive us if we call on him. But then . . . they don't know how to call on him. How should they? No one has taught them. They hardly know that he exists. Then how can one sin against a God one doesn't know? And if they've not knowingly sinned . . . how should they feel the shame, and why . . . oh why . . . should such punishment fall upon them? God . . . God . . . but who is to blame then for so much misery?

Enrique Sister Gracia . . . Sister Gracia!

Sister Gracia What am I saying . . . what have I said? Oh, forget it please. And God forgive me . . . blessed Jesus! . . . thy will be done . . . and as you have willed it . . . then so it should be. As it is . . . it is right . . . although we cannot understand. Have pity on us and forgive us all . . . Lord . . . Lord!

Enrique But . . . why are you crying then?

Sister Gracia Oh, indeed I'm not . . . well . . . no, I'm not quite myself yet. That girl . . . like a mad creature . . . like some fury from another world. You mustn't think I'm generally so impressionable as this. But today . . . well, you'll forgive such foolishness . . . and . . . another time. . . .

She starts to go.

Enrique Wait . . . wait a little.

Sister Gracia No, really . . . there is so much to be done. . . .

Enrique Wait . . . please . . . just for a minute. I want to speak to you . . . of something that may touch you very nearly.

Sister Gracia That may touch me . . .!

Enrique Well, then . . . that does touch *me* very, very nearly . . . that means more to me than anything in the world. (*At a gesture from her.*) No . . . for God's sake don't be offended.

Sister Gracia Let me go, please.

Enrique You guess what it is?

Sister Gracia No.

Enrique Ah . . . but you do. (*He is deeply moved for all that he speaks quietly and stands very still; she, trembling rather, stands as still, to listen.*) Sister Gracia . . . you can't go on leading this life. How can you endure to be sunk here in this pit of bitterness and despair? Well, then . . . I can't endure that you should be. For three years now I've been coming here and seeing you every day . . . and from the first day I've cared for you . . .

Sister Gracia Oh, God in heaven, don't say that . . . hush, hush!

Enrique Why? I have cared for you . . . felt for you more and more . . . and more deeply. For you are all that I believe a woman should be . . . you are good, you are true, you have sense . . . and you are full of joy . . . you were when I knew you first. And if you're unhappy now . . . why then, indeed, you are not yourself. You are a sick woman now.

Sister Gracia I . . .!

Enrique Yes . . . the foul breath of this place has poisoned you. All the tears that you have seen shed are heavy on your heart. And all the suffering you've seen and all the blasphemies you've heard have beaten back into your body and your mind. But you need the bright sky above you and the fresh air to breathe . . . and on your horizon some gleams of hope.

Sister Gracia No, no . . . oh, no!

Enrique Yes, yes . . . and that's what I bring you when I bring you . . . my love.

Sister Gracia Oh, for God's sake. . . .

Enrique My love. We must call things by their names.

Sister Gracia And you dare to speak to me of love . . . here . . . where we see how it all ends.

Enrique It isn't love that comes to such an end . . . that has eaten like a cancer into these lives. True love between men and women is health and strength to both.

Sister Gracia That is enough!

And she turns away determinedly.

Enrique No, don't go away . . . listen . . . there's nothing I'm saying that need offend you. Love that is worthy of the name brings peace of mind and harmony . . . clear thoughts and steadfastness. And work to be done . . . and shared . . . oh, anxious hours enough . . . but with their burden lightened by just half. Day after day of toil and weariness . . . but at the end of each the comfort of a heart that beats near yours. Come out of this prison and learn to laugh again. Take off that habit which is black like death and that coif . . . it's like the cloth that you lay on a dead woman's face . . . and honour me by trusting me to make you happy.

Sister Gracia I am happy. God knows it.

Enrique But won't you be as happy with me? And I should be so happy with you. Ah . . . forgive that from a man who really isn't used to being selfish. I'm not offering you what's called a life of pleasure . . . mine's austere. I'm not well-off, and I'm a doctor and you'd be brought close enough, if you were my wife, to all the ills of mankind. Don't be afraid that you'd have no chance of doing good. I live for my work . . . and though I don't worship science for its own sake . . . I do believe it can help me to help my neighbour. Won't you help me too? You have grown wise in charity. Working together we could give such life to our work . . . won't you try? I'm a free man . . . and you are free . . .

Sister Gracia I . . . free! How can you say that?

Enrique Why, you wouldn't be the first to leave the hard road you chose when you were young and full of illusions for a simpler way . . . the human way, you know, that love makes easier.

Sister Gracia I have given my love once and for all. I abide by that vow. I live for that love and I will die in it.

Enrique Sister Gracia. . . .

Sister Gracia Oh yes, you're right . . . I am unhappy . . . unhappier than you can think. And I'm tired, and perhaps I'm ill . . . poisoned . . . oh no doubt, as you say. But God, who has my love, is with me. I may not see him, but he is with me. And while I love him he will not leave me. Oh yes, it's true that just now he has put bitterness in the cup . . . but he has given me so much other happiness . . . that I have so little deserved. And he will again . . . I know that he will. And even if he does not I have given myself for ever.

Enrique Sister Gracia . . .

Sister Gracia For ever . . . for ever. And no one has the right to try and turn me from my way. My love and my sorrow are my God's. No, don't speak and don't come near me. Don't ever speak or ever think of this again.

Enrique Is that your last word?

Sister Gracia My last . . . and my only one. Goodbye.

She is more than a little shaken by all this, by the violence she is doing to herself. Once again she turns to go.

Enrique Well, at least let me as a doctor give you some advice. I really think you are ill . . . you are worn out.

Sister Gracia Don't let that trouble you. The Superior is responsible for my good health. What I need she will order. Goodbye.

Enrique Goodbye.

He bows and goes without turning his head. **Sister Gracia** *turns now to go out on the left and so she has to cross the whole patio. She is quite broken with emotion and physical fatigue; she moves very slowly and rests wherever she can, by a tree, a chair, a pillar. Half-way across she can hear the impudent, sensual voice of* **Candelas** *singing.*

Candelas I asked a sick man the complaint
  Of which he was to die,
  'Of loving you . . . of loving you,'
  The sick man made reply.

Sister Gracia *stops to listen and there comes over her, like an agony, all the temptation of love and its happiness. She wrings her hands, then crosses them on her breast, and stands there trembling. Then she lets her arms fall and stands for a moment with closed eyes. Then she pulls herself together, takes the crucifix from her sleeve, looks at it for a little, presses it to her breast and says*:

Sister Gracia Jesus . . . beloved saviour . . . do not leave me without help!

She starts on her way again, and, as she reaches the door, meets the Superior coming out.

Sister Gracia Sister Cristina.

Sister Cristina What is it? Why, what's the matter? You're shaking all over. Are you ill?

Sister Gracia No, indeed. But I want to ask a favour. Will you be so kind as to write today . . . today, please . . . to the authorities and ask them if they will transfer me . . .

Sister Cristina But . . .

Sister Gracia Please . . . please! I want to leave here at once . . . and without anyone knowing . . . or knowing where I go! I beg you . . . for the love of God! It is a case of conscience . . .

Curtain.

Act Three

The kitchen of an orphanage. It is a large white washed room, divided in two by a wooden barrier. In the back part, which is a little higher than the front, separated from it not only by the barrier but by one or two steps, is a great stove with large saucepans fitted into it; and they have taps in them. On the ground, close to stove, are four large two-handled pots.

The front of the room is arranged as a dining-room, with tables and benches of plain deal. There are two of these tables, one on each side of the room.

In the wall on the right is a large doorway; the door stands open all the time and through it one can catch a glimpse of the great patio. In the left wall are two smaller doors which lead to other dining-rooms, one for the girls, the other for the little boys; it is the big boys that eat in the kitchen.

At the back are high windows through which trees and sky can be seen. Beneath the windows is a shrine, and in it an image of the Virgin and Child. Two flower-pots with artificial flowers also adorn the shrine. **Sister Dionisia** *is in the kitchen; a Sister of Charity, aged about thirty-five, a country woman, uneducated and taciturn, but full of common sense and sturdy practical virtue possessing, too, great physical powers of work. She is by the stove and has just finished putting the four large pots in a row.*

Engracia *and* **Lorenza** *come in carrying a deal box with cord handles which is full of hunks of bread. They are inmates of the orphanage, very poorly dressed, cotton skirts, hemp sandals, sleeved aprons of striped cloth, and on their heads cotton handkerchiefs which they take off once they are in the kitchen and tie loosely round their necks.* **Engracia** *is very pretty and delicate in her movements,* **Lorenza** *is a rather ugly country girl.*

Engracia Here's the bread for supper.

They carry the box, which they had dropped for the moment while they untied the handkerchiefs from their heads, towards the door.

Sister Dionisia You've cut very little.

Lorenza (*sullenly*) That's all the bread there was.

To this **Sister Dionisia** *makes no reply.* **Lorenza** *and* **Engracia** *start taking out the bread with two great metal scoops, and putting it into the four great pots.*

Sister Dionisia Put a few extra in that . . . it's the little ones'.

Lorenza Yes, Sister.

Engracia (*looking at the stove*) Is the water hot?

Lorenza Not boiling yet.

Sister Dionisia Lots of time . . . it's only four o'clock.

Engracia I'll go and fetch the plates.

She goes out by one of the doors on the left.

Sister Dionisia   Get the ladle . . . and we'll put in the dripping.

Lorenza *takes out of a cupboard in the corner the vessel containing the dripping, and a large iron ladle.*

Sister Dionisia   Take care you don't burn yourself.

Lorenza *starts to ladle in the dripping. Then she stops, surprised.*

Lorenza   Sister Dionisia!

Sister Dionisia *knows what the matter is, and in self-defence looks severe.*

Sister Dionisia   What's the matter?

Lorenza   You've forgotten the peppers.

Sister Dionisia   No, I've not forgotten them.

Lorenza   Oh yes, Sister. Look, the dripping's not coloured at all.

Sister Dionisia   I tell you I've not forgotten them . . . there aren't any.

Lorenza, *horror struck, puts down the dripping and stands with the ladle in the air.*

Lorenza   No peppers!

Sister Dionisia (*ill-humouredly, to hide her own vexation*)   No, child, there aren't any. We used up the last this morning.

Lorenza   Well . . . we needn't waste time making the broth then . . . for they won't eat it.

Sister Dionisia   What else can they do . . . if it's all there is?

Lorenza   I know the big boys won't eat it. They'll go to bed starving. If there aren't peppers in the broth . . . they won't eat it.

Sister Dionisia   Come along now . . . the dripping will be cold . . . and if it's put with the bread like that the whole thing turns to glue.

She goes on apportioning the dripping to the pots. **Lorenza** *puts it in while* **Sister Dionisia** *stirs it.* **Engracia** *now comes back with a pile of tin plates which she puts on the table.*

Engracia   The plates!

And she goes out again.

Sister Dionisia   Now, put the lids on.

She carries the dripping back to its corner.

Lorenza   If you've things to do we'll look after the water boiling.

Engracia *comes back again with a basket full of tin mugs and wooden spoons.*

Sister Dionisia Well . . . even if it does boil don't pour it out or you'll burn yourselves . . . you'd better call me. I'm going to the bakehouse to see if they've done kneading.

She goes out through the wide open door. **Engracia** *has been setting out the plates, with a mug and a spoon by each.*

Engracia (*mocking*) The table's laid . . . the silver plate is on.

Lorenza (*coming from the back*) And as for the banquet . . . why, the King himself never had the like. Bread soaked in hot dripping just for a change . . . and no peppers with it either.

Engracia I don't know which way makes me sicker . . . with them or without them.

Lorenza (*philosophically good-humoured*) My child, when you can dip your bread in good pepper broth that turns it red, at least you can pretend that it tastes of sausage.

Engracia Sausage! You're a nice one.

Lorenza Oh my . . . what wish would I have if . . . ! Now look . . . suppose the blessed Saint Cayetano were to work a miracle, so that when we put in the ladle instead of bringing out hunks of bread and water we got . . . sausages . . . and boiled codfish . . . or beans and bacon . . . or lentils. Holy Mother, I want to forget there's such a thing as lentils in this world.

Engracia *is sitting on a bench, her elbows on the table, looking fixedly at some sort of little card she has taken from her pocket.*

Engracia Oh . . . there are such a lot of things in this world that you want to forget about.

Lorenza What's that you're looking at?

Engracia Nothing . . . a picture out of a matchbox.

Lorenza Let's see. (*She takes it and reads.*) 'Juanita la Serana'. Oh, my dear . . . isn't she handsome? Is she an actress?

Engracia Yes . . . one of those that sing and dance and have motor-cars and silk dresses!

Lorenza And how her hair's done! Now who is it she looks like?

Engracia Like me.

Lorenza (*scandalised*) Like you! Well . . . yes she is . . . if you wore your hair right high up like she does . . . and your skirts short. Oh . . . !

Engracia What are you laughing at?

Lorenza Oh . . . think of all the lentils you could have to eat, if you were an actress with your picture put on matchboxes.

Engracia Hold your tongue . . . someone's coming.

Lorenza   Only The Innocent.

Engracia   Here . . . give it me!

She seizes the picture and puts it back in her pocket. **The Innocent** *comes in. She is what is sometimes called a 'natural', a grown woman with the undeveloped brain of a child. She has, however, an old woman's face and her hair is grey and bristly. She is dressed like the other orphans. As she comes in she produces a screw of greasy paper, and takes from it after a moment the drumstick of a chicken.*

The Innocent   Girls . . . want some chicken?

Lorenza (*in fascinated amazement*)   Chicken!

The Innocent (*with all the pride of great possession*)   Chicken! Don't it smell good. (*She holds it close to* **Lorenza**'*s nose, and as suddenly snatches it away again.*) Ah . . . don't you wish you may get it! (*Then turning generous.*) All right . . . take it, greedy. But don't eat it all . . . give her a bit . . . she looks pretty hungry.

Lorenza (*to* **Engracia**)   Have some?

Engracia (*in great disgust*)   No, thank you!

The Innocent   Not like chicken! Have a cutlet.

She now produces from the screw of paper a cutlet bone with a little meat left on it. **Engracia** *looking upon this no more favourably she goes on cheerfully.*

The Innocent   Try some fish!

And out comes a bit of fried fish.

Engracia   No, no . . . take it away.

The Innocent (*amazed*)   No? Well, have a sweet?

Engracia (*a little moved*)   Oh . . . well . . . perhaps.

The Innocent   Here you are . . . cokernut!

Engracia *takes the sweet delightedly, puts it to her mouth, then takes it away again.*

Engracia   Oh, no . . . it makes me sick!

The Innocent   What . . . the sweet too!

Engracia (*with growing excitement*)   The sweet too . . . and everything else besides. Yes, I'm hungry . . . like everybody else here . . . well, I was . . . oh no, I'm not. I haven't been able to get through a meal for these two days . . . and it does turn me sick to see you with all that. Goodness knows I'd like something to eat . . . but not food! I'd like something very sour and very sweet . . . and cold . . . no, hot . . . oh, I don't know. Coffee with lots of sugar! Salad with lots of vinegar! No, nothing to eat . . . I'd like to sleep. Mother Mary, if I could go to bed this very minute and not ever have to get up again. For oh, I am sleepy!

Lorenza (*with rough kindness*)   Now you just listen to me. People that don't eat die . . . and that's what's going to happen to you . . . going on like this. And I tell you . . . that if you throw your supper under the bench again I'll tell Sister Dionisia, so I will . . . and she'll get it down you . . . see if she doesn't!

Engracia *bursts into tears.*

Lorenza   Oh . . . don't cry!

Engracia   Let me be!

Lorenza   Where are you off to?

Engracia   Let me alone, can't you?

She goes to the end of the table, sits down, hides her face in her hands and quietly proceeds to have her cry out. **Lorenza**, *much distressed, turns to* **The Innocent**.

Lorenza   There . . . she's all upset again. Some days she fires up at you because she's sure she must be a Marquis's daughter . . . or why are her hands so white, and her feet so something or other? Other times she's wild because she can't go on the stage! And last night in the dormitory she jumped out of bed in her sleep and was walking about with her eyes tight shut . . . a bit more and she'd have been out of the window. She's going off her head . . . that's what I think.

The Innocent   Where's the sweet? Don't let it get lost.

She takes the sweet from the table where it has dropped – it is a sugar-coated one – and gazes at it almost with adoration.

The Innocent   Yes, you'd like it yourself, wouldn't you? Don't you wish you may get it? But it's for Morenito. (*She fishes out another.*) Though this is even nicer . . . it's got rum inside.

Lorenza   Where did you get all this?

The Innocent *carefully puts the sweet away again and screws up her parcel.*

The Innocent   Don't you tell the Superior! I went out to take a letter to the Warden's daughter's sweetheart who's from Madrid, and stopping at the New Inn. And the cook there said she'd make me a present . . . because they'd had a big dinner on for the Town Council. Oh, my girl . . . but don't they just stuff themselves! Rice . . . chicken . . . cutlets . . . fish . . . ham in syrup . . . cheese! And all because a gentleman they call a Minister has come down . . . and they'd made him a free something or other of the city . . . and then this morning to celebrate it they've given him a funeral.

Lorenza (*amazed*)   A funeral!

The Innocent   Well, it must have been. They put him in a coach and took him all through the streets in a procession . . . and there's been a stone put up with his name on it in gold letters . . . just like the ones in the cemetery. And they hung wreaths . . . and everybody was in black clothes and high hats . . . all the Council and the Mayor . . . and the College professors and the Governor of the province and the Bishop. And I suppose it was just to make it all not seem so dreadful that they gave him a dinner.

And there's a bullfight too . . . just for him. They've gone there now. And, what's more . . . Juan de Dios, that used to be here, is fighting.

Engracia Juan de Dios!

The Innocent Look here . . . it says so.

She produces a crumpled handbill and they all three scan it excitedly.

Engracia The Bullring . . .

Lorenza In honor of His Excellency . . .

Engracia Six magnificent bulls . . .

Lorenza Bullfighters . . .

The Innocent Here . . . here!

Engracia . . . whose place will be taken by Juan de Dios Garcia, the Foundling . . . from the Orphanage of San Vincente de Paolo.

Lorenza From our orphanage . . . does it put that?

The Innocent Yes . . . and he made them put it . . . so as to show that he wasn't ashamed of being brought up here.

Engracia (*enviously*) Fancy flourishing it back at them like that when they meant it as a disgrace. Foundling! And perhaps his father will be watching him fight . . . and he may see him killed! He'll be one of those in a black coat and a high hat who's been at the dinner. Foundling! That's what I'll call myself, Engracia the Foundling . . . and if I'm a success I'll make some of the gentlemen in high hats pay pretty dear for the use of the name. Foundling! Foundling!

Most of this is muttered between her teeth. Meanwhile from the patio the sound of a quarrel can be heard; a man's voice, unsteady, half sober; a boy's, high in indignation; and the frightened cries of a child. This is **Morenito**. *It is* **Vicente** *that calls out, 'What are you up to . . . hitting a child like that?' and* **Policarpo** *that replies, 'I'll hit him if I choose. Take that! I'll learn you to laugh at me . . . on the other side of your mouth!' Then* **Morenito** *screams again.*

Engracia What's the matter . . . what's happening?

The three girls all rush to the door.

Lorenza It's that tailor! He's thrashing one of the little ones . . .

The Innocent It's Morenito! (*She calls out in great distress.*) Morenito . . . Morenito . . . come here.

Morenito, *a little boy of ten who seems even younger he is so pallid and fragile, runs helplessly in.* **Policarpo**, *the tailor, is close at his heels. He is a hunchback, a drunkard, debased, almost ape-like in his movements.* **Vicente** *comes too, one of the orphans, a well set up boy of sixteen.*

Vicente . . . And I'll break your head open because *I* choose. So now!

76   The Kingdom of God

Policarpo (*in great disdain*)   Oh, you will, will you?

Vicente   Yes, I will. Let that child alone. Let him alone, I tell you.

Morenito *yells with terror.*

Vicente   Will you let him alone . . . ?

Vicente *sends* **Policarpo** *flying. He staggers and falls against the screen.* **Morenito** *escapes and takes refuge with* **The Innocent**, *who comforts and pets him, and stops his crying by giving him a sweet.* **Policarpo** *struggles to his feet and scowls at the five of them.*

Policarpo   Scum! Charity brats!

Vicente   D'you want another? Oh yes . . . you're plucky enough to hit a poor child like that . . . you won't stand up to a man.

Policarpo   Him and you and all the lot of you . . . sons and daughters of trollops and thieves . . . that's what you are!

Vicente   Say that again!

Policarpo   I'll say it whenever I choose.

Vicente   Say it again, and I'll throttle you.

Policarpo   Aha . . . that gets you on the raw, does it? Yes, my lad . . . because it's true. You're the sons and daughters of . . .

Vicente, *with a yell, flings himself upon* **Policarpo**. **Lorenza** *and* **The Innocent** *rush to separate them.* **Engracia** *shouts with joy.*

Engracia   Throttle him, Vicente . . . throttle him!

Lorenza   Vicente . . . Vicente!

The Innocent   Help . . . help!

Engracia   Throttle him!

Lorenza   Now you be quiet!

While **Morenito**, *still quietly sobbing a little, looks on and sucks his sweet as if it were all no affair of his. At this moment* **Sister Gracia** *comes in. She is now an old lady of seventy. She supports herself with a stick, suffers from rheumatism and wears spectacles, but she is lively and merry all the same. As a rule she speaks gently enough, but she can get excited and be very angry too. And happening on this quarrel she raps out with great authority.*

Sister Gracia   What's going on here? Policarpo! Vicente! Get away from each other at once. What is all this about?

The fighters separate. **Lorenza** *and* **Engracia** *hang their heads. Only* **Morenito**, *feeling quite safe now that* **Sister Gracia** *is there, breaks out into renewed lamentations.*

Morenito Aie . . . aie . . . aie! He hit me . . . so he did!

In response to **Sister Gracia**'s *severely questioning look, both* **Policarpo** *and* **Vicente** *break out angrily.*

Vicente The coward . . . he was thrashing the child . . .

Policarpo The young blackguard . . . trying to throttle me!

Morenito Aie . . . aie . . . aie!

Sister Gracia (*to* **Morenito**) Keep quiet now.

Then she thumps the floor with her stick.

Silence!

There is dead silence. Then she turns to **Policarpo**.

Sister Gracia Whatever could such a child do to you to make you ill-treat him like that? Answer me.

Policarpo (*sullenly*) What they all do . . . all the time. Sit idling and laughing in a man's face.

Morenito (*perking up*) He tries to make me learn to sew with a needle that's got no point.

Policarpo You broke the point, you mean . . . so that you needn't learn to sew.

Morenito (*to* **Sister Gracia**) Oh . . . you tell him that's a lie. He gave me a needle that hadn't any point just so that I couldn't sew and then he hit me, he did . . . because he hates me because he says I called him a name. And I didn't call it him . . . and it's not a name, what's more . . . for it's true and everybody calls it him . . . the Sisters call it him. Policarpo the hunchback. Hunchie . . . hunchie . . . hunchie! (*He jumps up and down as he cries it out.*)

Policarpo See if I don't twist your neck for you!

Sister Gracia Quiet now. (*She raps with her stick again. The child's indignation amuses her, though she does her best to look severe.*) Morenito, I'm surprised at you. Go and stand this very minute with your face to the wall till you have learnt to be respectful to your elders. Is that the way a child should talk? Take care I don't shut you up in the cellar and let the rats eat you.

Morenito Aie . . . aie . . . aie!

Sister Gracia And as for you, my good Mr Tailor . . . I have told you a thousand times that the children are not to be beaten.

Policarpo Oh, I'll give him goodies!

Sister Gracia When they misbehave you are to come and complain to me . . . and I will punish them as they deserve.

Policarpo Why . . . you and the Sisters are all the same . . . always backing them up . . . and so they do just as they please. A pretty state my workshop would get into if I didn't take them in hand a bit myself!

Sister Gracia There are four workshops besides yours . . . and none of the other masters find they have to ill-treat the children before they can make them behave.

Policarpo Then they're cleverer than I am.

Sister Gracia Or less fond of brandy perhaps.

Policarpo There you go . . . always bringing up the brandy against me.

Sister Gracia Well, my friend . . . don't you put it down and then I shan't have to bring it up. Heavens . . . what a man!

Policarpo (*muttering*) Heavens . . . what an old woman!

Sister Gracia What's that you say, you insolent fellow?

Policarpo (*insolently indeed*) What I do in my workshop is my own affair. I'm not the Sisters' servant. I'm an employee of the Board. Let's understand that.

Sister Gracia Really. And have you never heard of an employee of the Board being out of employment sometimes?

Policarpo I've got some influence there though . . . and you may as well know it.

Sister Gracia And so have I . . . and you may as well know it. You lay another finger upon one of these children and we'll see who counts for most . . . your friends the publicans, or mine in the Church. And now you take yourself out of my sight.

Policarpo So one's to treat these charity brats as if they were the sons of dukes . . .

Sister Gracia They are the sons of God . . . and that's a higher title still.

Policarpo (*to* **Morenito**) Oh, well . . . come along now, you little imp.

Morenito Aie . . . aie . . . aie!

Sister Gracia No, Señor . . . he'll not go along . . . he'll stay here with me.

Policarpo Going to teach him his trade, are you?

Sister Gracia That's no concern of yours.

Policarpo (*as he goes angrily to the door*) Women's place is in the kitchen . . .

Sister Gracia Quite so . . . and men's in the tavern . . . and there we have the world nicely divided up, haven't we? (*Then she turns to* **Vicente**, *who has been standing quietly in a corner.*) And you now . . . what are you doing here?

Vicente (*a little uneasily*) Nothing . . . oh, nothing. I was just walking across the patio . . .

Sister Gracia I know that. But how did you come to be walking across the patio at this time of day . . . past the tailor's shop where you have no business to be? Who gave you permission? Who opened the door for you?

Policarpo, *who had about disappeared, suddenly thrusts his head back with a jeering laugh.*

Policarpo He didn't need it opened . . . he's got a key . . . a skeleton key . . . like a burglar.

After spitting this out he vanishes.

Vicente Curse him . . .

He starts to pursue **Policarpo**, *but* **Sister Gracia**'s *voice brings him to a stand.*

Sister Gracia Stop! A skeleton key. Is that true?

Vicente (*meekly*) Yes, Señora.

Sister Gracia (*drily*) Give it to me.

Vicente *takes a key from his pocket and hands it over.*

Vicente Here it is.

Sister Gracia And what are you doing with a skeleton key? Answer me.

Vicente *stands silent.*

Sister Gracia Let's see now. Oh . . . I understand. You come across the patio past the tailor's shop to get to where the girls are working. So we have a sweetheart, have we? Answer. Who were you going to see? Don't make me angry now, Vicente, or it will be the worse for you. Who did you come here to see?

Vicente *looks on the ground and does not reply.* **Sister Gracia** *turns to the girls, who are a little disconcerted.*

Sister Gracia It'll be a miracle if you're not concerned in this, Engracia.

Engracia (*hastily*) No, Señora . . . it wasn't to see me . . . no, Señora, indeed.

Sister Gracia But you know who it was. I can tell by your looks . . . all three of you know. Come along now . . . let's have it . . . quickly.

The three of them hang their heads and stay silent. **Sister Gracia**, *with a gesture of impatience, raps on the ground with her stick.*

Morenito (*piping up from his corner*) The Innocent won't say because Vicente has promised to stand her a glass of anisette presently.

Vicente *glances at the child as if he could murder him, but* **Morenito** *goes on quite imperturbably.*

Morenito But she knows . . . because she's the one that takes the letters to Paca . . .

Sister Gracia (*to* **Vicente**) To . . . to which Paca?

Morenito To little Paca . . . that works in the bakery . . . she's his sweetheart.

Sister Gracia Send Paca here to me at once . . . and you (*to the girls*) run along . . . run away.

Engracia *and* **Lorenzo** *vanish precipitately, and* **The Innocent** *is following when* **Sister Gracia** *stops her.*

Sister Gracia   No, no . . . you stay. I've to settle accounts with you too. Letters . . . glasses of anisette, indeed! A pretty business. This is what comes of trusting you and letting you go out. You carry letters to Paca, do you?

Morenito (*very pleased with himself*)   I took her one one day . . . and she baked me a little loaf of bread for it . . . all to myself.

Sister Gracia   Hold your tongue! Do you know what happens to children who speak when they're not spoken to? They have their tongues cut right out. Into the corner and down on your knees this very minute.

Morenito, *much taken aback, kneels down in the corner and weeps.* **Paquita** *appears in the doorway, a pretty girl of seventeen, dressed like the others. She is evidently a little troubled, but as evidently has her mind made up. She does not venture in, but stands, glancing sideways, first at* **Sister Gracia** *and then at* **Vicente**.

Sister Gracia   Come in . . . you.

Paquita *comes in.* **The Innocent**, *who had retired to a corner, little by little, edges her way to* **Morenito**, *and sits down on the floor to comfort him. After a while they are to be seen playing knucklebones together.*

Sister Gracia   Well . . . (*nodding to* **Vicente**) here he is. And can you tell me why he was making his way through the second patio by the help of a skeleton key?

Paquita (*seeing that denial is useless*)   Yes, Señora . . . to see me.

Sister Gracia   Well, I'm glad you confess it. You're pluckier about it than he is.

Paquita (*with childish petulance*)   I suppose I love him better than he does me.

Vicente (*just as childishly distressed*)   Oh . . . you've no right to say that!

Paquita   Well . . . if you're ashamed to say that you love me . . .

Vicente   I'm not . . . why should I be? And if I didn't tell, it was so as not to get you into trouble. And you know perfectly well that I love you every bit as much as you do me . . . and more, if it comes to that!

Paquita (*with a shy smile*)   Well . . . if you say so . . .

It would seem that they had completely forgotten **Sister Gracia**, *who with a burst of half-humorous anger interrupts them.*

Sister Gracia   That's right . . . that's all right, children! Go on sweethearting . . . don't attend to me! Well, this is the last straw!

Vicente   Oh . . . we don't mean to be rude. But we . . . she . . . you see . . .

Sister Gracia   Yes, I see her . . . and I see you . . . and a pretty pair of noodles you are! And what do you think is going to happen now, I should like to know?

She starts to get up, and with her rheumatism that's not easy, so **Paquita** *goes to help her. But with all the impatience of an old lady who hates to be reminded of her infirmities.*

Sister Gracia Let me be . . . let me be! Well . . . I like your impudence. One little angel of light mentions quite casually that he has made himself a skeleton key . . . and this girl confesses as calmly as you please that it's for clandestine meetings with her! And instead of being ashamed of yourselves and asking forgiveness . . .

Paquita But it isn't a sin to love people.

Sister Gracia But it's hardly a virtue, is it . . . to go making skeleton keys?

Vicente Oh . . . she knows I never wanted to.

Paquita No . . . because you haven't the courage of a mouse.

Sister Gracia (*banging on the ground with her stick*) Goodness gracious me . . . what a pair of children! May I ask if I'm to be allowed to get a word in edgeways?

Vicente Yes, Señora.

Sister Gracia Much obliged, I'm sure! Well, now . . . how long have you two been romancing like this?

Vicente It's since St James' day . . . that's the Warden's birthday . . . and Paquita went there with the Innocent to wait at table . . . and I was there seeing to the lock of the cupboard. And we started talking and I said to her . . .

Sister Gracia Thank you. I can guess what you said to her . . . and what she answered.

Paquita (*with great dignity*) No, Señora . . . I didn't answer him at all till the Eve of Our Lady's Day, when I was in the bakehouse with the Innocent . . . and he came in with the chopped wood . . . and then I said. . . .

Vicente She said I could make the key.

Sister Gracia Excellent! And now what happens?

Paquita We're going to get married.

Sister Gracia At once?

Paquita Yes . . . just as soon as he can get fifty dollars to buy the furniture.

Sister Gracia Oh . . . and then what?

Paquita Then . . .! We're used to going hungry. It won't be so bad to go hungry together.

Vicente And I'm sure I don't know why you need say you'll have to go hungry . . . when you know perfectly well you won't have to with me there to look after you. I can work . . . and though I say it that shouldn't, I know my trade with the best . . . I'm worth five pesetas a day anywhere. And I'd be earning it now and have the fifty dollars saved if it wasn't . . .

Sister Gracia That's the thing. Tomorrow we'll find you some work and we'll get you a lodging.

Paquita   What . . . send him away!

Sister Gracia   Yes, if you please. It doesn't suit me at all to have such a good locksmith living here.

Vicente (*to* **Paquita**)   There . . . what have I always told you!

Paquita   Send him away! Yes . . . you'll save your fifty dollars right enough . . . but who'll you spend them on then?

Vicente   Why, whatever should I want fifty dollars for . . . but to spend it on you?

Paquita   Oh, you say that now . . .

Vicente   I say it now . . . and I always shall . . . and God may strike me dead else.

Sister Gracia (*very angrily*)   And we've learnt to swear, have we? I've had enough of this. You be off to the bakehouse again . . . and you (*to* **Vicente**) get back to your work. Hurry up. Tomorrow I shall have a talk to the Warden about you . . . and that's the end of that.

Vicente (*meekly*)   You won't tell him about the skeleton key, will you?

Sister Gracia (*pretending to be very angry*)   I shall tell him just exactly what I choose. Of all the impudence! Get along with you.

Vicente *and* **Paquita** *linger, gazing at each other.*

Sister Gracia   Will you both be off . . . when I tell you?

Vicente (*very meekly*)   Yes, Señora. (*He turns to go and then back to* **Paquita** *with* . . .) Goodbye, Paquita.

Paquita (*as she turns away unresponsive*)   And a nice mess we've got into! This is what comes of trying to be happy!

As she goes out she meets **Sister Dionisia** *in the doorway.*

Sister Dionisia   Well . . . and where have you been hiding . . . and what about your oven? Oh, I beg pardon, Sister Gracia.

Sister Gracia   That's all right.

Sister Dionisia   May we serve supper? Come along . . . come along.

This last to **Engracia** *and* **Lorenza** *who are behind her with a basket filled with hunks of bread. They put it on the table, and join* **Sister Dionisia** *at the stove where they all three serve out the dripping-bread and broth.* **Sister Gracia** *sits down on a bench, crosses herself and says a Paternoster in a low voice. On ending it, she takes a little stone from her pocket and throws it out into the patio.*

Sister Gracia   Eah! The first Paternoster I've been able to say all day. (*Picking up the crucifix from her side and smiling at it lovingly.*) Ah . . . sweet Saviour, it's little time we get to talk to each other, you and I. But we're an old couple now.

She kisses the crucifix in simple affection, then, as in sudden reminder, turns to **Sister Dionisia**.

Sister Gracia   Sister Dionisia . . . did the peppers come?

Sister Dionisia *leaves the girls at the stove.*

Sister Dionisia   No, Señora.

Sister Gracia   Didn't you send for them?

Sister Dionisia   I went to the shop myself . . . with the Innocent.

Sister Gracia   And they wouldn't give them you?

Sister Dionisia   No . . . the man said that if it was for anyone of position or for the Sisters even he'd give credit . . . but that he wouldn't trust the Orphanage Board because they owed him for fourteen bags already and he's sure they won't pay.

Sister Gracia   God's will be done. But the flour . . . that came?

Sister Dionisia   Yes, Señora . . . yesterday afternoon.

Sister Gracia   Well . . . that's something.

Sister Dionisia   But you can't knead the dough it makes. Half of it's the commonest rye and half of it's nothing but bran. Just look what the bread's like.

She takes a bit of the black bread from the basket.

Sister Gracia   Mother of God!

Sister Dionisia (*lowering her voice*)   And there were cockroaches in some of the bags.

Sister Gracia (*her temper rising*)   Then it must all be sent back at once.

Sister Dionisia   But we sent it back last time . . . and it did no good. The contractor's on the Board, you know . . . and, as if that wasn't enough, his brother-in-law's the Party chairman.

Sister Gracia   I'm going to the Town Hall this very minute . . . and they shall hear what I have to say . . . yes indeed. Here . . . Innocent . . . give me my cloak . . . and you're to come too.

Sister Dionisia   You won't find anyone . . . they're all at the bullfight.

Sister Gracia   That's true . . . oh, very well then.

She sighs. **The Innocent** *who has jumped up, goes back to her corner.* **Lorenza** *comes from the stove to the bell-rope by the door.*

Lorenza   Supper's ready. Shall I ring?

Sister Dionisia (*to* **Sister Gracia**)   Do you think perhaps we'd better wait till everyone's back? Some of them, you know, had leave to go and stand near the bullring, to hear about the fight.

Sister Gracia (*a little fussed*)   What? . . . oh yes . . . certainly, we'd better wait. To stand near the bullring! I don't like it a bit. They'll come back excited as usual . . . and so difficult . . .

Sister Dionisia *is back at the stove.* **Engracia** *and* **Lorenza** *stand looking out of the patio door, while* **Morenito** *has come to sit at* **Sister Gracia**'s *feet.*

Sister Dionisia (*half to herself*)   He's fighting today.

Engracia (*to* **Lorenza**)   And won't he be proud . . . all dressed up like that!

Sister Dionisia   Come along now . . . take the basket . . . put out the bread for the children. Innocent . . . you can come with me.

Engracia *and* **Lorenza** *carry off their basket and* **Sister Dionisia** *goes off by the other small door with* **The Innocent**. *Seated on her bench,* **Sister Gracia**, *though still a little fussed, begins to pray in a low voice, while* **Morenito**, *at her feet, fingers her rosary and looks at her in silence for a little.*

Morenito   Are you saying your prayers?

Sister Gracia *smiles and nods.*

Morenito   Are you praying for Juan de Dios to do well?

Sister Gracia *still smiles.* **Morenito** *hesitates a little and then asks a most important question.*

Morenito   Tell me . . . is there any saint that was a bullfighter?

At this moment a great noise of cheering begins to be heard. As it grows, **Sister Dionisia**, **Engracia**, **Lorenza**, **The Innocent** *and a lot of the girls come out of the other dining-rooms. The sound of the cheering comes nearer; the crowd is evidently in the patio itself by now, and one can hear the shouts of 'Hurrah for Juan de Dios! Hurrah for the Foundling!' and* **Juan de Dios**'s *voice 'Where's Reverend Mother?' and cries of 'This way . . . she's here!'*

Sister Gracia   What's all this . . . who's making all this noise? Go and see, Sister Dionisia.

Sister Dionisia, *obeying, meets* **Juan de Dios** *at the patio door.*

Juan de Dios   Where is she? Reverend Mother . . . Reverend Mother . . .

Sister Dionisia   Oh . . . it's Juan de Dios!

And the girls cry out his name too. He is an attractive lad of twenty, dressed in a bullfighter's gala costume, which has lost its freshness, for indeed it is one that he has hired for his first fight.

Juan de Dios   Sister Gracia . . . oh, Reverend Mother . . . where are you?

He runs and kneels at her feet and puts his arms round her waist. **Sister Gracia**, *surprised and a little embarrassed, but very pleased, pushes him away, exclaiming.*

Sister Gracia   Here . . . here! What is all this? Get away!

Juan de Dios   I've come . . . oh, congratulate me!

Sister Gracia   Juan de Dios! There . . . get up.

He sits on the bench by her side. She leans on him a little.

Juan de Dios Why . . . what is it? You're not ill?

Sister Gracia (*smiling*) No . . . no . . .

Morenito (*jealously, pulling at her skirts*) Reverend Mother . . . Reverend Mother!

The girls at the back are all exclaiming among themselves, 'Oh, what clothes!' 'Oh, doesn't he look handsome!'

Juan de Dios The porter didn't want to let us in. A fine thing to have had the door shut in my face . . . today of all others!

Some of the bigger boys of the orphanage that were with **Juan de Dios** *come in from the patio, some little ones come from the other dining-room. And the crowd that followed him helps fill up the patio door. And they all cheer him, 'Hurrah for the Foundling!'* **Juan de Dios** *is beside himself with joy.*

Juan de Dios D'you hear that . . . d'you hear that? 'Hurrah for the Foundling!' And in the bullring . . . you should just have heard them shouting it there. They threw me cigars and they threw their hats in . . . and all the beautiful young ladies in the boxes stood up and applauded me . . . they did. And before you can say 'knife' I'll have all Spain applauding me . . . and adoring me . . . and shouting . . . every one of them . . . 'Hurrah for the Foundling' . . . and that's me . . . that's me . . . who hadn't any father or a name of his own . . . but went hungry and cold . . .! Oh, Reverend Mother, I have dreamed of this day . . . and I've kept myself for it . . . yes, I have . . . like one of God's blessed angels.

Sister Gracia Hush, hush . . . don't talk like that.

Juan de Dios (*very seriously*) But I have . . . I swear it. And look here . . .

He now proceeds to show **Sister Gracia** *by a lively pantomime how he disposed of his bull, the present spectators cheering him at every point with cries of* 'Olé! Olé!' *He pulls out his handkerchief for a muleta* (*the red cloth by which the bull is distracted*).

Juan de Dios The muleta . . . so! One pass . . . over his head to blind him. Then a high one to get my position. That leaves me exposed . . . so four more over his head, quickly, one after another. Then one to turn him . . . one from down on my knees right at his horns. And then . . . the thrust! And you should have heard them shout. I tell you . . . they went mad! And if you had only been there too . . . with a white mantilla on . . . and I could have dedicated my bull to you.

Sister Gracia Quiet . . . quiet . . . you heretic!

Juan de Dios But for all that, I've brought you . . . a present. Give it here . . . give it here.

One of the boys gives him something that is carefully wrapped up in a silk handkerchief. **Sister Gracia** *hesitates a moment before she takes it.*

Juan de Dios Take it . . . you deserve it . . . better than anyone else does. Open it . . . open it.

Sister Gracia *undoes the handkerchief, and discloses a bull's ear . . . all bloody still.*

Sister Gracia   Mother of God . . . what's this?

Sister Dionisia (*innocently*)   Why . . . it's an ear off a cow!

Juan de Dios (*very offendedly*)   What d'you mean by a cow? It's the bull's ear, Señora . . . my bull that, I killed . . . and this is his ear to prove it!

Once more the whole assemblage bursts into cheers.

Juan de Dios   And there were fifty people at least came and asked me for it as a souvenir. But it's for you. . . . just for you . . . to hang in your room . . . and everyone that sees it there will envy you.

Sister Gracia   Thank you . . . my son.

She cannot think what to do with her present, but **Engracia** *takes it and does it up again with the greatest care.*

Juan de Dios   And look . . . look at the tie-pin his Excellency threw me. Isn't it wonderful . . . isn't it, Sister Dionisia . . . and all of you . . . aren't you proud . . . and happy . . . isn't this a wonderful day for our orphanage?

The boys and girls agree enthusiastically.

Juan de Dios   But do look happy, Reverend Mother. (*He puts his arm round her and calls to the people in the doorway and out in the patio.*) For she is my mother . . . she is . . . she is! The other one left me in a basket on the doorstep . . . but she took me in and brought me up and cared for me. And Hurrah for our Reverend Mother . . . she's all the mother I ever want.

Tremendous cheering.

Sister Gracia   Be quiet now. Tell them all to be quiet.

Juan de Dios   But why don't you look happy? Oh, . . . haven't you made up your mind yet to my being a bullfighter? I know . . . I know! Oh wasn't she just set on my staying a carpenter all my life!

Sister Gracia   But suppose a bull kills you, my son?

Juan de Dios   Well . . . if a bull kills me after I've done my duty by him, they'll give me a finer funeral than they would the Prime Minister.

Sister Gracia   Mother of God!

Juan de Dios   And whether or no . . . I have a good time and everybody talks about me and all the women go mad about me and I get lots of money . . . yes, I'm going to be rich . . . do you know that? I got nothing for fighting today . . . because it was the first time. But I did so well that for next Sunday they're giving me a thousand pesetas . . . one thousand pesetas!

This creates an enormous sensation. The orphans stare and comment upon the marvel in low, impassioned tones. And **Juan de Dios** *adds impulsively:*

Juan de Dios And fifty of them for you . . . and then Sister Dionisia can cook you such a dinner. Hurrah, girls, hurrah! Meat for dinner next Sunday!

They all cheer ecstatically.

Juan de Dios But I must be off . . . they're waiting for me. (*To* **Sister Gracia**.) Oh . . . come as far as the gate with me, so that everybody can see us together.

Sister Gracia My son . . . I never heard of such a thing!

Juan De Dios Please . . . please . . . for it's the happiest day of my life. Goodbye, everybody . . . goodbye!

Engracia *suddenly darts up to him.*

Engracia Well . . . good luck to you, Juan de Dios!

Sister Gracia *lets him lead her to the door, where everyone makes way for them, and out into the patio, where the cheers are tremendous. 'Hurrah for the Foundling! Hurrah for our Reverend Mother!' Gradually the crowd disperses and the cheers die away.* **Sister Dionisia**, *the girls, the little ones and* **Morenito** *are left in possession of the room.*

Sister Dionisia Come now . . . come everybody . . . back to work. Back to your refectory. (*Then to* **Lorenza** *and* **Engracia**.) You can serve supper.

Engracia *does not stir.*

Sister Dionisia And what's the matter with you, stupid? D'you want to be a bullfighter too? Ring the bell now.

Engracia, *without a word, goes to the bell-rope and pulls it.* **Morenito** *likewise stands very aloof.*

Sister Dionisia And what's come to you, pray? Sit down in your place.

Morenito And aren't I a foundling too?

He seats himself at the head of one of the tables. The bigger boys now begin to filter in again through the patio door. And in the further rooms can be heard the chatter of children who will have come in to their meal by some other way. The big boys talk and gesticulate excitedly as they make their way to their places at the table, jostling and stepping over each other or crawling even under the tables.

First Boy Get out . . .

Second Boy Get out yourself!

Third Boy Stop it, will you . . .

First Boy That's my place.

Sister Dionisia (*rapping upon the screen with a wooden spoon*) Order there . . . order . . . keep order and silence. Take your proper places at once.

Second Boy Precious stuck-up, wasn't he?

Felipe   And well he may be! He's going to get more rosettes off bulls yet . . . and make millions at it.

First Boy   Well, we shall see . . . or perhaps we shan't!

Felipe   We've seen enough to know, señor!

Second Boy   Oh, don't tell me! He's only a phenomenon.

First Boy   Anyone can be that!

Felipe   Can they? Well, let's see anyone else that can give the last thrust like he did . . .

He proceeds to illustrate the way it was done and all the others applaud him with cries of 'Olé! Olé!'

Sister Dionisia   Silence there!

First Boy   Well . . . if he keeps on doing it that way see how long it'll be before he finds himself stuck on the horns of the bull.

Felipe   Don't you believe it!

First Boy   A bit of a suicide . . . that's what he'll be!

Second Boy   Still, he's a plucky fellow.

First Boy   Being plucky isn't bullfighting.

Felipe   It's being a hero.

Third Boy   It's being a man anyhow.

Second Boy   Hurrah!

First Boy   Oh, stop it!

Sister Dionisia (*in despair*)   Now . . . now . . . now! Do sit down and be quiet . . . your supper's getting cold.

Third Boy   You know just as much about bullfighting as a potato!

Second Boy   I know more than you do, anyway.

Sister Dionisia   Silence . . . silence! Now. In the name of the Father and of the Son and of the Holy Ghost . . . Amen.

And she crosses herself, as do the girls. Some of the boys do so, carelessly enough, and some go on talking.

First Boy   I bet anything you like that he started in to kill the bull too soon . . .

Sister Dionisia   Silence!

And now she prays while the boys mumble after her.

Sister Dionisia   Bless, Lord, the food that we are about to receive. Preserve us from the sin of gluttony. And be thou unto us, by thy grace, the eternal food of our souls . . . Amen.

Boys (*in a hurry to begin talking again*)   Amen.

Lorenza, **Engracia** and **The Innocent** *have been serving out the supper.*

Sister Dionisia   Be careful with that saucepan now!

Engracia (*to a boy who has joggled it*)   Look here . . . you keep your hands to yourself.

Third Boy   Me!

Engracia   Yes . . . you!

Third Boy   You're off your head, my dear!

First Boy   Well . . . she's not all there anyway . . . poor girl!

Engracia   Clumsy lout!

Third Boy   Why, how much more do you want of her?

Sister Dionisia   What's all that now? Don't you hear me tell you to be quiet?

First Boy   Where's my bread?

Third Boy   Who's got my spoon?

Morenito   Aie . . . they've taken my mug!

Sister Dionisia   Will you start your suppers . . . yes or no?

Felipe (*having dipped his spoon in*)   Look here . . . what sort of stuff is this?

First Boy   It's got no peppers in it!

And several of the boys repeat protestingly, 'No peppers! It's got no peppers!'

Sister Dionisia (*gently apologetic*)   Now my children . . . what difference does it make?

Felipe   Well . . . I'm not going to eat it.

He gets up in protest and all the others do the same, crying, 'Nor am I!' 'Nor I!' . . . all but **Morenito**, *who says nothing, but stays in his corner calmly eating away.*

Sister Dionisia (*very distressed*)   But, my children, if there's nothing else . . . why, for the love of God . . . eat this!

Felipe *stands upon a bench and shouts.*

Felipe   We don't want it and we won't eat it! We've had enough of eating bread and water for the love of God!

A chorus of shouting approbation.

Sister Dionisia   But boys . . . boys . . . boys!

Felipe   Always shaking a crucifix at you . . .

More approbation.

Felipe . . . whenever they want to cheat you out of something!

There is enthusiastic agreement with this.

Sister Dionisia Oh boys, do be quiet . . . just because I ask you to. You're quite right . . . but do eat your supper. What good will it do you to go to bed hungry? You shall have something better tomorrow. Now be good . . . be patient . . . sit down . . . oh, please do as I tell you!

Some of them, thus appealed to, are sitting down when **Felipe** *says:*

Felipe The boy that puts his spoon in his plate is a coward.

Sister Dionisia Now you be quiet!

Felipe I won't be quiet. I say that he's a coward and a sneak.

Those that are down get up again and thus reinforced they all protest loudly, 'We won't! No, we won't!'

Sister Dionisia Sit down . . . sit down!

Felipe And the boy that sits down to table again is a disgrace to us all!

A great clamour; cries, stamping and hammering on the tables.

Sister Dionisia (*to* **Felipe**) Will you be good enough to leave the room this very minute?

Felipe Oh, I'm going! But I'm not going alone. Come along, all of you! Anyone that's not afraid and wants something to eat . . . follow me!

They cheer him and cry that they will, and they are moving off. **Sister Dionisia** *darts to the door and tries to block the way.*

Sister Dionisia But where are you going . . . what are you going to do?

Felipe What men do . . . take by force what we can't get by asking nicely.

Loud cheers and great readiness to be gone.

Sister Dionisia No . . . no . . . no!

Felipe Now you stop interfering or it will be the worse for you. Come on, boys! They keep us penned up here as if we were brute beasts. We may shout as loud as we like and we shan't be heard . . . they've forgotten us. And we're just starved. Well . . . there's bread outside . . and there's meat outside . . . and there's wine outside . . . so come outside and get it. If it has to be stolen we'll steal it . . . and if killing's what's needed . . . well, we'll do some killing!

Tremendous enthusiasm.

Sister Dionisia Blessed Jesus . . . Ave Maria . . . help!

Felipe (*beside himself*) Into the street with you! We'll let them see . . . we'll let them hear. It's an everlasting disgrace the way that we're treated. Well, then . . . let's make them treat us better. Throw their bread and water back in their swine's faces! We weren't born different to anyone else, were we? Well, then . . . we've a right to be as well fed as everyone else is.

They cheer wildly and are marching off. **Sister Dionisia** *struggles with them in vain, crying, 'Get back! Get back!' and then rushes to the bell-rope and pulls it violently. The girls scream.* **Felipe** *turns back to them.*

Felipe Well, aren't you coming too? All of us . . . all together . . . where are the rest? Let's have the whole orphanage out in the streets to demand its rights. If we're nobody's children . . . why, we're everybody's children. Come along then . . . March!

At this moment **Sister Gracia** *appears in the doorway.*

Sister Gracia What's all this?

At the sound of her voice and the sight of her, there is something of a lull in the storm, and voices can be heard exclaiming 'Reverend Mother! . . . Sister Gracia!'

Sister Gracia Oh yes . . . it's Sister Gracia! And what is all this terrible fuss about?

The girls have drawn back already and so have some of the boys. The rest stand their ground and the noise has by no means ceased.

Sister Dionisia Aie . . . Sister! People must have been giving them wine in the Plaza . . . and there's no holding them.

Sister Gracia So I see. Well . . . we live in a revolutionary age! (*To the girls.*) What . . . you too! (*Then she faces the malcontents.*) Have you had your supper yet?

Sister Dionisia They . . . they didn't like. . . .

Sister Gracia Let me talk to them. Have you had your supper yet?

Felipe That's where we're going . . . to get our supper. Well . . . what are you all waiting for? Come on!

Sister Gracia Tsch . . . tsch! (*Looking* **Felipe** *squarely in the eyes.*) To get your supper indeed? Where, pray?

Felipe Wherever it's to be found.

Sister Gracia And when you've found it . . . do you fancy its owners'll give it you?

Felipe If they don't, we'll take it.

The few enthusiasts that are left reinforce this with what boldness they can muster.

Sister Gracia People keep things that they value locked up, my son.

Felipe Then we'll break open the locks.

The enthusiasts applaud this also.

Sister Gracia (*quietly now and kindly*) And do you think if there were any locked door that would open I shouldn't have been there by this to knock at it for you?

Felipe Yes . . . but you go asking so prettily. We're going to try if a few stones won't make them attend.

Sister Gracia My son . . . the answer to a stone is often a bullet.

Felipe (*defiantly*) So much the better! Far better to be left dead in the street once and for all than to stay here and starve to death bit by bit.

Sister Gracia (*sternly*)   You don't know what you're talking about. And none of you know what you're doing. Now, there has been enough of this . . . and everybody will be quiet and sit down . . . because I tell them to. *(They are quiet . . . but they can't make up their minds to obey altogether.)*

Sister Gracia   Did you hear what I said? Sit down.

The boys go slowly towards the benches.

Sister Gracia   Come now . . . be quick about it.

They slowly sit down.

Sister Gracia (*to* **Felipe**)   And you.

Last of all and much against his will **Felipe** *sits down too.*

Sister Gracia   Now, Sister Dionisia . . . is there any more broth in the kettle?

Sister Dionisia (*who is still rather frightened*)   Yes, Señora.

Sister Gracia   Well, then, serve that out . . . then they'll have their supper hot. And let everyone keep quiet. I don't want to have to punish anybody tonight.

Sister Dionisia *and the girls put more broth in the plates. Then after a moment* **Sister Gracia** *goes on talking . . . quietly and kindly now, but masterfully still.*

Sister Gracia   And d'you think you're the only folk in this world who don't get all that they want to eat? No, my children, no. There are people worse off than you. . . . some of them so poor that they'd think your plate of supper a luxury. You'll have a roof over your head tonight and a mattress to sleep on and a blanket to cover you. Think of the people who'll sleep in a ditch by the roadside with no roof but the sky, and only the hoarfrost to come down and cover them. Think of the sick people . . . of people without a friend . . . stumbling through the world with not a hand held out to them . . . nobody caring. While you have a home and all the love we can give you. You are sheltered . . . you are taught . . . you are kept in right paths. And then think if you don't owe a few thanks to God after all.

Felipe   To God . . . to God! There is no God!

A stir of horror among the children. **Sister Dionisia** *crosses herself and exclaims, 'Blessed Jesus!'*

Sister Gracia   And whatever do you think you mean by that, you little fool?

Felipe   Because if there were . . . would he think this was all right?

Sister Gracia   God does not think this is right. Men break his laws. He made them brothers. Is it his fault if they turn wolves and devour each other? God does not think it right that his children should go hungry . . . and the innocent are not ever disgraced in his eyes. It is by no will of his that some are poor and neglected while some are set up in pride. For God is Love and he loves us all and to each one he gives a share in heaven and in this earth.

Felipe   Don't listen to her . . . she's just preaching lies to you. Nuns have all sold themselves to the rich. Do they ever go hungry? And as long as they can get us to keep up the sham they're let stuff themselves with food in peace.

Sister Gracia I am not lying to you. I am telling you the truth and the whole truth. God does not smile upon the injustice of this world. He endures it . . . for how long? . . . ah, that we do not know. But he does not think it right.

Felipe Well, then . . . let's go and break the heads of those that do . . . and God will thank us for that.

A few of the boys cheer up at this and approve.

Sister Gracia Ah, no, no . . . all that can be done for this wicked world is to help to make it good.

Felipe And who's going to?

Sister Gracia You . . . you . . . not by hating but through love. Yes, all of you will help do that. For, when you are men . . . and go away from here, it will be because you have suffered from injustice that you'll know how to make . . . and want to make . . . laws that are just. Oh yes, my sons yes . . . the world is yours . . . for you have won it by hunger and by suffering and pain. So when you hold it in your hands, make it what it ought to be. God is watching you . . . his hopes are all in you. You suffer now that you may succour his world then. God sees you . . . God hears you. Now say with me. Lord, Lord, we thank thee for this food which is given us in thy name. There is not much of it, it is not very good, and we will not forget the taste of this bitter bread. And by thy precious love we swear that thy children on this earth shall eat of it no more . . . say it with me . . . say it . . .

The boys repeat after her solemnly and quietly.

Sister Gracia Jesus, Son of God . . . Christ, son of man, by the divine blood that thou didst shed for us we swear to spend our own to the last drop when we are men . . . that children may not be forsaken anymore . . . that no more mothers may be wronged and go hungry and be ashamed to carry their children in their arms. My sons . . . my sons, promise me that when you are men you'll try to bring these things to pass . . . that you'll help to build on earth the Kingdom of God.

Very quietly, very solemnly, they murmur 'Yes'.

Sister Gracia Thank you, my children . . . thank you. And now . . . supper's over . . . go to bed and sleep in peace.

The boys go slowly out. Only **Felipe** *does not move. He is sitting on his bench, head buried in his arms and crying.*

Sister Gracia *goes to him and puts a hand upon his shoulder.*

Sister Gracia Don't cry . . . for men don't cry, you know. And they don't complain. They suffer . . . but they work and hope.

Curtain.

The Romantic Young Lady
(Sueño de Una Noche de Agosto)

A Comedy in Three Acts

Teatro Eslava, Madrid (1918)
Royalty Theatre, London (1920)
The Neighborhood Playhouse, New York (1926)

Royalty Theatre, London (16 September 1920) cast included:

The Apparition	Dennis Eadie
Doña Barbarita	Mary Rorke
Rosario	Joyce Carey
Emilio	Harry W. Furniss
Mario	Tarver Penna
Pepe	Lionel Westlake
Don Juan	A. Scott-Gatty
Guillermo	Joynsen Powell

Producers: Frank Curzon and Dennis Eadie
Production overseen by: Helen and Harley Granville Barker

Neighborhood Playhouse, New York (4 May 1926) cast included:

The Apparition	Ian Maclaren
Doña Barbarita	Dorothy Sands
Rosario	Mary Ellis
Emilio	Marc Loebell
Mario	Otto Hulicius
Pepe	Albert Carroll
Don Juan	Harold Minjer
Guillermo	George Hoag

Director: Agnes Morgan

Characters

Rosario
Emilio
Doña Barbarita
Mario
María Pepa
Pepe
Irene
Don Juan
Amalia
Guillermo
The Apparition

The action passes – at the present time, more or less, and in Madrid – between one August evening and the next, at Doña Barbarita's house and at the abode of the Apparition.

Act One

The scene is in a room in **Doña Barbarita**'s *house. It is a study furnished modestly but in good taste. There is a table with books, papers, periodicals: a large bookcase full of books; an easy chair; a chaise-longue or a large sofa placed against the table; other chairs of course; some prints and engravings on the walls, of small value but well chosen. There are doors at the back and on the right. The one on the right leads to a bedroom. The one at the back communicates with the rest of the house. At the left is a large window; it must be obvious that it is not a very great height above the street. An electric light fixture hangs from the ceiling; another, movable, with a blue shade is on the table, in such a way that its light is useful to anyone seated, or lying, on the sofa, and that it can be turned out from there without moving.*

At the rising of the curtain, **Pepe**, *who is about twenty-one, in evening dress but without having yet put on his dinner-coat, is standing before the mirror over the mantelpiece, trying to tie his tie, but not succeeding very well.* **Emilio**, *his brother, eight or nine years older, at the table is writing a letter and showing signs of impatience because the pen and ink are not working as well as he would like, and hunting among the papers on the table to find a sheet which he can substitute for the one he has just blotted.*

Pepe Oh, this tie, Rosario!

Rosario (*from the bedroom*) I'm coming.

Emilio What a pen! What ink! Another blot . . . that sheet's done for now. Where on earth is the writing paper? Rosario!

Rosario I'm coming! I'm coming! (**Rosario** *comes in. She is a very pretty girl of twenty-three.*)

Rosario What *is* the matter?

Pepe Tie my tie for me.

Emilio Where *is* the writing paper?

Rosario (*affectionately*) Come here . . . clumsy! What useless creatures men are! (*She ties his tie.*)

Emilio And why, may I ask, is the baby of the family to be attended to first?

Rosario Because he howled first. Don't mix up those papers, or Mario will be angry. (*Finishing the tie. To* **Pepe**.) There!

Emilio And suppose Mario is . . . Does Mario own the whole house?

Rosario Not the house – but the table.

Emilio And may I ask why that dearly beloved brother of ours is to keep to himself the only place in the house where one can write?

Rosario Because he's the only one in the house who does any writing. If anyone else had a claim, what about mine, to the table and the room, too?

Emilio And am I not writing . . . or trying to – Heaven help me!

Rosario Writing a love letter is not writing. (*She searches the table quickly and methodically.*) Here you are . . . paper, envelope, blotting paper . . . stamp. Now, shall I dictate the letter as well?

Emilio No, thank you.

Rosario That's something.

Pepe The clothes brush?

Rosario I'll lend you one.

She goes into the bedroom and comes out almost immediately with a clothes brush in her hand.

Pepe One never can find anything in this house.

Rosario Because you never look in the right place. And haven't you a bedroom to dress in?

Pepe (*looking at himself in the glass*) I can't see myself in the bedroom.

Rosario You're very smart tonight. Where are you off to?

Pepe The theatre.

Rosario Bent on conquest?

Pepe Yes, indeed.

Rosario Of the leading lady?

Pepe Of someone far more important . . . of the leading lady's backer.

Rosario Really!

Pepe He's an American and a millionaire. And he's looking for a private secretary, and I'm to be introduced to him tonight. If he takes a fancy to me, isn't my fortune made? Off to America, I shall work myself to death for him, and, in a year or two's time, when he can't do without me, he'll give me a share of his business . . . Say a prayer for me, my child . . . my foot's on the ladder. And when I'm rich, think of all the chocolates I'll buy you.

Emilio Could you stop talking just for one minute? I've made three mistakes already.

Rosario (*as she leans over the writing table*) Passion spelt with one 's' again. Give her my love. Oh, but I wish you'd get married.

Emilio Not more than she does.

Rosario Not more than you do, I hope.

Emilio Well, you know, personally, now that we've waited five years . . .

Rosario Yes . . . and why have you waited five years? She has to wait till you're rich enough to get married. If I'll kindly wait till you're rich I shall have chocolates.

Doña Barbarita *and* **Mario** *have come in. She is a very old lady and leans on her grandson's arm. He is twenty-seven or so.*

Mario No, my dear, not till then . . . not all that time! Wait till I'm editor of my paper . . . till I've had a few plays produced . . . Then you shall see. As you go along the street you'll hear them whispering: 'That's Mario Castellanos' sister, Castellanos, the dramatist!

While he is talking, he has crossed the room and helped his grandmother to sit down on the sofa near the window.

Rosario It's quite like a fairy tale. Once on a time there were three brothers – famous, rich and happy. And they had a sister. Well, what about her?

Mario You?

Emilio How do you mean? . . . what about you?

Rosario What happens to me when you're all such thrilling successes?

Pepe I suppose you'll marry.

Mario Won't you?

Rosario Suppose I don't?

Emilio But why shouldn't you? You're very pretty.

Mario And clever enough . . . to be anybody's wife.

Rosario Thank you. (*She curtseys ironically to all three.*)

Mario How old are you now, Rosario?

Rosario Can't you remember? Twenty-three last birthday.

Emilio Well . . . it is time you were looking around.

Rosario (*very much offended*)   What do you mean?

Pepe Don't worry, my child. I'll find you a husband.

Rosario Thanks. I'm not sure I'd trust to your taste.

Pepe Why not?

Rosario Well . . . if I'm to judge by the cigarette girl I saw you out walking with yesterday . . .

Pepe Oh, did you? I must be off or I shall miss my millionaire. Goodnight, Grandmamma. (*He kisses her hand.*) You were married three times, weren't you? Tell this silly girl how to catch a husband before she's past praying for. (*As he goes he tries to kiss* **Rosario**.) Goodnight, ugly duckling.

Rosario Run away, idiot!

Doña Barbarita Don't come walking in at half past nothing o'clock now . . . for I'm awake and I hear you.

Pepe (*at the door*) But, my dear Grandmamma, if I'm going to conquer America you must expect me to be late home.

He goes off gaily, and outside is heard singing some popular song.

Doña Barbarita That young gentleman is riding for a fall!

Emilio Goodnight, Grandmamma. (*Kisses her hand.*)

Doña Barbarita Are you off too?

Emilio To post my letter.

Rosario And then to find consolation till the answer comes. That's what you call being in love.

Emilio My good child, what do you know about being in love? I shall be a model husband.

Doña Barbarita Are you taking lessons in the art?

Emilio Well . . . anything to forget one's troubles, you know. Goodnight.

He goes out, embracing **Rosario** *as he passes her, while she shakes her fist at him affectionately.* **Rosario** *then picks up the torn papers which have been left on the table. She then sets all the table in order, picks up the clothes brush which* **Pepe** *has left on a chair and goes into the bedroom, and comes back again.* **Doña Barbarita** *remains seated on the sofa.* **Mario** *walks about idly, looks out of the window at the street, takes another turn and sits down in a chair.*

Rosario Aren't you off, too?

Mario I wish I weren't! But what would my respected editor say if he had to go to press without my column of spiteful gossip about the great ones of the earth? Wait till I'm one of them! Patience . . . patience. (*To* **Rosario**.) Goodnight, my precious. Ten years hence, on such a night as this – the poor wretch doing the comic chippings in my stead will be racking his brains to think – 'What can I say this time about Mario Castellanos?' – which is precisely my trouble at the moment over my favourite dramatist. Goodnight, Grandmother.

He kisses her hand and goes out.

Rosario (*looking out of the window*) What a divine night! How the jasmine smells. (*Waving her hand.*) Good luck!

Doña Barbarita Whom are you waving to?

Rosario Mario. (*To the unseen* **Mario**.) What? Wait, I'll see. (*As she goes to the table she says to* **Doña Barbarita**.) His fountain pen! Here!

She leans over out of the window to hand it to **Mario** *who is down below.*

Doña Barbarita Take care, you'll fall.

Rosario I shouldn't kill myself . . . tumbling six feet into the street.

She waves to the disappearing **Mario**; *then sits on the window seat with a sigh.*

Doña Barbarita Why are you sighing?

Rosario Envy, I suppose. Off he goes . . . so happily!

Doña Barbarita To his work.

Rosario Well . . . one to his work, another to amuse himself . . . another to look for his lucky chance. But the thing is that they go . . . and here we stay. (*There is a short pause, then quickly.*) Have you ever noticed, Grandmamma . . .?

Doña Barbarita What?

Rosario How quickly men walk off once they reach the door? While we stand buttoning our gloves, and look up the street and down and hesitate . . . as if we feared someone might stop us. It's as if they went off by right but we were stealing out of jail. (*She looks out into the street and takes a deep breath of the perfumed air.*) Oh, what a wonderful night! (*She leaves the window and takes her grandmother's hand sitting close by her.*) Grandmother, suppose I should say to you . . . I'm a free woman. I can make a will, run a business, commit suicide, go off to America, go on the stage. Therefore I want a latchkey, just as my brothers have. And I want to come and go as I like just as they do . . . by day or night without questions asked. What would you think of that?

Doña Barbarita I should think it quite a natural caprice.

Rosario (*a little astonished*) Would you give it to me?

Doña Barbarita Why not? The cook's key will be hanging behind the back door. Go and get it, and go out by all means if you want to. (**Rosario** *jumps up.*) Now, I wonder where you'll go.

Rosario (*perplexed . . . brought to a standstill*) I know . . . that's just it. Where can a girl go alone at this time of night without fear of being thought something she isn't? Fear! That's a woman's curse.

Doña Barbarita Perhaps it's her blessing. (*Smiling.*) If we feared as little as men do what the world would think of us we should soon be as shameless as they. And that would be a pity, for if we lost *our* sense of decency where else in the world would you find it?

Rosario (*sitting down by her grandmother again*) Do you believe, Grandmamma, that all men who go off at night so gaily . . . behave wickedly?

Doña Barbarita No doubt some of them do . . . and some try to. But most of them only want to pretend that they are being wicked. And I expect that oftenest they all get cheated out of their money and their wickedness both. And that's why they come back so depressed. (*Stroking her hair.*) I shouldn't envy them, my dear, if I were you.

Rosario (*with a great deal of feeling which, little by little, changes into a pretty anger*) Oh no, not their wickedness, or even their fun, as they call it. But their courage and their confidence. They're so ready to fight and so sure that they'll win. 'I mean to get on – you must get married . . .' to some other bold gentleman who has got on, who can afford to buy me and keep me. 'And when we're all rich what a good time we'll give you.' Suppose I don't want to be given a good time. (*Imitating* **Mario**.) 'That's Mario Castellanos's sister' (*With much dignity.*) I don't want to be anyone's sister, or anyone's wife . . . I don't want to reflect someone else's fame. I want to hear them say: 'That's Rosario Castellanos.' Why can't I be myself? Are you laughing at me?

Doña Barbarita I seem to remember that while the sun is masculine the moon that reflects him is a lady.

Rosario Yes, in Spanish, but in German the sun's a woman and the moon's a man, and in English, which is a most commonsensical language, sun is sun and moon is moon and each is itself and no one thinks of being masculine or feminine until . . . well, until that particular question arises. (*Sits down yet again by her grandmother.*) You're laughing again. You don't understand – you belong to the past – you all liked being slaves.

Doña Barbarita No, my dear, only masters like *having* slaves . . . but while you want to be free of the tyranny we were satisfied by being revenged on the tyrants now and then.

Rosario How?

Doña Barbarita We just made their lives unbearable. (*She takes from her neck a sort of triple locket which she opens. Smiling tenderly.*) My three masters! Ernesto my first, Enrique my second and your grandfather, my dear . . . the third. How they loved me . . . and how I loved them!

Rosario (*somewhat scandalised*)   All three?

Doña Barbarita Yes . . . each in turn. And how I plagued them!

Rosario Did you?

Doña Barbarita (*very pleased with her conjugal recollections*)   I was jealous of every woman my first husband looked in the face . . . and he was a portrait painter, do you remember? My second husband suffered tortures from his own jealousy . . . of your grandfather. That was premature, but prophetic, for your dear grandfather was our neighbour in those days and he used to stand and look at me from his balcony. And then he in his turn tortured himself, poor man, with jealousy of my second husband, who was dead by that time to be sure . . . but that only seemed to make it worse. When I think of the times I've walked into my first husband's studio, shaking all over, to see what sort of a woman he was painting this time . . . and how much of her, and of the times when I'd glance up at your grandfather on his balcony and let my dear second husband imagine . . . God forgive me . . . that I was smiling at him; and then when your grandfather would catch me looking at my poor second husband's portrait . . . my first husband had painted it while they were both alive . . . and if I wanted to drive him to fury I'd only to give one sigh. Well, now they're in heaven all three and I'm almost sorry I worried them so. (*And she kisses the three pictures.*)

Rosario Oh, Grandmother!

Doña Barbarita But never forget that I was an obedient wife, gentle and loving, an angel of the fireside, an angel in crinoline. No doubt it's far nobler to 'live your own life' (isn't that what you call it?) but I fear you'll never find it so amusing.

María Pepa, *a maid – a family servant, nearly as old as* **Doña Barbarita** *herself – appears. She remains planted in the doorway with folded arms and doesn't speak.*

Doña Barbarita (*rather ill-humouredly; she knows the footstep so well*) And what do you want?

María Pepa It's past eleven.

Doña Barbarita What of it?

María Pepa You've to put in your curl papers and say your prayers – a special one tonight, too, for tomorrow was Señor Emilio's birthday – and if you stop here talking much longer you won't be in bed before midnight.

Doña Barbarita What of it?

María Pepa You have to be up early tomorrow for Mass, and if you don't get your eight hours and a half you'll have another of your attacks.

Doña Barbarita (*slyly*) What sort of an attack is it *you* get when you try to sit still for five minutes without coming to hear what we're talking about?

María Pepa (*very offended*) Little I care what you're talking about!

Doña Barbarita How long have you been listening at the door?

María Pepa Listening? Holy saints!

Doña Barbarita I heard you tiptoeing up the passage like a ghost.

María Pepa And if one walks like a human being you say the noise upsets your nerves.

She turns to go with extreme dignity.

Doña Barbarita Where are you going?

María Pepa To the kitchen . . . my proper place. Where else?

Doña Barbarita Sit down.

María Pepa Thank you. I'm not tired.

Doña Barbarita Sit down!

María Pepa *sits stiffly and haughtily on the edge of a chair.*

Doña Barbarita And don't start a grievance when no one has done a thing to you. We're not talking secrets. I was just telling my granddaughter –

María Pepa What an angel you were to your three husbands – I heard you.

Rosario (*bursting into a hearty laugh*) Oh, María Pepa!

Doña Barbarita (*ironically*)   Don't laugh, my dear, please. She'll take offence and then what shall I do! Has the cook gone to bed yet?

María Pepa   What on earth would the woman be doing sitting up to this hour?

Doña Barbarita   Good heavens, you talk as if it were three in the morning. Why can't you say at once that you're dead with sleep yourself?

María Pepa (*as if she had been accused of a crime*)   I . . . dead with sleep!

Doña Barbarita   Oh, come along, come along. (*Getting up.*) When my maid is tired of course I must go to bed. Goodnight, my child.

María Pepa   Sit up till daybreak if you like. You suffer for it, not I!

Rosario (*kissing her*)   Goodnight, Grandmamma.

Doña Barbarita (*patting her cheek*)   But don't sit up till all hours reading.

Rosario   No, Grandmamma.

María Pepa   She will, she will! If food failed I believe the women of this family could eat books. It's an unnatural appetite.

Doña Barbarita   Well, you're no glutton. Sixty-five years I've been trying to teach you your letters.

María Pepa   Thank you. I hear enough lies as it is without splitting my skull getting more out of books.

Doña Barbarita   Get back to your tub, Diogenes, and don't talk so much.

The two go out, arm in arm without its being quite clear which one is supporting the other. **Rosario**, *with her characteristic instinct of order, puts the furniture in place almost unconsciously, afterwards she sighs, stretches herself lazily, yawns, sighs again, yields to the little clock which is on the mantelpiece, begins to unhook her dress. When she has it nearly unhooked, she goes into the bedroom, and comes out after a minute with a kimono half put on and some slippers in her hand. She finishes putting on the kimono, sits down on the sofa, takes off her shoes, and puts on the slippers, puts the shoes carefully under the sofa, takes her hair down serenely, lights the lamp which is near the sofa, puts out the other light; throws herself comfortably on the sofa and begins to read.* **María Pepa** *comes back and goes towards the window.*

Rosario (*without looking up from her book*)   What are you doing?

María Pepa   I must shut the window. There's going to be a storm. There's a big wind blowing up.

Rosario   I'll shut it when I go to bed. (*Goes on reading.*)

María Pepa (*hovering near the writing table for a chance of conversation*)   Your brother's verses mustn't be blown about, or there'll be trouble.

Rosario   Put a paper weight on them.

María Pepa   I'll put the sheep dog on them. That's heavy.

Rosario It's not a sheep dog; it's a lion.

María Pepa (*placing the paper-weight which is, indeed, a bronze lion*) When first I saw it I thought it was a sheep dog. I've always called it a sheep dog and, I *always shall*. (**Rosario** *goes on reading, but* **María Pepa** *goes on talking nevertheless.*) It was a present from Señor Enrique – that was your dear grandmother's second husband, but before he was her husband, to Señor Ernesto – that was her first husband – given on her birthday. She was twenty-three and she wore a Scotch plaid poplin with a green velvet coat hemmed with gold acorns which was a sight for sore eyes and I have it still put away and not at all moth-eaten. Your poor grandfather . . . God rest his soul . . . hated the sight of it.

Rosario (*interested in spite of herself*) The green velvet?

María Pepa No, the sheep dog. Because your grandmother whenever she went into the room where it stood on the table, always stroked it . . . so. (*Stroking the bronze lion.*) And one day when he would have her go to the theatre with him on the very anniversary as it was of her second husband's death which, of course, she couldn't, he changed into a basilisk as soon as she had left the room crying like a Magdalen, and he took the sheep dog and threw it at Señor Ernesto's – no, at Señor Enrique's portrait which hung over the mantelpiece and, as it is a bronze dog, of course the glass was broken so he had to have a new frame made carved with a crown of laurel and bevelled glass and that cost him a lot of money.

All this **María Pepa** *says without taking breath.*

Rosario Grandmamma liked her second husband, didn't she, the best of the three?

María Pepa (*with disdainful and Olympian superiority*) I can tell you this much . . . that your poor dear grandfather was the worst.

Rosario Oh, María!

María Pepa (*with resentful calm*) God forgive him . . . a jealous, obstinate, stingy tyrant; and the only way to manage him at all was just to keep on reminding him what a perfect angel the one before him had been. Though he had given us trouble enough, heaven knows, for he was a gambler. And when he lost – which was always – the way we had to pinch and screw! And that didn't come easily at all because Señor Ernesto – he was her first – though he wasn't a practical man being an artist and he told lies worse than the newspapers – still he was generous and while he was alive your dear grandmamma never put her foot to the ground. 'Angels mustn't tread on the dust of the earth,' he'd say, and not a yard did we go without our own carriage. Though for all that we might go to bed without supper sometimes because, if he didn't paint why he didn't earn anything, and there'd be times when he lacked inspiration – so he said, and he'd lie on the sofa for weeks at a stretch in a state of artistic torpor – smoking, just smoking. But a kinder, refineder, more considerate and gentlemanly man . . .

Rosario There's grandmamma's bell.

María Pepa That means she has finished her beads. Will you turn out the lights?

Rosario Yes, I'll put out the lights. And I'll close the window. Take away those shoes, please.

María Pepa (*picking up the shoes with a sigh*)   Well, pray God you may never know the troubles of a married life.

Rosario   Thank you! (*She is very offended.*)

María Pepa   Ah! . . . you mean to get married, do you? And to half a dozen, I daresay, just to outdo your grandmother . . . Well, if you make your bed you must lie on it. (*With compassionate superiority.*) We shan't be able to help you. We shall be snugly in heaven. Though what's going to happen there when they all three come out to meet us, each one expecting to have us all to himself for eternity . . .! They'll fight it out, I suppose.

Rosario   María, that's the third time the bell has rung.

María Pepa (*calmly*)   I hear it. No doubt St Peter will settle things somehow. I'll shut the door, there's a draught.

She goes out slowly, having closed the bedroom door. **Rosario** *tries to return to her reading, but she can't do it because* **María Pepa's** *reminiscences have distracted her attention from her book. She meditates incoherently.*

Rosario   Half a dozen! (*She starts reading her book aloud, though in a low voice, so that she may enjoy the poetry of it more.*) 'Love is a solitary flower of an exquisite evanescent fragrance.' How true – a *solitary* flower. 'It blooms but once in the life of the soul and then the soul which this triumphant lily has enriched . . .' This triumphant lily? What a wonderful phrase . . . 'dies when it dies, but ony for love's single service can it wish to live.' Ah yes! But then how could Grandmamma have been really in love with all three of them? 'But into a life may come visions and phantoms, envoys and heralds of the true love that still delays . . .' (*Meditating.*) That might explain it. Grandpapa came last, so her first and her second were heralds and phantoms perhaps. 'But on that divine night, when the love of Carlos and Esperanza . . .' (*She goes on reading in an undertone for a minute, but interrupts herself almost immediately turning over and supporting herself on an elbow.*) Or was Grandpapa a herald and a phantom, too, and did Grandmamma only think she loved all three because she really never loved anyone at all? I wonder! (*Reads.*) 'But on that divine night . . .' (*Impatiently.*) Oh, I can't read.

The wind can be heard blowing.

What a wind! I'd better go to bed. But then I shall only dream of all three of them fighting over Grandmamma at the gate of heaven. I'll lie still for ten minutes and think.

She switches off the light without moving from the sofa and lies down again. The room remains in the dark, lighted only at intervals by the light, not very brilliant, which comes in by the window. The wind goes on howling.

Rosario   I do believe there will be a storm. What a dust! I'd better shut the window. . . . Too much bother.

By this time she is half asleep. Suddenly a straw hat, carried on the violent wind, blows in the window and falls beside the sofa.

Rosario (*opening her eyes*)   What's that? Something flew in at the window? (*Looking round her to see, but not getting up.*) A bird? A hat! A man's hat . . . what has happened?

She looks alternately on the floor, where the hat is, and at the window. She gets up with a certain timidity and goes slowly towards the window. At this moment there is a tremendous lightning flash, followed immediately by a terrifying burst of thunder, and in the really infernal resplendence of the lightning flash there appears at the window the figure of a well-dressed, but hatless man, who looks around the room a second, and then jumps. **Rosario**, *terrified and bewildered by the thunder and lightning, sees the man, and not knowing whether he is reality or a vision, remains frozen with horror and gasps in a low voice.*

Rosario   Jesu! Ave María! Virgén del Carmen! Blessed souls in Purgatory! Blessed Saint Barbara who art enrolled in heaven . . .

The Apparition (*observing that there is a woman in the room, and going towards her uncertainly, because an almost total obscurity has succeeded to the lightning flash*)   Don't be alarmed . . . please don't be alarmed.

There is another flash, then thunder and then a perfect downpour of rain begins. **Rosario** *sees by the light of the lightning flash that the man is directing himself towards her, and, horrified, stretches out her arms to keep him off.*

Rosario   Keep off! Keep away! Help!

The Apparition (*going up to her*)   Don't shout . . . for heaven's sake, don't shout. I'm not a thief. I am an entirely respectable person.

Rosario   Yes, yes . . . but go away!

The Apparition   I am going, Señora, this very minute.

But in the darkness he has accidentally come quite close to her and when he moves he finds that a piece of her hair is entangled in his sleeve link.

The Apparition   No . . . I can't!

Rosario   Why not?

The Apparition   Your hair has got twisted in my sleeve links.

Rosario (*impatiently*)   Then untwist it at once.

The Apparition   That's not so easy . . . in the dark. Could you turn on some light perhaps . . . where is it?

Rosario   On the table. (*She starts to move, and he follows her, but in spite of his precautions, he pulls her hair.*) Aah! . . . You're pulling my hair. It hurts.

The Apparition   Ten thousand apologies! (*He stops, and as she is going on, he pulls it a second time.*)

Rosario (*angrily*)   But come with me . . . then it won't.

The Apparition I'm coming . . . I'm coming.

But as they go towards the table in the pitch dark he stumbles; and to save himself – and her – puts his arms round her. They fall on the sofa together.

Rosario How dare you? This is outrageous. How dare you put your arms round me?

Another lightning flash discloses the situation.

The Apparition (*very calmly*) I assure you I did not put my arms round you. I fell . . . and you fell in them. And I have bruised my shin most confoundedly. This is quite as unpleasant for me as for you.

She makes a gesture of protesting amazement . . . whether at the supposition that any man could find it disagreeable to have his arms around her or not.

Rosario Then if you realise that please move away . . . as far as you can . . . till I've turned on the light.

The Apparition (*calmly*) But now your hair has caught in my studs and if I move at all I shall hurt you extremely. Until you can turn on the light I'm very much afraid there's no real alternative . . . to this.

Rosario (*impatiently*) Very well then, don't move. I mean . . . do move . . . when I move. Now.

She tries to find the light, but her hair is badly pulled in spite of precautions.

Rosario Oh – oh – oh!

The Apparition I told you so.

Rosario (*as she manages at last to turn on the light*) Thank heaven!

The two then look at each other for a moment in silence and with not a little curiosity. Then he speaks, very much at his ease.

The Apparition Now perhaps we can undo the tangle. If you'll try the stud I'll do the sleeve-links.

They devote themselves to the job in silence. After a moment he says quite casually.

The Apparition You really have most infernal hair.

Rosario (*offended*) I beg your pardon?

The Apparition I meant for present purposes. Does it often get caught up like this. And do you always wear it floating in the breeze?

Rosario (*offended*) I wear it as I choose.

The Apparition Quite so . . . and of course it's not very long. I beg your pardon. That again is not criticism. If I had to criticise I should say only that you must find it most inconveniently fine. But a charming colour.

Rosario (*furious*) Thank you.

The Apparition   And it smells of . . . what is it, violets? Violets.

Rosario   How dare you?

The Apparition   Don't move please . . . it'll hurt you horribly. But it does smell of violets surely.

Rosario (*now at the height of her indignation*)   Does that concern you?

The Apparition   I never said it concerned me. I said it smelt of violets. I'm sorry that offended you – but it does.

Rosario   As you please. Have you finished? (*She has by this time got the studs free.*)

The Apparition   Not nearly.

Rosario (*reaching to the table for some scissors*)   Take them! Cut it!

The Apparition   Cut it! But what a pity!

Rosario   Cut it! Give them to me, then. (*She cuts herself free.*) There! (*She rises with dignity and turns to him.*) And now.

The Apparition (*who rises too and bows to her most formally*)   Señora . . . or Señorita . . .

Rosario (*without noticing either the bow or the interruption*)   Would you please explain why a thoroughly respectable person – as you say you are – (*She looks at him up and down and observes that he is, indeed, very well dressed in informal evening clothes.*) has presumed to enter a stranger's house like this? (*The beginning of the sentence is said with great violence but at the end it has been modified to something like suavity.*)

The Apparition   Certainly. This high wind which preceded this storm blew my hat off my head, but thoughtfully blew it in here. I came in to find it. Having found it I will, with your kind permission, take my leave.

Rosario (*angry again, because his calm manner makes her so nervous*)   And so, for the sake of a miserable straw hat, you jump in at a window like a burglar at this time of night.

The Apparition   Señora – or Señorita . . .?

Rosario (*shortly*)   Señorita.

The Apparition (*bowing and smiling*)   Señorita . . . so much depends upon one's point of view. To you my hat – (*he picks it up*) and I grant you aviation is not a suitable career for it – is naturally a thing of no consequence. But to me it was . . . and on this occasion particularly so, for I was on my way to keep a most important appointment.

Rosario   Indeed!

The Apparition   And I prefer not to walk through the streets in this weather bareheaded and arrive looking like a pursued pickpocket. Sooner than take the liberty of ringing the bell of a strange house and waking everyone up I climbed in at the window. The room was dark, I thought no one was here. I meant to get my hat and go on my way and, if you had not made such a needless noise . . .

Rosario   Do you expect –

The Apparition   . . . I should have gone as I came, quite quietly, quite discreetly.

Rosario (*convinced, but a little annoyed with herself for having let herself be convinced*)   Very well, I accept the explanation. And now, having recovered the priceless object will you be good enough to show your discretion – by going as you came – and at once.

She makes a magnificent gesture towards the window and then sits down with her back to it. He goes and looks out, then turns.

The Apparition   Señorita!

Rosario (*without moving*)   What is it?

The Apparition   It's pouring in torrents.

Rosario   And what of that?

The Apparition   Well, I haven't an umbrella; it was quite fine when I started. If I launch myself into this flood in two minutes I shall look like a drowned rat.

Rosario (*with completely unreasonable but entirely feminine animosity*)   And quite unfit to be seen by the lady you are going to visit.

He is startled for a moment. Then he smiles and sits by her on the sofa.

The Apparition   And who told you it was a lady?

Rosario (*rising indignantly*)   Go away at once. The rain is stopping.

The Apparition   The rain is not stopping.

And indeed it is pouring harder than ever. **Rosario** *makes a gesture of despair.*

The Apparition   Besides, look at the concierge standing at the door of the house opposite. If he sees me jump out of the window he'd either think I'm a thief and arrest me . . . or he will not arrest me thinking . . . that I'm leaving by the window for reasons best known to both of us. And then you will be horribly compromised.

Rosario (*dismayed*)   So I shall be!

The Apparition (*most respectfully*)   Therefore, with your approval, I'll wait till he has gone in, and that will prevent any possible scandal.

Rosario (*in a voice of anguish*)   Please sit down.

The Apparition   Thanks. (*He sits at a most respectful distance.*)

Rosario   We must certainly prevent any possible scandal. (*There is a pause. Then* **Rosario***'s anguish develops into anger again and she speaks, half to him, half to herself.*)

Act One   111

Rosario   When is one allowed to forget one's misfortune in being a woman!

The Apparition   Do you find that a misfortune?

Rosario   Isn't this a good sample of it? You jump out of my window, with my connivance, so people think, and my reputation is gone. Mine . . . but not yours . . . oh no! Do you call that fair?

The Apparition (*humbly*)   No, Señora.

Rosario (*aggressively*)   Does it seem to you just that men should have all the rights and women none?

The Apparition   You feel you should be free to jump in and out of windows if you want to?

Rosario   Not at all . . . But I think the man who jumps out of windows should be as much dishonoured as the woman who remains within.

The Apparition   Yes, there's something in that.

Rosario   There is everything in it. Equal rights . . . equal obligations.

The Apparition (*with a slight twinkle, with the least touch of irony in his voice – she is so very young*)   I see that you are very advanced in your ideas.

Rosario (*getting up with great dignity*)   I hope so. (*He smiles.*) Do you doubt it?

The Apparition   Forgive me for questioning it just a little, when I see that you waste your time reading . . . this sort of stuff. (*He points to the book that she has left on the sofa.*)

Rosario (*bridling*)   Really! Do you happen to know what that book is?

The Apparition   Yes, it is a sentimental novel called 'A Spring Romance'.

Rosario (*challenging*)   Have you read it?

The Apparition   Yes, I have read it.

Rosario (*sarcastically*)   But it doesn't please you?

The Apparition (*with a slight grimace of contempt*)   Well . . . it isn't so badly written.

Rosario (*indignant*)   It is beautifully written.

The Apparition   But the writer's conception of life –

Rosario   What's wrong with that, pray?

The Apparition   The fellow hasn't any sense.

Rosario   Señor!

The Apparition   His heroine's a fool of a girl with not an idea in her head except love; all she wants is to be lied to in the moonlight by a young man who is, if possible, a bigger fool than she. Every half dozen pages or so they are swearing their love will endure for eternity . . . which is absurd; and that they'll be faithful to death . . . which is almost as unlikely.

Rosario   Good heavens!

The Apparition   The situations are ridiculous. Now, that 'divine night of love' in a gondola . . .

Rosario   . . . When they float through the narrow canals of Venice.

The Apparition   Well, now, have you ever floated at night through the narrow canals of Venice? They smell most abominably, and anything may be thrown out of windows on your head . . . I assure you, anything.

Rosario (*scandalised*)   You are very vulgar.

The Apparition (*politely*)   I am a man of ordinary common sense. I like the realities of life. And, if you were what you like to think yourself – a 'modern' woman instead of being – forgive me – a girl trying to balance herself between new ideas and traditional sentiments . . .

Rosario (*interrupting him*)   Señor, doesn't it occur to you that one needs now and then a dream and a little poetry to compensate, perhaps, for those more real things which will never come one's way? This man can probe the depths – the very depths – of a woman's heart. (*She tries to make these speeches sound imposing . . . but she is very young.*)

The Apparition   Do you really think so?

Rosario   Do you deny it?

The Apparition   I think that the poor wretch writes his stories as well as he knows how and stuffs them full of all the pretty lies he can invent in the hope of selling as many as possible to that vast crowd of old-fashioned, romantically minded women who . . .

Rosario   Please don't talk such libellous nonsense. He is a genius. And womanhood – all that is best in it – owes him a deep debt of gratitude. And I wish I could tell him so . . . old fashioned and romantic though I may be.

The Apparition   Well . . . I think that could be managed.

Rosario (*marvelling*)   Do you mean that you know him?

The Apparition   Oh yes, I know him!

Rosario   You're not friends?

The Apparition   Well, I could introduce you both to each other. I'll write him a letter.

Rosario (*enthusiastically*)   Oh, will you? It isn't asking too much?

The Apparition   Not a bit. (*He sits at the table and starts to write.*) Now then . . . 'I very much want you to know Señorita . . .' By the way, what's your name?

Rosario Castellanos. (*But her face has fallen; and he notices it.*)

The Apparition What's troubling you?

Rosario Nothing . . . that is . . . no, nothing. (*Distressed but still determined.*) Please go on with the letter. What are you laughing at?

The Apparition You, a strong-minded, up-to-date woman sitting quaking at the mere thought of going to call on a distinguished author . . . just to tell him how much you admire his work. Come, come, now . . . equal rights, equal responsibilities, you know.

Rosario (*angry*) I am not quaking. I don't in the least mind going. It's only for fear he should misunderstand.

The Apparition What . . . that expert in women's hearts misunderstand?

Rosario (*exceedingly angry*) Please go on writing the letter.

The Apparition Still – he's a lucky fellow!

Rosario (*flashing resentment at his mischievous tone*) Please do not write that letter.

The Apparition But why disappoint yourself – ?

Rosario That is my business.

The Apparition Well, let's think of some other plan. Ah!

Rosario What?

The Apparition Have you this morning's newspaper?

Rosario *takes it from a heap of papers, gives it to him and he starts searching among the advertisements.*

The Apparition Because I rather think that . . . yes. Read that.

Rosario (*reading*) 'Wanted, well-educated and responsible lady as secretary to a literary man. Typing, not shorthand.' (*Without taking breath.*) Do you think that is . . .

The Apparition I know it is. . . . That's his address. A fortnight ago I heard him say he'd be wanting a secretary – and this morning I saw this. What luck! You can take him the letter. I'll change it a little – on the pretext of applying for the place. (*He sets himself to finish his letter.*)

Rosario Thank you . . . I think that I will apply for the place.

The Apparition (*astonished*) What did you say? Apply for the . . . seriously?

Rosario Why not? I'm quite responsible and fairly well educated. I know French, German, English – besides Spanish.

The Apparition Splendid!

Rosario Well, what is astonishing you then?

The Apparition (*looking round the room*) It is only that I fancied – to judge by the way you live – that you had no need to –

Rosario   Earn my living? I needn't. I have brothers quite ready to earn it for me. (*Pathetically.*) There again . . . that's the bitter humiliation of being a woman. One must rise above that. I want to work – to earn the bread that I eat. I am tired of being a parasite.

The Apparition (*as he writes*)   Talk like that to him and, as a literary man, he will engage you at once. (*He gives her the letter while he writes an envelope.*)

Rosario (*reading it with great delight*)   Oh, how kind you are. (*When she reaches the signature she makes a slight grimace.*) Your name is Obdulio . . .?

The Apparition (*resigned and meek*)   Yes, Señorita, Obdulio Gomez. Commonplace, isn't it? But we're not all lucky enough to be called, as your hero is, Luis Felipe De Córdoba. Ah, well!

He sighs, puts the letter in the envelope and hands it to her.

Rosario   Thank you a thousand times. (*She puts the letter in her dress and gives him her hand.*)

The Apparition (*holding her hand and bowing*)   Not at all. I shall be proud to have helped a little towards raising you from the humiliation of being merely a most attractive young lady.

They shake hands smilingly. At that moment **Pepe** *and* **Emilio** *can be heard letting themselves into the house and rather noisily.* **Pepe** *is singing.*

Emilio's Voice   Shut up, man, for heaven's sake. You'll rouse the house.

Rosario   Good heavens . . . there are my brothers.

She starts to run. **The Apparition** *catches for a minute at her wrap.*

The Apparition   But . . . please . . .

Rosario   Let me go . . . let me go.

She bolts into her bedroom, losing a slipper as she goes. **The Apparition** *picks it up and stands for a moment holding it. The two boys are in the passage now, so he moves to the window. But before he can reach it, they are in the room.* **Pepe** *is still singing sotto voce.*

Emilio   Oh, do be quiet.

Pepe (*seeing* **The Apparition**)   What's that? A man!

Emilio   Catch him!

They proceed to try. But **The Apparition** *is too much for them. He throws them both off and to the floor. Then he jumps out of the window.*

Pepe   Thief!

Emilio   Stop thief.

The noise brings in **Doña Barbarita** *and* **María Pepa** *in their dressing gowns. They may look a little odd, but* **Doña Barbarita** *is as dignified as ever.*

Doña Barbarita Whatever is happening?

María Pepa What is all this?

Rosita *appears from her bedroom, limping because she has only one slipper but with the most innocent air in the world.*

Rosario What on earth are you shouting about?

Emilio (*who has succeeded in getting up*) A man.

Pepe In the room.

María Pepa A man!

Rosario (*with the greatest innocence*) Nonsense.

Emilio Was it indeed?

Rosario How could he have got in?

Pepe By the way he went out . . . The window.

Rosario Impossible!

María Pepa This comes of getting too merry. You see things.

Emilio Well, I like that!

Pepe The rain has gone to our heads, I suppose.

Emilio (*to* **Pepe**) Didn't you see him as plainly as . . .

Pepe (*rubbing his arm*) I felt him.

Doña Barbarita Well, I daresay, I daresay –

But suddenly **Emilio** *sees on a chair . . . the straw hat.*

Emilio And here is his hat.

Doña Barbarita, Rosario *and* **María Pepa** (*together*) His hat!

Emilio and Pepe (*together*) So now, what do you say?

Rosario Let me see it.

She takes it and then . . . deliberately throws it out of the window.

Pepe and Emilio What are you doing?

Rosario Sending it after its owner.

And now, as if in exchange for the hat, there sails in **Rosario**'s *slipper, which falls at her feet.*

María Pepa What's that?

Pepe and Emilio A slipper!

Rosario (*completely off her guard*) My slipper!

Doña Barbarita (*who has been watching her keenly*)   My dear child . . . think what you're saying.

Emilio   Your *slipper.*

Pepe   *Your* slipper.

Rosario (*losing her head completely*)   Yes . . . it is – but . . . that's to say.

Emilio and Pepe   How did he get your slipper?

Rosario   I don't know.

Pepe   You must know.

Emilio   Explain.

Pepe   Tell us at once.

Rosario   But I . . . it is my slipper . . . but – (*She gasps.*)

Emilio and Pepe   Go on.

Emilio   Will you go on, please.

Rosario *finding no way out, falls flat on the sofa.*

María Pepa (*running to her*)   She has fainted.

Doña Barbarita (*to herself*)   Thank God . . . I was afraid that it wouldn't occur to her.

Emilio   Don't faint!

Pepe   Don't be a fool.

Emilio   Tell us what has happened.

Doña Barbarita   Keep away from her – let her be. When a woman sees fit to faint . . . there's no more to be said.

Curtain.

Act Two

The scene is the working-room of the novelist Luis Felipe De Córdoba. It is a room with bright walls, and a great deal of light which comes in by two large windows with balconies; it is furnished with much comfort, but without any pretensions to fashion. A big writing table – not a desk – is placed near one of the two balconies, on it the disorder of a table where anyone works; sheets of papers, books, periodicals and reviews – among them three or four foreign ones – of fashions and women's affairs. Near the other balcony is a typist's table, with its typewriter and sufficient work ready on it, shorthand tablets, papers ready for the machine. Nearly all the left wall (except the space where a door opens on the inside rooms) is occupied by a wide and comfortable divan. Near it there is another small table, also full of books and papers; but in perfect order. Over the divan are some small pictures and a little mirror of porcelain or carving; the only one there is in the room. On the right wall there is another door which is supposed to lead to the vestibule, and by which people coming in from the street enter. The rest of the wall is occupied by a low bookcase, full of books; on the top of the bookcase some well-chosen china. On the walls some few good modern pictures and old engravings. On the big writing-table a gold fish bowl with gold fish swimming in it. On the floor, before the divan the working-table and the typist's table are bright-coloured rush mats. There are some very comfortable English chairs and armchairs.

On the rising of the curtain **Irene** *and* **Don Juan** *are discovered.* **Irene**, *the secretary, is an attractive girl of twenty-two. She is wearing a simple tailor suit and a black apron.* **Don Juan** *is a gentleman of fifty, well dressed and rather foolish. The secretary is at her table, putting her notes and papers in perfect order.* **Don Juan** *walks up and down while he is talking. Although he is paying a visit, he has neither hat nor stick, because he has left both of them in the hall.*

Don Juan   Our distinguished novelist is a long time.

Irene (*very occupied*)   Yes.

Don Juan   Do you know where he has gone?

Irene (*still very occupied*)   No.

Don Juan   Doesn't usually go out in the morning, does he?

Irene (*even more occupied*)   No. (*With a gleam of hope.*) If you'd like to leave a message –

Don Juan   I'd rather wait if it doesn't disturb you.

Irene   Not in the least.

Don Juan (*who is one of those people who cannot keep quiet even though they know that they are annoying other people by talking*)   Is that work you are doing?

Irene   No. (*She has finished, and is now putting her papers in order*)   Work is over.

Don Juan   For today?

Irene For ever and a day. That was my last 'official' job. (*Rises.*)

Don Juan 'Official'?

Irene Well, I must look in unofficially for a few days to put the new secretary in the way of things.

Don Juan Oho! A new secretary?

Irene (*laughing*) Don't rejoice too soon . . . she's not engaged yet. He put aside a whole lot of applications this morning, too.

She goes up to the table and puts the books and papers in order.

Don Juan Am I likely to rejoice at the thought of losing you? Irene, Irene . . . how dare you desert us!

Irene (*smiling*) How dare I get married?

Don Juan Is he *very* fond of you?

Irene (*laughing*) Scandalously.

Don Juan In the army, isn't he? And twenty-four?

Irene (*very well content and enumerating prettily*) He's an engineer, he's very good-looking and he's an only son. Anything else you'd like to know?

Don Juan (*going close to her*) Why wouldn't you marry me?

Irene (*moving away from him and looking at him with mocking seriousness*) It would have seemed so . . . disrespectful.

Don Juan What a delicate reminder that I'm too old.

Irene (*very modestly*) Not at all . . . but there's a limit even to my daring.

Don Juan (*going close to her again*) But tell me –

Irene (*moving away from him again and profoundly respectful*) Well?

Don Juan (*mischievously, pointing to the chair which undoubtedly is that of the novelist, and as if he were present*) Why haven't you married the 'great man'?

Irene (*laughing*) How many more?

Don Juan (*impudently*) Didn't you ever find yourselves falling the least little bit in love?

Irene (*a little drily, because the conversation is beginning to annoy her, but forcing herself to keep up her jesting tone*) It never occurred to us.

Don Juan Not to him?

Irene Not to my knowledge.

Don Juan I can't believe it. For three years you've been typing out these love scenes for him.

Irene Just three years.

Don Juan Why, if it was only to get a fresh idea or two for them.

Irene (*very serious and annoyed*) Do you mind my telling you that the 'great man', as you call him, is not only a distinguished novelist but a distinguished gentleman as well . . . who knows the difference between a secretary and an . . .

Don Juan I beg your pardon.

Irene Not at all.

She gets to the typewriter again.

Don Juan (*incorrigible*) You said you'd finished work.

Irene (*very drily*) I've some letters of my own to write.

She writes violently.

Don Juan You want me to go?

Irene (*without looking at him*) I don't think Señor De Córdoba will be in before lunch.

She continues writing violently and making a great deal of noise with the machine.

Don Juan Well, if that's so . . . good morning.

Irene (*without changing her attitude*) Good morning.

Don Juan (*hoping even yet to renew the conversation*) You will excuse me?

Irene Certainly.

Don Juan I hope you will be very happy.

Irene Thank you.

Don Juan *prepares to leave, but at the door stumbles on* **Guillermo**, *who is the novelist's servant.* **Guillermo** *is a man of more than fifty, of a type, half servant, half professor. He is completely bald, and is scrupulously well dressed, not in livery, but in a suit of good material, and well cut, though evidently not made for him; he is in fact dressed in his master's cast-off clothes. He is amiable, smiling, discreet.* **Don Juan** *pauses on seeing him come in, because he likes to know everything that is going on, and wants to find out who has come.*

Guillermo Señorita Irene, there's a young lady come in answer to the advertisement.

Don Juan (*pleasantly excited*) Aha! . . . a recruit to replace a deserter. – (*To* **Guillermo**.) Is she pretty?

Guillermo *does not answer and looks imperturbably at* **Irene**.

Irene Show her in. (*To* **Don Juan** *who, as a pretext for awaiting the candidate's entrance, looks from one side to another as if in search of something.*) If you are looking for your hat it is in the hall.

Don Juan (*ironically*)   Thank you!

He is preparing to leave, seeing there is nothing else for it, when **Guillermo** *shows in* **Rosario***, who is shy and a little inclined to take* **Don Juan** *for the novelist. He'd be willing enough, but* **Irene** *interrupts with:*

Irene   Guillermo, please give Señor *Don Juan* Medina his hat.

Guillermo   Sí, Señorita. (*He holds the door for* **Don Juan** *who goes out, furious with* **Irene**.)

Rosario   Oh, I thought –

Irene (*amiably*)   That he was Señor De Córdoba . . . not he, indeed. Señor De Córdoba won't be long . . . if you don't mind waiting. Do sit down.

Rosario (*without sitting down*)   Are you . . . Señora de –

Irene (*smiling*)   I'm his secretary.

Rosario (*nervously*)   Oh . . . then it's no use my waiting. I came . . .

Irene   No, no . . . do sit down please. I should have said 'I was'. I'm only staying on till my successor can take possession. (*She evidently takes to* **Rosario** *in a flash, as a young girl may.*) I hope he'll engage you. I would.

Rosario   Thank you *so* much.

Irene (*looking about the room almost maternally*)   Well – I should hate to leave all this . . . that I've grown so fond of . . . to anyone who wouldn't appreciate it.

Rosario   Why are you giving it up?

Irene   Change of profession. I'm getting married.

Rosario   To . . . him?

Irene   Oh no. You've never met him?

Rosario   Señor De Córdoba?

Irene   Yes.

Rosario   No . . . is he married?

Irene   No.

Rosario (*wishing to show how casual she is about it*)   I admire his work immensely. (*She emphasises the 'work'.*) I've tried so often to get a picture of him, but they're not to be had.

Irene   No, he won't be photographed. He prefers, he says, to have his woman readers picture him each for herself, and he doesn't want to spoil any one of their illusions.

Rosario   Is he so ugly?

Irene (*with all the indifference of a young lady who is going to be married*)   Oh no, I shouldn't call him ugly – not bad looking – for a civilian.

Rosario   He's not young?

Irene   Thirty-eight.

Rosario   Is this where he works? What a charming room – and so beautifully kept!

Irene (*drily*)   Yes . . . he's the untidiest man in the world, and the one thing he won't stand is untidiness. That's where his secretary comes in. He'll go out leaving his writing strewn all over the place, pages unnumbered, books on the floor, torn-up paper in the drawers and his notes in the waste-paper basket. But when he comes back, he likes to find everything just so. Have you ever done this sort of work before?

Rosario   Not just this sort.

Irene   You've been in an office?

Rosario   I – I saw the advertisement. I came with a letter.

Irene (*interested*)   Oh!

Rosario   Here.

She takes the letter which **The Apparition** *gave her out of her bag and offers it to* **Irene**.

Irene   Better leave it on the table.

She takes it and puts it there, then, at the sight of the handwriting, gives a jump.

Irene   Well!

Rosario (*alarmed*)   What is it?

Irene (*puzzled, looking at the letter and at* **Rosario**)   Who gave you this letter?

Rosario (*a little curtly*)   A friend.

Irene (*still watching her*)   Gave it to you . . . personally?

Rosario   Yes. Why?

Irene   I thought I knew the handwriting.

She leaves the letter on the table.

Rosario   It's from Don Obdulio Gomez.

Irene (*full of amazement*)   Then you know . . . Señor Gomez.

Rosario   Why not? Is it any disgrace?

Irene (*smiling*)   No, of course not.

Rosario (*doubtfully*)   He told me he was a friend of Señor De Córdoba's. Isn't he?

Irene   His best. (**Rosario** *gives a sigh of relief.*)

Irene By the way, talking of friends, (*She sits by* **Rosario** *confidentially.*) If you get this place . . .

Rosario D'you think I shall?

Irene With that letter . . . yes, I think you're sure to.

Rosario Oh!

Irene Well, then . . . look out for that fat gentleman I was getting rid of when you arrived.

Rosario (*opening her eyes wide*)   Did I hear you calling him Don Juan?

Irene Yes, his name is Don Juan and he's always trying to live up to his name. He'll make love to you without ceasing. He'll bring you sweets, he'll interrupt your work to tell you stupid little jokes . . . But that doesn't matter . . .

Rosario (*opening her eyes wide*)   Doesn't it?

Irene But what does is that he has a horrible influence over Señor De Córdoba. It's a secret, but you'll soon find it out. The man's mad enough about women in real life . . . but when it comes to literature he loathes us all . . .

Rosario Does he?

Irene And he plots against us.

Rosario How?

Irene You've read 'A Spring Romance'?

Rosario Of course.

Irene You remember the girl with fair hair who sells carnations and oranges on the banks of the Arno at Florence?

Rosario (*as if she were speaking of her dearest friend*)   Bettina?

Irene (*as if Bettina were her dearest friend too*)   Yes, Bettina Floriana, who falls in love with the handsome English painter –

Rosario And then throws herself into the river . . .

Irene Because she finds out that he doesn't love her . . . that's to say he does love her . . .

Rosario But he's married already.

Irene Well . . . *he* was to blame for that.

Rosario Who?

Irene Don Juan!

Rosario That nasty fat man?

Irene (*much excited*)   Yes. The Englishman wasn't married at all to begin with. But he insisted, if you please, that it was much more artistic for a rich painter to deceive a poor flower girl than that they should get married and live happily ever after.

Rosario (*indignantly*)   And Señor De Córdoba let himself be persuaded?

Irene   Yes . . . and why? Because Don Juan's a critic and writes for the newspapers! A critic! (*Contemptuously.*) Why he can't even spell. He sent me a love-letter one day – hid it under the typewriter . . . said my pretty hands as I worked looked like Carrara marble.

. . . and spelt it with one *r*. Well, and now – not content with that – he's trying to have Juanita Llerena – are you reading 'The Budding Pomegranate'?

Rosario   In the *Revista Gráfica* . . . yes of course.

Irene   The dunderhead has made up his mind that Juanita . . . you remember she's studying chemistry – such a good idea – because she means to be independent, to earn her own living and marry Mariano Ochoa –

Rosario   Such a nice boy!

Irene   But he is determined that she shall fail in her examination and then marry that rich old man who has been making love to her for years.

Rosario (*horrified*)   Don Indalecio!

Irene (*with fatal affirmation*)   Don Indalecio!

Rosario (*on fire with indignation*)   But it must be stopped.

Irene   I'd like to know, he says, how a girl with her head full of poetry and stuff is ever to remember a dozen chemical formulae correctly.

Rosario (*combative*)   That's the sort of silly thing they all say.

Irene   And besides, he asks, what girl nowadays will take a poor young man when she can get an old rich one?

Rosario   Disgusting!

Irene   And, to crown all, won't it be time enough for her to be in love with the young man once she's married to the old one.

Rosario   The man is a shameless cynic.

Irene   So now you see. And next week the chapter in which Juanita decides has to go to press.

Rosario (*terribly anxious*)   Is she going to marry the old man?

Irene   It's still unsettled. Yesterday Señor De Córdoba gave me two sheets to copy in which she said yes . . . but when he saw the expression of my face he told me not to go on with them.

Rosario (*with great relief*)   Ah!

Irene And I simply hate to go away in this uncertainty. Over poor Bettina – well, after all, death's a poetic end, one could make up one's mind to it. But this about Juanita is horrible.

Rosario Revolting.

Irene (*suddenly seeing the clock*) Oh, good heavens – half past eleven! Paco has been waiting half an hour.

Rosario Perhaps I'd better go, too.

Irene No, no – Señor De Córdoba will be in directly. He told me to wait till eleven, but he knew I had to go then. Would you tell him that I'll be here by nine in the morning.

She takes off her apron and puts it away; takes out a clothes brush and generally puts herself to rights.

Guillermo, I'm going now! You don't know what a nuisance a wedding is, especially for me. I've no mother. I have to do everything myself. Paco is an angel and helps all he can, but like all men, he loathes shopping. Today we're going to buy saucepans.

Guillermo *brings in her outdoor things.*

Irene Thanks, Guillermo. This young lady will wait.

Guillermo Yes, Señorita Irene.

Irene If Don Juan comes back before Señor De Córdoba does, don't let him in.

Guillermo No, Señorita Irene.

Irene If the printer sends . . . the proofs are on the table.

Guillermo Yes, Señorita Irene.

Irene Don't forget to change the water for the goldfish.

Guillermo *through this has waited on* **Irene** *like a perfect valet, handing her hat, veil, gloves, parasol, bag, etc. She goes to the goldfish.*

Irene (*putting her hand on the glass globe*) Poor little things! I hate to leave you, too. (*To* **Rosario**.) But you'll take good care of them, won't you? They only eat flies. We'll meet tomorrow.

Rosario Thank you so much.

Irene And I trust you about Juanita. I think you can save her.

Rosario (*fired with excitement*) Do you?

Irene Yes, I do. (*Mysteriously.*) Tomorrow I will tell you why. Good morning, Guillermo.

She departs.

Guillermo Good morning, Señorita Irene. (*He notices that* **Rosario** *is standing by the goldfish.*) Are you wondering what the goldfish are for, Señorita? Señor De

Córdoba always has them on his table while he works; he says that their twisting and turning helps him to think out the plots of his novels . . . especially the love episodes. (*Philosophically.*) Art must find inspiration somehow . . . and he drinks nothing but water as a rule. I bring them their flies every morning . . . a bagful – the boy at the grocer's catches them for me. (*A bell buzzes in the distance.*) The telephone! Excuse me a minute, Señorita.

He goes out. **Rosario** *left alone looks curiously about and studies the typewriter with some apprehension. Then she returns to the goldfish and says half unconsciously.*

Rosario They do twist and turn – especially in the love episodes.

Without her hearing him **The Apparition** *of the night before comes in. Seen in the full light he is an attractive man, close on forty. He puts down his hat and stick, closes the door softly and comes over to her and says with the most perfect suavity.*

The Apparition Do you like goldfish?

Rosario *turns and sees him, and is quite as surprised and almost as alarmed as when he came through the window.*

Rosario Oh!

The Apparition (*reassuredly*) Señorita.

Rosario (*backing away*) Don't come near me.

The Apparition (*smiling*) Do you still take me for a ghost?

Rosario (*passing from fright to indignation*) Don't add mockery to persecution, sir.

The Apparition (*bowing with even greater amiability*) I do most honestly protest . . .

Rosario Isn't it enough to compromise me?

The Apparition I . . .!

Rosario What on earth made you throw my slipper in at the window?

The Apparition You threw my hat out of it.

Rosario Because I was sorry you should be going through the streets in the rain with nothing on your head.

The Apparition (*bowing, very pleased*) Thank you . . . and I could not bear to think of the little foot, companion to that merciful hand, unshod.

Rosario I had to pretend, and tell lies . . . and even to faint.

The Apparition Was that very difficult?

Rosario (*much offended*) I am accustomed to speaking the truth.

The Apparition I have heard that women sometimes do.

Rosario (*with immense dignity and emphasising the name with a certain contempt*)   Señor Don Obdulio Gomez . . . (*He starts at the name, then recollects and recovers himself.*) I think that you have some very mistaken ideas about women.

The Apparition (*meekly*)   Possibly.

Rosario (*very much the superior person*)   You seem to imagine that it flatters a woman to persecute her . . .

The Apparition (*interrupting her, with a certain seriousness*)   Forgive me . . . you have used that word twice in two minutes. As far as I am concerned it is quite uncalled for . . .

Rosario   !

The Apparition   Even at the risk of accusing you of . . . I am sure the most pardonable vanity . . . I protest that I have never had the least intention of persecuting you.

Rosario (*in a challenging tone*)   Do you mean to tell me that you didn't come today knowing that I should be here?

The Apparition (*meekly*)   Yes, I can't deny that. (**Rosario** *makes a gesture equivalent to 'There, you see'.*)

The Apparition   I expected . . . if you insist upon greater exactness, I hoped that you would be. Are you offended? You have a most offended air, but somehow I don't believe you are. (*She starts to protest, but his mischievous, insinuating voice checks her.*) But what would you have thought of me if, when I'd met you so romantically, I had by the next day forgotten all about it?

Rosario (*with intense scorn*)   Romantically!

The Apparition (*good-humouredly*)   Now don't be a hypocrite.

Rosario   Sir!

The Apparition (*going up to her with an agreeable 'calinerie' as if her indignation was nothing at all*)   Can't you imagine how easily in a tangle of hair black as a black cat's . . .

Rosario (*unable to resist it*)   Such an 'infernal tangle' of hair!

The Apparition (*continuing, as if he had not noted the aggressive tone of the interruption*)   . . . one's heart may be caught, for all that one twists and turns.

Rosario (*her eyes straying to the goldfish*)   Twists and turns . . .

The Apparition   . . . trying to escape from the snare. Not that one really wants to, perhaps.

Rosario (*who, as soon as she scents the merest whiff of a declaration in the air, feels apparently that she is behaving like an idiot*)   Please don't talk like this . . .

The Apparition (*going a little closer and speaking in an insinuating tone, half tender, half mocking*)   Not that you really want me to either.

Rosario It is most insulting.

The Apparition You know you really are a terrible dragon. How is a man to guess that you'll take a few casual compliments in the course of a friendly conversation so seriously as this? What would happen if anyone started making love to you?

Rosario (*desperately disillusioned at this and at heart disappointed*) In the course of –

The Apparition But you don't take them seriously ... or did you? Oh come now, you don't think I'm so simple as to fall in love with a woman just from seeing her with her hair down. Hardly!

Rosario (*now really on the point of throwing something at him*) You dare say that to me ... you dare remind me of that!

The Apparition I, also, am accustomed to speaking the truth.

Rosario (*with immense dignity*) Leave this house immediately.

The Apparition (*with mock resignation*) Good heavens! Last night by the window ... this morning at least it's by the door. But do you mean to spend your life in ordering me out of the house?

Rosario Certainly, if you spend yours coming in when you are not asked!

He goes towards the door, then as if he could not bring himself to leave without a humble protest.

The Apparition Women are so ungrateful.

Rosario (*falling into the trap*) What have I to be grateful to you for?

The Apparition The first real thrill of your life.

Rosario (*contemptuously*) Seeing you jump through that window. You flatter yourself.

The Apparition (*with affected modesty*) Not because it was me you saw ...

Rosario (*childishly*) I wasn't in the least thrilled.

The Apparition (*trapped in his turn*) Then, what in Heaven's name would thrill you I'd like to know.

Rosario (*pleased to have exasperated him, even a little*) When I know I'll tell you. Perhaps it does take more than one has imagined.

The Apparition (*sarcastically appealing to the heavens*) Save me from the innocence of young ladies who read books like 'A Spring Romance'!

Rosario (*she shows the first signs of a serious attack of nerves*) Oh do be quiet ... and go away. (*He grows a little alarmed, puts down the hat which he had taken up and goes towards her. This makes matters worse.*) Don't come near me!

But he fears she is going to faint and goes nearer still.

Rosario   If you touch me . . . I shall scream.

More alarmed still he puts out his arms to support her, and at this she does scream.

Rosario   Guillermo! Guillermo! Guillermo!

Guillermo *appears, calm and smiling.*

Guillermo   Did the Señorita call? (*He looks alternately at the 'Señor' and the 'Señorita' and smiles.*)

The Apparition   Bring a glass of water.

Rosario (*recovering her school-girl dignity*)   And please show this gentleman out.

Guillermo *quite dumbfounded can only look at 'this gentleman'.*

Rosario   Don't you hear me?

Guillermo *remains speechless.*

Rosario   Then will you be good enough to do as I tell you?

The Apparition (*coming to the rescue*)   He hears but is in rather a difficulty. For, if he shows me the door, I shall certainly kick him down the steps.

Rosario (*half comprehending*)   You'll kick him down –

The Apparition (*smiling*)   And we'd be sorry to part with each other, Guillermo and I.

Rosario (*with alarm*)   So that you are – ?

The Apparition (*bowing meekly*)   . . . and your favourite author.

Rosario (*amazed*)   You? (*Then with more wrath and astonishment.*) You! (*In the anguish of disillusion.*) You!

She throws herself in a heap on the sofa. This time **De Córdoba** *is really frightened.*

The Apparition   Guillermo, get that glass of water – and put some orange flower in it.

Guillermo *goes.* **De Córdoba** *sits by her on the sofa and soothes her as if she were a child.*

The Apparition   Forgive me. There, there! And don't cry, please. It's not worth it.

She goes on crying, without answering but is growing quieter, little by little, lulled by his caressing voice.

The Apparition   Is it really such a shock? Are you so disappointed that the Apparition has materialised into . . . me? Do look at me, please, and answer. Come now, little Rosario.

Rosario (*like an angry child, but taking out her handkerchief, to dry her tears, nevertheless*)   Don't call me Rosario.

Act Two   129

The Apparition   I'm sorry, it came so naturally. (**Guillermo** *brings in the glass of water and goes out again, discreet and silent.*)

The Apparition   Drink a little water . . . there's some orange flower in it.

Rosario   Thanks; I don't need it.

She gets up.

De Córdoba   Where are you going?

Rosario (*like a lost child*)   Home.

De Córdoba (*getting up still holding the glass of water*)   No, no, no! Not till you are quite yourself again.

She has her parasol. He takes it from her. She glares at him.

De Córdoba   Please. (*She faces him aggressively.*) What will the concierge think if he sees you looking like this?

Rosario   Yes . . . I suppose I'm a perfect fright.

Furiously she proceeds to put her hair tidy, and has to fling off her hat to start with.
De Córdoba *still clings to the glass of water.*

De Córdoba   You really don't need the water . . . with a little orange flower?

Rosario   No!

He drinks it off – she sees him in the mirror.

Rosario   You do!

De Córdoba (*putting down the glass* on *the table*)   I tell you you gave me a scare.

Rosario (*sarcastically*)   Forgive me.

De Córdoba (*recovering his slightly mocking courtesy*)   I will exchange forgiveness with you . . . and I need yours rather more.

Rosario   Why did you tell me last night your name was –

She turns on him and they stand face to face.

The Apparition   Obdulio? Alas, it *is*!

Rosario (*who wishes, at all costs, to go on being angry and can't because* **De Córdoba**, *in spite of everything, is extraordinarily attractive*)   Then Luis Felipe De Córdoba is a fraud you practise on the public?

De Córdoba   It's called a pseudonym usually. I ask you . . . how could a man named Obdulio set out to write romantic novels? Obdulio! With Gomez to follow! What woman of really refined taste would ever open a book with that on the cover? Think how it shocked you last night!

Rosario   You could at least have told me who you were.

De Córdoba (*lowering his eyes*)   I didn't dare.

Rosario (*sarcastically*)   You were too shy? You are very shy!

De Córdoba   I was ashamed to. What! After you'd lauded my wretched books to the skies to say, 'I wrote them?' What an anticlimax! I am only human. I really could not bear to have you disillusioned under my very eyes.

Rosario   But then . . . why did you give me the letter?

De Córdoba   Once again, I'm very human. And I was tempted.

Rosario (*looking at him askance*)   By what?

De Córdoba   Promise you won't fly out again.

Rosario   Don't be afraid.

De Córdoba   Well then . . . (*While he speaks he is stepping backwards and away from her as if he was afraid of her.*) I gave you the letter because I wanted so much to see you once more. And if last night – the moment we had cut ourselves loose – I'd asked might I call on you, you'd probably have said no.

Rosario *looks at him cryptically, but says nothing.*

De Córdoba   And if . . . advertisement for a secretary or no . . . I had asked you to call on me . . .

Rosario *gives an indignant exclamation.*

De Córdoba   You see! You'd certainly have said no – so what else could I do?

Rosario (*with a certain soft bitterness*)   Having got me here though, you don't seem to mind how disillusioned I am.

De Córdoba   I mind very much. But . . . the fact is . . . I thought the horrid business would have been got over . . . I wasn't at home, you know, when you came.

Rosario   Did you think that I'd not have the courage to come?

De Córdoba   I was sure that you would. I went to the café at the corner and waited till I saw you pass. . . . Didn't you find my secretary here?

Rosario   Yes.

De Córdoba   Didn't you tell her why you came?

Rosario (*beginning to see the point*)   Yes!

De Córdoba   Didn't you give her my letter?

Rosario   Yes!

De Córdoba   But what did she say when she saw the handwriting?

Rosario   Nothing . . . the little wretch!

De Córdoba   Nothing! Good God! (*Quite overcome by the revelation he lifts his hands to his head.*) I have found a discreet woman.

Rosario (*tartly*)   A pity to lose her.

De Córdoba (*smiling*)   I must make a note of this.

Rosario   Well, I am glad I have helped you discover that there was something about women you didn't know. May I go now? Am I calm enough not to scandalise the concierge?

De Córdoba   Quite. And, therefore, there is now no need for your going at all. Please (*with caressing insistence*) be generous . . . say you forgive me.

Rosario (*with some bitterness*)   For your practical joke?

De Córdoba   For a harmless bit of fun. I am older than you . . . but there are times when I do badly want to behave like a child. Do sit down.

Now she obediently does so and he takes her hat from her.

Thank you. Do you think you could smile?

She can't help smiling.

Thank you so much. Besides, it was a bit your fault, you know. You did seem such a little girl . . . with your hair down . . . and those slippers which wouldn't stay on.

She frowns.

Don't frown. I know how you dislike being treated like a child . . . a plaything – an inferior being; that – though you may not always look it – you are a very serious-minded person, an advanced thinker. Well, let's make a fresh start on that basis.

He sits at his table in a most business-like way. She is on the other side of it.

You have most kindly come in answer to my advertisement, and we have been more or less introduced. Or shall we leave that intruding busybody, Obdulio Gomez, and his confounded letter right out of it? Anyhow Luis Felipe De Córdoba has great pleasure in asking Señorita Rosario Castellanos this important question . . . Will you be my secretary?

*At this moment **Amalia** and **Guillermo** are heard in the hall and a moment later **Amalia** comes in.*

Guillermo   But he's at work!

Amalia   Then he can stop for a minute.

She is a woman of thirty, dressed with aggressive elegance. Although it is morning she is wearing an exaggerated hat and an afternoon dress. She is handsome, although one immediately feels that the square shawl and the high comb would suit her better than the hat and frock of a fashionable dressmaker. She walks in a little as if the room were her own.

Amalia   Well, what happened to you last night? (*Then seeing **Rosario**.*) Oh sorry, sorry, sorry – Am I in the way?

Rosario, *on seeing her, jumps up.* **De Córdoba**, *who has received a rude shock, gets up also, but dominates the situation almost immediately.*

De Córdoba   Didn't Guillermo tell you I was at work?

Amalia (*divided between confusion and impertinence*)   Yes, but not with . . .

De Córdoba (*without making any introduction*)   My secretary.

Amalia (*quite indifferent to secretaries*)   Oh . . . is she? I want a word with you.

De Córdoba (*to* **Rosario**)   Excuse me.

Amalia   Come here!

They go towards the window.

Amalia (*quite good-temperedly*)   D'you think it the right thing to keep a good woman waiting supper for you till daybreak and never even write her one of the usual lies to say you can't come? Why didn't you?

De Córdoba   I was caught in the storm and lost my hat.

Amalia   Well, as long as you'd turned up with your head on – but don't lose that, will you? I shall so miss it . . . it's a handsome head.

She taps it with her fan. **De Córdoba** *steals a horrified glance at* **Rosario** *who is studying the goldfish.*

Amalia   Oh, how cross we are when we're interrupted in the middle of a chapter!

Rosario *makes a movement to go.*

De Córdoba (*to* **Rosario**)   Please don't go yet . . . I hadn't finished.

Rosario *snatches the hat and parasol wrathfully and takes up a position where she can look out of the balcony.*

Amalia   But as for me . . . please do.

De Córdoba   If you don't mind.

Amalia   I don't mind . . . I'll go one better and take you with me. Ain't I forgiving? You cut me for supper and I ask you to lunch. Hurry up . . . the car's waiting.

De Córdoba   I can't!

Amalia   Why not?

De Córdoba   You know I work all the morning.

Amalia   Very bad for you.

De Córdoba (*very seriously*)   I must finish what I'm doing.

Amalia   Well, finish, my lad . . . (*She drops suddenly in a chair.*) I'll wait.

De Córdoba   How much work shall I do with you sitting there? I'll come along in half an hour.

Amalia Word of honour?

De Córdoba (*rather nervous*)   On the word of – a novelist.

Amalia (*getting up*)   Ain't I an angel? With my best halo on too! 200 pesetas, straight from Paris . . . what do you think of it? I don't believe a word you say and I'm going to pretend I do and leave you to finish your chapter. Half an hour? I'll give you three-quarters . . . and if I have to come back and fetch you, it's not your hat you'll lose this time but your hair . . . I'll pull it out bit by bit.

De Córdoba You shall do anything you like. Goodbye. (*He gets her to the door.*)

Amalia (*to* **Rosario** *who does not respond*)   Good morning. (*In the doorway.*) Nice manners, hasn't she? Why do you have a woman for a secretary?

De Córdoba Why do you have a man?

Amalia Because I can't spell. But at least he's my brother.

She goes out.

De Córdoba (*to* **Rosario**)   One moment.

He follows to see her safely away. **Rosario** *furiously jams on her hat and pulls on her gloves, seizes her parasol and, when he returns, is on her way to the door, too.*

De Córdoba (*feigning a scandalised surprise*)   . . . You're going?

Rosario (*drily*)   Good morning.

De Córdoba (*putting himself between her and the door*)   But you've given me no answer.

Rosario (*wishing to pass*)   My answer is good morning.

De Córdoba (*with comic despair*)   But I've no secretary.

Rosario Let me go . . . *please.*

De Córdoba But who is to type my first chapter of a brand new story – such a good story, seething in my head – and I'm going to call it 'The Romantic Young Lady'.

Rosario (*unable to conceal her jealous anger any longer*)   That . . . 'lady'!

De Córdoba Now I ask you – !

Rosario Then try her brother . . . since he can spell.

De Córdoba Little Rosario . . .

Rosario Don't dare call me by that name again!

De Córdoba (*with humorous inflection*)   It's such a pretty name.

They might really be two children playing 'tag' or 'bullfighting' because she is always turning about trying to get out, and he is always putting himself in her path, with slow, but mathematical movements. He does not lose his self-possession, but she grows more and more upset.

Rosario Let me go!

Here she is on the point of getting out; but he detains her with a question.

De Córdoba Do you know who that was?

Rosario (*pausing for a moment, which he takes advantage of to obtain a desirable position*) The person, I presume you were on your way to last night when you unfortunately lost your hat.

De Córdoba And when I'd so fortunately found my hat I did not go on my way. Well, who is to be blamed – or shan't we say thanked . . . for that?

Rosario (*sarcastic and aggressive*) Me?

De Córdoba Not precisely the indignant lady that I see now before me but – if I may disobey just once . . . little Rosario. But you prefer to be treated as an up-to-date woman! Then cultivate some common sense.

She, however, taps the ground with her foot and looks at him with a dangerous expression.

De Córdoba That's the first qualification, believe me. My quite friendly relations with Señorita Amalia Torralba . . . professionally known as La Malagueña –

Rosario (*furiously*) – don't concern me in the slightest.

De Córdoba (*serenely*) Then why are you so angry? Even a fairy princess, you know, straight out of a story book and worthy of any man's most loyal love, cannot expect a poor novelist, no matter how bewitching the curls are, to be faithful and true *before* he has had even a chance of rescuing his hat and losing his heart in the tangle. Last night, when I set out to supper, I didn't even know you existed. Now – I want you to be jealous . . . I love you to be jealous.

Rosario (*flaming with wrath*) Jealous!

De Córdoba (*wishing to calm her*) Señorita!

Rosario (*wishing to slay him*) Did you say jealous?

De Córdoba (*defending himself*) *Not that you* were – but that I *wished* you were.

Rosario (*stammering and trying hard to control herself*) Why should I be?

De Córdoba Quite so – you've no cause.

Rosario I'm not talking of that woman!

De Córdoba Ah, but I am – for the moment.

Rosario And I think you're going to lunch with her.

De Córdoba One should keep one's promise. I made it to get her to go.

Rosario I did not want her to go.

De Córdoba You only wish that she hadn't come.

Rosario Not at all. I am glad that she came! And now, if you please, for the last time, before I call for help, will you let me go?

De Córdoba But listen to reason. Pretend, just pretend, for a moment that you are a strong-minded, cynical, up-to-date woman –

Rosario (*approaching hysterics again*) I won't. Very well then, I can't – can't if you like . . . and don't want to be.

She flings out. He calls after her, 'Rosario! Little Rosario.' But the street door slams violently. Then he sighs and smiles, first with resignation, then with mischief, then tenderly; goes towards the balcony and remains looking out on the street, along which it may be supposed she is going away from him – all with the absorption of the true lover – until she may be thought to have turned the corner. Then he again sighs and smiles and after ringing the bell seats himself at his writing table. **Guillermo** *enters.*

De Córdoba Guillermo, I want you to go yourself to Señorita Amalia's and explain why I can't lunch with her. I've been suddenly called out of town – I've gone already – and you might add that, as far as you know, I shan't be back for a fortnight.

Guillermo Very good, sir.

He goes.

De Córdoba A new story . . . 'The Romantic Young Lady' – No, no – too good to write – too good to spoil by writing it.

Curtain.

Act Three

We are at **Doña Barbarita**'s *house again. It is evening. The window stands open.* **Rosario**, *her three brothers and* **Doña Barbarita** *are present.* **Doña Barbarita** *is seated in an armchair near the table, smiling as always. She is looking at an illustrated weekly.* **Rosario**, *buried in the sofa, wears an expression of profound ill-humour, which she tries neither to conquer nor conceal. The three brothers once more are all about to go out, but this time they are all in morning clothes.* **Emilio**, *standing near the table, has just finished sealing a letter to his absent fiancée.* **Pepe** *is carefully smartening himself.* **Mario** *is by the window, looking out.*

Pepe (*to* **Mario**) Is it going to rain again tonight?

Mario I don't think so . . . not a cloud.

Doña Barbarita Nor a breath of air.

Emilio If there is a storm it'll get cooler.

Mario There won't be.

Doña Barbarita (*fanning herself with her newspaper*) One can't breathe!

Rosario (*aggressively*) Dear grandmamma . . . if there's no air at least there's lots of cigarette smoke . . . and the boys enjoy that even if we don't. (*And she beats the air with her handkerchief.*)

Mario Hullo, how long have you disliked tobacco?

Rosario Ever since I first smelt it.

Emilio You might have mentioned it earlier.

Rosario Who am I to interfere with your pleasures?

Mario *throws his cigarette out of the window.*

Rosario Oh, please don't start being unselfish – *now!*

Mario *looks at her with amazement, but says nothing.* **María Pepa** *comes in with a letter.*

María Pepa A letter.

Rosario (*rousing suddenly*) Give it me.

María Pepa It's for Señor Pepe.

Rosatuo *flings back on the sofa again.*

Pepe (*slyly*) Were you expecting one?

Rosario I? Who ever writes to me?

Mario (*astonished*) My dear Rosario, what's the matter with you?

Rosario Nothing. What should be?

Emilio (*to* **María**)   Nothing for me?

María Pepa   Nothing.

Emilio   Nor by the afternoon post. Sure?

Maria Pepa   Nothing.

Emilio   It's very odd. Two days running . . . no letter!

Rosario (*unpleasantly*)   Perhaps she has heard how well you amuse yourself without her . . . so why not without your letters as well? If I were she I'd throw you over tomorrow.

Emilio   My dear girl!

Mario *goes to* **Rosario***; takes her wrist with one hand – feels her forehead with the other.*

Rosario   What are you doing?

Mario   Pulse rapid . . . head hot. I thought this bad temper wasn't natural.

Rosario (*rises and goes from settee*)   So now I'm bad tempered, am I?

Mario   No, my dear, with all your faults you are not . . . that is why this exhibition of it alarms me.

María Pepa   It's the heat.

Rosario (*yielding a little*)   I'm not ill nor cross . . . really I'm not . . . but bored, bored, bored!

Pepe   Then let's go out somewhere. Come along. What about the Winter Garden? La Malagueña is doing some new dances.

Rosario   Is she?

Emilio   Ever seen her?

Doña Barbarita   Here's a picture of her. (*In the paper she is reading.*)

Three Men   Graceful creature, isn't she?

Pepe   I love her. I love her!

Mario   Yes . . . she has got that spice of something . . .

Rosario *rages but nobody notices.*

Emilio   But they say she's getting quite spoiled. All these painters and writers that crowd round her only make her do things that don't suit her at all.

Mario   Nonsense . . . she dances better than ever she did.

Emilio   She's a Spanish gypsy, and while she's content to remain one she's perfect. But look at her dressed up as Madame Pompadour – absurd!

Pepe Let her dress in a blanket with a rope round her waist – let some one introduce me to her – that's all. Now do you know why one wants millions of money? I love her . . . I adore her . . . I worship her! When she steps on the stage I feel funny all over. Come along, my child – hurry – we shall be late.

Rosario (*drily*) Thank you – I think not.

Pepe *Not!*

Rosario If you're going to swoon with ecstasy when you see her I should have to carry you out.

Emilio I'll help. What a tribute to the lady!

Rosario Oh . . . you're going, too.

Emilio Good! (*Then to* **Mario**.) Aren't you?

Mario Worse luck . . . no. I've got work to do.

Rosario Why don't I fall in love with a lion comique of the music halls?

Three Men (*highly scandalised*) Really, Rosario!

Doña Barbarita Well, why shouldn't she? Bullfighters, singers, actors, dancers have always had great success with the ladies.

Mario With a certain sort of lady, no doubt.

Emilio A rather foolish, hysterical sort of lady.

Rosario I see. If I lose my head over Nijinsky that's hysterics . . . but when you go stark mad about Pavlova you're just three normal, sensible, healthy young men.

Pepe Oh, it's quite different.

Mario There *is* a difference.

Emilio Which I think I can explain.

Rosario (*with a grim smile*) Well?

Emilio Well – it goes rather deep . . . (*He stops, not knowing indeed how to go on.*)

Pepe If we lose our heads . . . (*He stops too.*)

Mario But I don't admit that we do. We are conscious . . .

Emilio It's the difference of temperament.

Rosario Don't get too tied up. There isn't any difference. But, for all that, you needn't be afraid . . . I shan't make that sort of a fool of myself. Still what puzzles me is how a man of real genius . . .

Pepe (*bowing*) Thank you.

Rosario . . . I'm not speaking of you . . . can go mad over a face that – well, look, it's nothing wonderful, and a pretty trick of kicking her heels up.

Pepe Well – are you coming or not?

Rosario (*a little more amiably*) Not. Thank you all the same, but I'm tired.

Emilio (*insinuatingly*) Did you take too long a walk this morning?

Mario You were very late back to lunch.

Rosario (*with renewed ill-humour*) And last night I fancy you were not back at all – late or early.

Pepe Really, my dear girl – you're impossible.

Emilio We'd better be off – she'll be throwing things at us. Goodnight, Grandmamma.

He bids goodnight to his grandmother, kissing her hand.

Pepe Shut the window tight in case the ghost comes back.

Emilio Yes . . . I'm afraid these nocturnal alarms upset poor Rosario rather.

Pepe What annoys her is that the ghost didn't stay.

Mario Or abduct her. Remember the Rape of the Sabines. The Sabine ladies liked it.

Emilio Oh, some fellow came after the forks and spoons and made a mistake in the window . . .

Pepe And got nothing but Rosario's slipper!

Mario And that he threw back!

Pepe Well, it was too large for him!

The three young men laugh heartily.

Rosario Oh, do go away and leave us in peace.

Mario I'll be home early, Grandmother.

Doña Barbarita Oh yes, you're a wonderful watch dog.

Mario Well, you wouldn't let me tell the police.

Doña Barbarita What's the use? There's nothing missing – we've looked.

Emilio Very well . . . goodnight.

Pepe Till tomorrow.

Emilio, **Mario** *and* **Pepe** *go out.*

Rosario (*who has gone sulkily up to the table, and picked up the illustrated paper that contains the picture of Loa Malagueña almost without knowing what she is doing*) All three of them . . . cracked about that worthless creature. I detest men! (*Throws down the paper.*)

María Pepa *has just come on again.*

María Pepa *That's right.*

Doña Barbarita (*severely*) It is very wrong.

Rosario (*with the air of a little girl who is enjoying her own fit of temper*) Why wrong?

Doña Barbarita One doesn't alter things by hating them.

Rosario And is it an inevitable law of nature that some man should be able to poison one's whole life?

She sits down near the table, takes a lace-making pillow, which is on a chair, and begins to work furiously.

Doña Barbarita Is 'poison' quite the right word?

María Pepa They wipe their boots on us.

Doña Barbarita And you hold your tongue. You know perfectly well that I don't like to hear women abusing men. It is exceedingly vulgar.

María Pepa They abuse us enough. You don't know half the things they say – and none of us know the other half.

Doña Barbarita That makes it no better. If men and women can't share the burden of life between them –

María Pepa With the man sneaking out from under his share whenever he can!

Rosario *has been trying to work at the lace she has in hand. She now gives it up in despair. Throws the lace pillow violently on the table; the bobbins roll about mixing themselves up.*

Rosario I can't do this . . . I simply can't. The bobbins get mixed, the threads break, all the pins bend! Lace making is idiotic work!

Doña Barbarita (*severely*) My dear, this is like a spoiled child.

Rosario Oh . . . and who am I spoiled by I'd like to know?

Doña Barbarita By everybody.

Rosario I wish I were.

Doña Barbarita By me, by your brothers, by life itself. And because in twenty-two years you have never had a pain or a sorrow you think you've the right to behave like a baby when anything annoys you.

Rosario Nothing has annoyed me.

Doña Barbarita That makes it all the worse.

Rosario (*sitting down on the sofa and holding her head in her two hands*) It's only that I've got a most awful headache.

Doña Barbarita (*smiling*) Keep those excuses for your husband when you're married. They don't go down with other women – you have no headache.

Act Three 141

Rosario *looks at her a little alarmed, a little guiltily.*

Doña Barbarita I ask you no questions. But when a girl can't control herself she had better shut herself in her room and not make other people uncomfortable.

María Pepa (*firing up, as indignant and distressed as if she herself were being scolded*) That's right . . . now scold the poor child.

Doña Barbarita I am not scolding her. I'm trying to teach her to control her nerves – for she'll need to know how.

María Pepa I like to hear you talk about nerves; if I had as many pennies as you've had attacks of nerves in your life –

Doña Barbarita At the right moment. Never at the wrong.

María Pepa The poor dear child.

Doña Barbarita Don't make a fool of yourself . . . and what's more important – don't make one of her. There's no need for anyone to pity her.

Rosario (*suddenly showing both good temper and good sense*) I'm sorry, Grandmamma, I'm a fool . . . and unjust . . . and ill-tempered.

María Pepa Oh, well . . . if you're going to call yourself names – !

Rosario *smiles affectionately at* **María Pepa.** *Then sits down at her grandmother's feet, who strokes her hair soothingly.*

Doña Barbarita You'd better go to bed – you said you were tired.

Rosario But not *sleepy* – (*She looks at the window.*)

Doña Barbarita (*following her look*) Well, nor am I . . . so let's sit up together. (*To* **María Pepa**.)

You can go if you want to . . . my granddaughter will help me undress.

María Pepa (*touchy, as always*) And I should like to know why I must be supposed to get sleepier than you! But, of course, if I'm in the way –

Doña Barbarita Sit down then . . . and don't talk nonsense.

María Pepa *sits down again. There is a silence.* **María Pepa** *yawns.* **Rosario** *sighs.*

Doña Barbarita Won't you read aloud a little? That would distract our minds. What about the novel we began the other night?

María Pepa (*with profound contempt*) The one about the painter man who made a fool of the girl that sold oranges and she having no sense at all threw herself into the river? What's the use of a book like that? Pages and pages to tell me something that I can learn much better by sticking my own nose any day I choose into any corner of this miserable world. There was Encarna, the porter's daughter, taken in by just such another man . . . not a painter, he taught the piano, but it's the same thing. Off he went after a while and left her with something to remember him by. She didn't throw herself into the river because it's only a foot deep, but she drank half a bottle of disinfectant – and the wonder is that she and the baby were saved. Now that's true and the book was only lies!

Doña Barbarita   Have you quite finished talking nonsense?

Rosario   No . . . I think you're right, María. Novels are lies – and then men who write them laugh in their sleeve at us – and themselves, too.

Doña Barbarita   What do you know about it, my dear?

Rosario (*with sentimental bitterness*)   I should if I were they . . . at such fools of women.

María Pepa   Well, if you're not going to read I'll put out the light. They keep telling us to save all we can – and the metre ticks it up like a taxi-cab. Moonlight's cheap – (*She turns out the light. There is a bright moon.*) – and good.

There is another silence.

Rosario   Too hot to sleep!

Doña Barbarita   Shall we tell a rosary?

She takes out her rosary and, at that moment in through the window flies a man's straw hat, falling at their feet.

Rosario   Oh! – what's that?

María Pepa (*picking it up*)   A hat!

Rosario (*very agitated, but mischievously satisfied for all that the adventure is not over*)   Well, now we shall see!

Doña Barbarita   See what, my dear?

María Pepa   But there's no wind tonight.

Rosario (*frightened for her secret*)   Still – oh better shut the window, perhaps.

Doña Barbarita   Do nothing of the sort. Let them climb up and come in. Then we shall know what this is all about.

María Pepa   Come in! And we have our throats cut! There's not a man in the place.

Rosario   Come in . . . no! No!

Outside is heard the noise of someone climbing.

Doña Barbarita   Sh! They are climbing up.

María Pepa   Help! Help!

Doña Barbarita   Be quiet.

Rosario   Shut the window.

Doña Barbarita   Leave the window alone.

María Pepa   Help – thieves – police!

Looking in her terror for something to protect herself with she seizes the 'sheep dog' paper weight from the table and hurls it through the window just as a man's head appears there. It catches him full on the forehead. An exclamation follows that sounds very like a curse. Then silence.

Doña Barbarita   Now, what have you done?

María Pepa (*proudly*)   I threw it at him.

Rosario   At who?

María Pepa   How do I know . . . ? But it hit him hard!

Rosario   Oh, my God!

She drops on the sofa, half fainting – the two others go to her.

Doña Barbarita *and* **María Pepa**   What's the matter?

Rosario   Nothing . . . that is . . . (*Seizing her grandmother's hand.*) Grandmamma, there's something I'd better tell you.

Doña Barbarita   Yes, my dear, yes. (*Then, to get rid of* **María Pepa**.) – Now, you can shut the window.

María Pepa, *fully aware that she is being got out of the way, does so.*

Rosario   Grandmamma . . . last night . . . .

At this moment there is a loud knocking on the street door.

María Pepa   Someone at the door?

Rosario   The door?

Doña Barbarita   Obviously.

María Pepa   It's the police.

Doña Barbarita   That's all you've done by screaming.

María Pepa   Shall I go?

Doña Barbarita   Of course – and turn on the light.

María Pepa *goes and in a moment her voice is heard distressful and alarmed; also* **De Córnoba**'s.

De Córdoba   There's nothing wrong, I assure you . . . nothing at all.

María Pepa   Holy Virgin!

Doña Barbarita   Whatever is the matter?

Rosario (*calling*)   María Pepa!

María Pepa *appears again – her eyes starting.*

Rosario Who is it?

Doña Barbarita Is it the police?

María Pepa *shakes an agitated head.*

Rosario Is it – the thief?

María Pepa (*bursting into speech*) I don't think he is. It's . . . a gentleman!

Doña Barbarita Show him in.

María Pepa Oh, he's coming in! And don't be frightened. The poor thing . . . is wounded.

Doña Barbarita and Rosario Wounded?

Doña Barbarita *and* **Rosario** *hurry impulsively to the door, much alarmed, but before they can reach it* **De Córdoba** *appears quite at his ease, as usual. In one hand he has a handkerchief with which he staunches the wound in his forehead; in the other the 'sheep dog'.*

De Córdoba Nothing serious, dear ladies . . . please don't be alarmed. A slight contusion from this little 'objet d'art et vertu' which came flying out of the window as I was passing by . . . and which I now have the pleasure of returning to you – intact.

Doña Barbarita The 'sheep dog'! (*Reproachfully.*) María Pepa!

María Pepa (*in extreme affliction*) Don't say anything more to me. I feel dreadfully about it. It was sure to be that nasty animal, too . . . the first thing that came!

De Córdoba *shows no sign of knowing* **Rosario** *who, having given an exclamation, almost of triumph, on his appearance, now maintains an impersonal silence.*

De Córdoba I hope you will forgive my intruding on you in this rather unconventional way, but . . .

Doña Barbarita (*very distressed*) But it is we must ask your forgiveness. Dear me! you are bleeding dreadfully.

De Córdoba Well . . . if you had a bit of court plaster –

Doña Barbarita Plaster won't do. We'll take more care of you than that. Sit down, please. María Pepa, bring me some hot water and some lint and a bandage.

María Pepa *goes out.*

Doña Barbarita Child, don't stand there like a statue . . . come and help.

She says this, while through her glasses, she is examining **De Córdoba***'s wound.*

De Córdoba (*with a twinkle*) I do hope I haven't alarmed her. Is she very easily upset?

Rosario *makes an angry gesture, but approaches.*

Doña Barbarita The hair will have to be cut. I'll get my scissors.

Act Three   145

She goes out quickly. As soon as they are alone **De Córdoba** *seizes* **Rosario***'s hand.*

De Córdoba   Little Rosario . . . are you still angry at me?

Rosario   I consider you utterly contemptible.

De Córdoba   With my head cut open!

Rosario   I didn't cut your head open. But what else did you deserve?

De Córdoba (*half jesting and half supplicating*)   Rosario!

María Pepa *enters with a beautiful antique silver water basin and jug, and a basket with bandages, gauze, cotton wool, etc., and puts it all on the table.* **Doña Barbarita** *comes in after her with a pretty scissors-case, a little silver bowl, and a small bottle of collodion. Everything is very dainty and pretty, as is usual with old ladies who don't anymore have anything but details to live for, and who have always been accustomed to an infinite number of feminine refinements.*

Doña Barbarita   Now – let us see! . . . Water, María Pepa!

María Pepa *pours some water from the silver jug into the basin and comes up.*

Doña Barbarita   Child, you cut the hair. Your eyes are good.

Rosario, *seizing the scissors which her grandmother gives her, and treating* **De Córdoba***'s head with no great respect, cuts off a large lock of hair.*

Doña Barbarita (*scandalised*)   My dear . . . not all that!

De Córdoba (*slyly*)   Her hand is shaking. No wonder! What a shock to you all!

Rosario   Not in the least, thank you . . . but your hair is so . . .

De Córdoba   Tangled . . . infernally tangled. And it never used to be.

Doña Barbarita   That's all right . . . I can manage now. (*She puts* **Rosario** *aside and sponges the wound.*) Now a little collodion. (*She applies a little.*) Does it smart?

De Córdoba (*with an eloquent gesture*)   Doesn't it!

Doña Barbarita   All the better. Now the bandage, child. There – the scar will hardly show.

Rosario *has watched his sufferings with great composure, ignoring completely his appealing looks.*

María Pepa (*with deep sympathy*)   Think if it had been on the nose!

Doña Barbarita (*washing her hands and drying them with a towel*)   Now would you like a comb and a looking-glass?

De Córdoba (*rising*)   No, indeed. I've given you quite enough trouble for this evening. But if I might call on you at a more reasonable hour –

Doña Barbarita   Why of course! But we must introduce ourselves. I am Señora de Castellanos.

De Córdoba   And I am Luis Felipe De Córdoba.

Doña Barbarita (*with great surprise*)   The writer?

De Córdoba (*bowing*)   Yes.

Doña Barbarita (*looking at* **Rosario**)   The famous author of 'A Spring Romance'.

On hearing this **María Pepa** *stares at him as if he were a prehistoric animal.*

De Córdoba   Am I famous?

María Pepa   Wasn't it he wrote that beautiful story about the painter and the orange-girl? And you said you were dying to know him. Now I see him I don't wonder.

Rosario *thus appealed to is covered with confusion. But* **De Córdoba** *bows his acknowledgments to* **María Pepa**.

Doña Barbarita (*scolding her good-naturedly*)   María Pepa!

María Pepa   Well, he's very handsome. I'm old enough to be able to tell him so, God knows.

Doña Barbarita   Take all this away.

María Pepa *goes off with the bowl, jug, etc., smiling sweetly upon* **De Córdoba** *who, when she has gone, puts his hand to his head and reels slightly.*

Doña Barbarita   What is the matter?

De Córdoba   Nothing – I'm a little giddy.

Doña Barbarita   Of course . . . the blow and the loss of blood. Sit down – just keep quiet.

De Córdoba   Oh, señora!

Doña Barbarita   I'll get some brandy –

Rosario   I'll go.

Doña Barbarita   No, stay where you are – I have the keys.

She goes out. Once more **De Córdoba** *seizes* **Rosario***'s hand.*

De Córdoba   Let me kiss the hand that wounded me.

Rosario   It was María Pepa's.

De Córdoba (*with ironical pathos*)   I'd sooner think it was yours.

Rosario   I mightn't have aimed so well.

Doña Barbarita *comes back with a little decanter of brandy and a glass.*

Doña Barbarita   Here is the brandy.

She gives him some.

De Córdoba So many thanks! Excellent brandy!

Rosario (*sarcastically*) You prefer it to water? . . . with a little orange flower in it?

Doña Barbarita (*alert, but not knowing what on earth she means*) My dear!

De Córdoba I much prefer it. (*Smiling.*) And, for the future, I'll keep some in my study for the benefit of nervous, high-strung visitors.

Doña Barbarita Ah! . . . do many ladies come to call on you?

De Córdoba (*modestly*) Quite a number.

Rosario (*aggressively*) Actresses . . . and people of that sort?

Doña Barbarita (*a little scandalised*) My dear child!

De Córdoba (*smiling*) An actress will drop in sometimes.

Doña Barbarita Well, do you feel better?

De Córdoba Much better, thank you. Well enough to take my leave.

Doña Barbarita No, indeed . . . I insist on your resting a little longer.

De Córdoba Oh, but –

Doña Barbarita And, my child, I think we'll all have some tea or some chocolate and cake. María Pepa!

María Pepa *appears so quickly that she could only have been just on the other side of the door.*

María Pepa Well, which – tea or chocolate?

De Córdoba Oh, not for me, indeed!

Doña Barbarita We don't often have so distinguished a guest. (**De Córdoba** *bows profoundly.*) And it has been a most trying ten minutes for us all. We shall be the better for a little refreshment – I shall be.

She seats herself in her chair. **De Córdoba** *is standing by the writing table.* **Rosario** *manages to say to him sotto voce.*

Rosario You're caught now! Yes, it's very late . . . but you can't get to the theatre in time to see her new dances. Will her picture console you, perhaps?

She lays the illustrated paper in front of him.

De Córdoba Very like her, isn't it?

María Pepa *has now gone for the chocolate. There is a silence.*

Doña Barbarita Aren't you two going to sit down?

They do. And now the air of a formal call supervenes.

De Córdoba What a charming house you have!

Doña Barbarita Old fashioned, but convenient. This is my grandson's study. He is a writer, too.

De Córdoba *throws out a polite 'Ah', although he takes no interest in that whatever.*

Doña Barbarita We are all interested in literature and great admirers of yours. So, though we're sorry you were hurt, we can't but be pleased at the chance of meeting you.

De Córdoba Señora, the pleasure is mine.

Doña Barbarita But you have paid rather dearly for it.

De Córdoba Oh, *that* wound isn't mortal. (*He gives a glance at* **Rosario**.) And, even if it were – 'One man the less, one flitting ghost the more.'

Doña Barbarita Ah . . . I recognise that quotation. I have the whole passage in the album I kept as a girl written out in the author's handwriting. No, I didn't know him personally, but I imitated it from a facsimile there was in the newspaper. It was quite the thing in those days to keep an album and get famous men to write and draw in it – if you could –

De Córdoba It still is.

Doña Barbarita What a nuisance you must find it!

De Córdoba A perfect plague.

Doña Barbarita Yes, I feared you'd think so.

De Córdoba But for you . . . Good heavens – why nothing would give me greater pleasure.

Doña Barbarita (*delighted*) Child, get my album at once. The last verses were written, I'm afraid, in 1865. It was still possible then to call me young and golden-haired without taxing too much poetic licence.

The precious album is produced.

Write something romantic in it. I've not lost my love for romance.

Rosario *puts the album on the table.* **De Córdoba** *sits down and she silently hands him a pen. They are now hidden from the old lady in her chair.*

De Córdoba (*sotto voce, pretending to write*) You don't look nearly so pretty when you're cross.

Rosario I'm glad to hear it.

De Córdoba Couldn't you relax just a little?

Rosario No.

De Córdoba (*aloud to* **Doña Barbarita**) Shall it be in prose or verse?

As soon as she stopped talking, **Doña Barbarita**, *overcome no doubt by fatigue, had begun to nod. The voice rouses her, but only a little.*

Doña Barbarita Eh? Prose or verse? Prose, if you please . . . poetical prose.

She nods again.

De Córdoba If I were you d'you know what I'd do?

Rosario (*quite childishly*) Something stupid, probably.

De Córdoba I'd answer yes or no to the question we left unsettled this morning . . . Will you be my –

Rosario (*interrupting him furiously but without raising her voice*) I will be nothing whatever to you. Sh! Grandmamma!

De Córdoba She's asleep. (*Then with a good deal of feeling in the jest.*) And I was just beginning to fancy that you might be so much – almost everything.

Rosario (*very inconsequently*) Why 'almost'?

De Córdoba Do you think that any woman can completely fulfil a man's requirements . . . no matter how perfect she may be?

Rosario Are you wise then to be so particular?

De Córdoba Wise or unwise . . . I want you . . .

Rosario For a secretary?

De Córdoba I want you.

Rosario (*looking towards her grandmother in partly pretended alarm*) Good heavens – sh!

De Córdoba (*coaxing*) Won't you answer?

Rosario (*looking at him askance, but with a little smile*) What salary do you offer?

Da CÓrdoba To my secretary. Four hundred pesetas a month.

Rosario It's very small.

De Córdoba Six hours a day – and quite pleasant work.

Rosario But it costs so much to live in these times.

De Córdoba If you'll marry me as well I'll add board and lodging for nothing.

Rosario (*very haughtily*) Thank you, I want nothing for nothing.

De Córdoba Well, I'll raise your salary. Four hundred as secretary and three hundred and fifty as wife – with board besides – separate board. You might ask me to dinner sometimes. I shall ask you regularly on Thursdays and Mondays.

Rosario (*with a little quiet and rather happy laugh*) How absurd you are!

De Córdoba Thank God! I've heard you laugh again. Well, will you or not?

Rosario (*the modern woman with a vengeance*) What guarantee can you give?

De Córdoba For the money?

Rosario (*sentimentally*) That we shall be happy?

De Córdoba None.

Rosario What?

De Córdoba Well, what guarantee can you give me! Happiness, believe me, is a very strange thing. You may find it by looking for it, or it may come by pure luck. And, looking back you may find you weren't happy when you thought you were . . . or unhappy, for that matter, when you thought you were either. Guarantees are no good, oh yes, I know – people always promise each other a heaven on earth. There's no such thing.

Rosario (*protesting*) Isn't there?

De Córdoba In the last chapters of novels . . .

Rosario (*resentfully*) Your novels?

De Córdoba My last chapters are shockingly bad, don't you think? I'm always too anxious to finish. But life's not a novel.

Rosario (*now playing at disillusion*) Alas, no.

De Córdoba But a far better book than the best of us ever will write . . . such a good story, full of passion and thought, full of mysteries and revelation . . . worth living, and better, far better, worth sharing. No, little Rosario, I can't promise you, or you me that love will be heaven on earth. But it will be life. No more than life – but nevertheless, I mean well – but I've lots of faults. So have you.

Rosario (*a little peevishly*) Of course, I know that.

De Córdoba . . . Or you wouldn't be human. Well, shall we try the journey together? No doubt we shall stumble a bit – and one or the other may fall now and then. But that won't matter, will it? If the one that is up helps the one that is down. I don't think we'll both ever be down together . . . that would be awful luck.

Rosario (*whispering*) Yes.

De Córdoba We shall have troubles – who hasn't! but we'll laugh at them when they'll bear it. We'll work a great deal and we'll always have faith in our work – that's how one keeps young. We'll never think we're important people . . . so that a bit of success will always seem a little bit more than we deserve – and we'll be as pleased with it as a child with his new shoes . . .

Rosario (*like a vexed child*) That would be all very well if you loved me . . . But you don't love me.

De Córdoba How on earth do you make that out?

Rosario Because you've been mocking me all the time.

That's not like love. With the hat . . . with the letter you wrote yourself . . . and even when you walked in with the sheep dog.

De Córdoba And my head broken.

Rosario (*quite childishly*) Yes . . . that was one to me . . . though I didn't do it. But the only one.

De Córdoba And how beautifully I bear it! Little Rosario . . . I couldn't have slept tonight if I'd not made peace with you. Would you rather I'd sent you a letter in my best literary style. 'Señorita, since first I had the joy of looking in your face . . .' I thought you had a little more real imagination than that!

Rosario (*falling into his trap*) Indeed, but I have.

De Córdoba Oh, then, why is it that I . . . so old and serious . . . must be teaching you that the way to get the best out of even the most serious things in life is still . . . to keep your sense of humour about them?

She says nothing, so now he goes very close to her.

De Córdoba Well, which is it to be? Will you take the chance of being loved all your life by a man who gets his head broken so that he may sit here and talk a little real common sense to you?

Rosario *longs to say yes, and struggles . . . apparently just with her inability to say it. Then suddenly* **Doña Barbarita** *looks up.*

Doña Barbarita Oh, my dear child . . . do say yes or no.

The two of them jump out of their skins as she says this. They had quite forgotten her. But **Doña Barbarita** *continues coolly.*

Doña Barbarita Quite right to make difficulties up to a *point* . . . but –

Rosario (*stammering*) Weren't you asleep?

Doña Barbarita My dear . . . do you suppose that in eighty years I've not been able to learn when to go to sleep and when to wake up again?

Then **Rosario** *runs to her grandmother like a child, kneeling, her head hidden in the old lady's lap.*

Rosario Oh, Grandmamma . . . You say it to him . . . you say it.

Doña Barbarita (*caressing the child*) And last night she was asking me for a latch key! She hasn't a mother, you know. I've spoiled her a little . . . and I'm so old now, perhaps I've forgotten what the things are she wants most to learn about life. I haven't been able to teach her, you see . . . even how to say yes.

But **Doña Barbarita** *gives her hand to* **De Córdoba**, *who kisses it and the 'yes' is thus almost said. And, at the moment . . . as usual . . .* **María Pepa** *comes in.*

María Pepa Now don't you go away till she has said it . . . or she'll cry her heart out and give us a terrible time. For we all love you, all of us . . . even though it's not my place to tell you . . . that's true.

De Córdoba Rosario!

Rosario (*getting up and facing him, smiling, still shy, but bold*)   One condition! Juanita –

De Córdoba   Who's Juanita?

Rosario   You haven't forgotten . . . the girl in your new book!

De Córdoba   Good heavens! . . . I had!

Rosario   She's not to marry Don Indalecio . . . not on any account whatever.

De Córdoba   She shall marry her Mariano on the day that you marry me.

Rosario   And pass her examination?

De Córdoba   With honours?

Rosario (*holding out her two hands to him*)   You promise?

De Córdoba (*taking her hands*)   I promise!

The two old people gaze at them with entire delight and **María Pepa** *says, 'Pretty dears'.*

Curtain.

Take Two from One
(Triángulo)

A Farce in Three Acts

Haymarket Theatre, London (1931)

Haymarket Theatre, London (16 September) cast included:

Diana	Gertrude Lawrence
Faustino	Nicholas Hannen
Marcela	Peggy Ashcroft
Mario	Kim Peacock
Mr Turner	H. G. Stoker
Don Francisco	Marcus Barron
Milano	Douglas Burbidge
Astrid	Margaret Vines
Sussy	Elvira Henderson
Miss Turner	Gertrude Sterroll
Regina	Stella Rho
Finna	Elma Reid
Dona Dolores	Marguerite Cellier
Margarita	Margaret Hood
Lorenza	Evelyn Dane
Juliana	Olga Slade

Director: Theodore Komisarjevsky

Characters

Diana
Regina
Finna
Mr Turner
Sussy
Faustino
Mario
Astrid
Miss Turner
Second Officer
Six Young Ladies
Marcela
Doña Dolores
Don Francisco
Margarita
Milano
Lorenza
Juliana

The first act on a ship at sea; the second and third in Faustino's flat in Madrid.

Act One

The corner of the deck of a liner. She is on a tourist cruise and at the moment passing down the Red Sea. It is night. A group of passengers has gathered round a small table where **Regina** *sits telling fortunes by cards. It consists of* **Faustino**, *a good-looking young Spanish lawyer – he is on his honeymoon journey with* **Diana**, *who is young too and attractive;* **Mr Turner**, *an elderly Englishman, and* **Miss Turner**, *his sister;* **Mario**, *a young Italian, handsome but far too conscious of it, as he is also too smartly dressed;* **Astrid**, *a Swedish girl, who looks even younger and more inexperienced than she can possibly be; and* **Sussy** *and* **Finna**, *two sisters – probably – one of whom is fair and the other dark.*

Regina *herself is a woman of forty-five. She is very simply dressed, for she is employed in the ship's laundry, but she has tied a gay silk handkerchief round her neck, and wherever you met her, and however she was dressed, you would know she was not an 'ordinary' person. She has just finished one fortune and is ready to begin another.*

Diana   Mine next!

Sussy   Mine!

Finna   No, mine!

Mr Turner   One at a time, ladies! A little discipline . . . a little method. Even the Oracle at Delphi could not have prophesied to six people at once.

Regina   It is your turn, sir.

This to **Faustino**, *who is seated by* **Diana** *a little apart.*

Faustino   No, no! Let the ladies . . .

Regina   It is your turn.

Faustino   Very well.

Sussy   Your turn!

Finna   Courage! Come along.

Faustino *draws his chair in to the table and follows* **Regina**'s *directions.*

Regina   Breathe on them. Choose fifteen. Shuffle and cut. (*Then she reads.*) Long life! A very long life. (*General congratulations.*) Danger. Great danger. You escape it.

Faustino   Good!

Regina   Money. Unexpected money. A woman.

Faustino   True.

He and **Diana** *smile at each other.*

Regina   Another woman.

Diana   No, no!

Regina   Another woman. I'm sorry!

Mario   Don't be selfish!

Diana   I will be selfish. What's to happen to me?

Mario   There'd never be any difficulty about that!

Diana   Thank you! In Spain we don't take matters quite so easily.

Mario   Very silly of you. Now in Italy . . .

Mr Turner *tactfully intervenes.*

Mr Turner   Never mind, dear young lady. England can still boast of being a little behind the times too.

Mario   Really? I'd been told not.

Mr Turner   There is our notorious national hypocrisy to be allowed for, of course!

Faustino (*over the cards*)   Well, what next?

Regina   I can't make it out. You don't seem to die . . . you don't seem to die at all. And yet . . .

Faustino   Don't tell me I'm to turn into a Wandering Jew.

Regina   I can't make it out.

She gathers up the cards.

Diana   Now mine!

Faustino   Well, whatever else happens I shall grow to be a very old and a very venerable gentleman. So will you all please practise paying me some respect?

Regina   Breathe. Choose fifteen. Then shuffle and cut.

Finna   I see a white hair already. Shall I pull it out for you? Two! Three! Four!

Faustino   No, no, please! I scream if I'm touched.

The cards are cut again.

Diana   Well?

Regina   Long life . . . the very first card.

Faustino, *rather bored by* **Finna**'*s too obvious attentions, is standing over his wife.*

Faustino   That's right.

Diana   We'll be buried together.

Finna   Like an elderly Romeo and Juliet.

Regina   A handsome man loves you.

Faustino Thank you.

Diana Egoist! Other and much handsomer men may . . . once upon a time . . . have been in love with me. Who knows?

Mario Who knows?

Regina Here's a forest. And money. Precious stones. Yes, it's a forest. And black men.

Diana Dearest . . . have we put any money in the Congo?

Regina Danger . . . but nothing comes of it. I think that's all.

She gathers up the cards again.

Diana I've come off quite well.

Astrid Will you . . . would you be kind enough to do mine?

Regina Yes. Breathe. Choose fifteen. Shuffle and cut.

Finna Quite well! precious stones! I should think so.

Diana I make you a present of them.

Sussy You know . . . we can't be sure that all this isn't true. We can't be sure that anything isn't true.

Mr Turner No . . . it is an axiom in logic that one cannot prove a negative.

Sussy There! Thank you! (*To the rest.*) So I'm not quite the fool you all think me!

Mario (*to* **Diana**) I wish you were as generous with some things you've already got.

Diana (*coldly*) With what?

Mario (*subtly evasive*) The passing moment.

Astrid (*to* **Regina**) Well?

Regina There's someone you're very fond of . . . .

Astrid No, no! Why don't you tell me what that card says.

Regina It's not important.

Astrid Yes, it is.

Regina Not when it comes alone . . .

Astrid That's the death card, isn't it?

Regina Yes.

Astrid Then why don't you tell me. I'm not afraid. I don't think I want to live . . . to be old.

Mr Turner That, if I may say so, my dear young lady, is where you are wrong. It is great fun to be old. Life's much less troublesome . . . and far more interesting.

Sussy (*to* **Regina**)   Do you really believe all this?

Regina   I make mistakes . . . but the cards never lie. (*To* **Astrid**.) You come from the North?

Astrid   From Sweden.

Regina   I was there once.

Astrid   Were you?

Mario   On a cruise?

Regina (*turning the cards*)   A house by the water. Trees.

Astrid   That might be my home.

Mr Turner   There are a good many houses in Sweden . . . standing by lakes with trees round them.

Regina   Was it burnt down?

Astrid   No.

Regina   Because here's fire as well as water.

Mario   What took you to Sweden?

Regina   More water. And here's water.

Faustino   And here's lots more . . . all around us.

Mario   What took you to Sweden?

Regina (*giving* **Astrid** *a sharp look and then sweeping the cards together*)   I can't see anything else, I'm afraid. I went to Sweden with a circus.

Miss Turner   Dear me! Do they carry laundries with them?

Regina   I was in the circus. I did an equestrian act.

Diana   Riding bareback and jumping through hoops?

Regina   Oh, that's nothing! Anyone can do that. I used to throw up six glass balls and catch them with the horse at full gallop. I could do it with knives too. But that was stopped.

Faustino   Why?

Regina   It made the ring-master so nervous.

Diana   Good!

Finna   Why did you give it all up?

Regina   I married. And now I'm too old.

Miss Turner   What made you take to laundry work?

Regina   I must earn my living.

Act One   159

Mr Turner   Your husband should do that for you.

Regina   He'd rather I earned his.

Miss Turner   But . . . laundry work on a ship?

Regina   I like travelling. I got so used to it. Now there'll be trouble. I'm not allowed on this deck.

For the **Second Officer**, *a man of forty or so, has come along.*

Faustino   Nonsense. We made you come. I'll be responsible.

Mr Turner   *I* made her come. *I* am responsible.

Diana   *I* made the suggestion.

Miss Turner   *I* told you about her.

Second Officer (*to* **Regina**, *not unkindly*)   Now, now, now! This won't do.

Diana   It's our fault entirely.

Second Officer   But I can't discipline you, madam.

Finna   What's the punishment?

Second Officer (*mock serious*)   What will the Captain make it this time? Three days cells. He may put her in irons. Get along . . . get along. Or has anyone else to have his fortune told?

Sussy   Let her tell yours. Then you can't punish her.

Second Officer   Thanks. I know mine. To wear this uniform another twenty years . . . if I'm lucky.

Diana   But it isn't so dull cruising, is it, as going back and forth across the Atlantic week after week?

Second Officer   The Red Sea's a bit warmer, that's all.

Faustino (*his pocket-book out*)   What shall we . . .?

Mr Turner   Allow me. This is my affair.

Faustino   Certainly not.

They both proceed to pay **Regina**. *The ship's band can now be heard playing dance music.*

Diana   Will you tell me your name?

Regina   Regina. (*To* **Mr Turner**.) Thank you. (*To* **Faustino**.) This is too much.

Faustino   For such a fortune as you told me! Long life . . . lots of money . . . lots of love.

Regina   You mayn't always think so well of it. We can have too much of anything, can't we? Good night, ladies. Good night, kind gentlemen . . . and thank you. (*To the* **Second Officer**.) Am I to be put in irons?

Second Officer Wait and see. Gipsy!

Regina Yes, I am. And my mother was a queen among them. And so might I have been!

She goes off.

Second Officer She's a character.

Mr Turner She won't get into trouble, will she?

Second Officer No. It's against the rules and the Captain doesn't like it. But she amuses the passengers . . . and when things are a bit dull . . . five days between ports . . .

Diana I like her.

Mario It is hot tonight.

Second Officer Hot! You don't know what the Red Sea can do when it wants to be hot.

Finna Who's going to dance?

Diana I like her very much.

Mr Turner Heavens. What energy!

Sussy I dare say she does very well. I know a palmist in New York . . . who crystal gazes . . . and turns tables and all that . . . and makes . . . oh, thousands and thousands a year.

Miss Turner How scandalous!

Sussy Why?

Miss Turner To earn money . . . and all that money . . . by deceiving people.

Sussy But if they like it!

Miss Turner (*to the* **Second Officer**) D'you think it might be cooler on the left side?

Mr Turner The port side, Lilian, the port side!

Second Officer Yes, if there's any breeze at all you'll get it there.

Finna There aren't enough partners on this ship.

Mr Turner In this ship.

Finna What's the difference?

Mr Turner One is right, my dear young lady, and the other is wrong.

Finna Oh dear! Why don't you carry partners for us?

Second Officer There are the junior officers . . . now and then.

Finna Oh, they're always on duty . . . in duty.

Mr Turner   On duty.

Second Officer   (*ironically*)   It is a pity she can't navigate herself.

Miss Turner   Science makes such strides. I dare say in time the Captain will be able to sit in his cabin . . .

Second Officer   Or on shore . . .

Miss Turner   And just tap keys on a machine . . . .

Second Officer   Then sailors will have nothing to learn except two-steps and fox-trots.

Sussy   Well, it isn't nice for us . . . it really isn't . . . when there aren't enough men on board and a few over. We can't go competing for them!

Finna   Openly!

Sussy   And men are so lazy.

The **Second Officer** *has departed; and since* **Regina** *was disposed of the rest have been drifting in the direction of the dancing, though* **Faustino** *and* **Diana** *have lagged behind, and* **Mario** *has been hovering in the hope that he might detach her from her husband . . . and of this she is rather unpleasantly aware.* **Astrid**, *too, has stayed. She is standing by the rail, looking out to sea.* **Mr Turner** *goes up to her.*

Mr Turner   Star-gazing!

Astrid   They don't look as if they cared much what happens to us . . . do they?

Mr Turner   Why should they . . . when by the time they can see what has happened to us it is all over and done with years ago . . . if what the astronomers say is true?

Astrid   Yes, everything's over soon enough . . . from the stars' point of view.

Mr Turner   Are you feeling better tonight?

Astrid   I'm not really ill at all, you know.

Mr Turner   Well enough to help a decrepit old man twice round the dancing-floor?

Astrid   I ought to go down and look after my aunt.

Mr Turner   She'll be asleep.

Astrid   Are you afraid of death, Mr Turner?

Mr Turner   There are things I fear more.

Astrid   What?

Mr Turner   Let us think. There is an English poem that ends with

> He did not mind death
> But he could not stand tickling.

And it is on record, you know, that men have been literally tickled to death . . . .

They go off. **Diana** *and* **Faustino** *are alone.*

Diana   Shall we dance?

Faustino   No . . . let's stay here a little . . . by ourselves. What a night! And the sea . . . looks as if you could skate on it.

Diana   What a sky! Are you happy?

Faustino   Quite.

Diana   Oh dear . . . no happier than that?

Faustino   How much happier can one be?

Diana   What a question! I want you to be positively, ecstatically happy.

Faustino   With you . . . who wouldn't be?

Diana   But without me!

Faustino   That's a nice thing to suggest . . . with our honeymoon not half over.

Diana   Apart from me! Couldn't you be?

Faustino   How shall I ever be able to tell now?

Diana   Well . . . it has been a wonderful honeymoon so far, hasn't it? Tangier . . . Monte Carlo . . . Naples . . . Athens . . . Egypt! And over there now if we could see it . . . tropical Africa . . . shiny Black men stealing through the jungle . . . .

Faustino   Has that been in your mind this evening?

Diana   I dare say.

Faustino   Perhaps that was why it came out in the cards. I trust it's cooler in the jungle. And if I was a shiny Black man at least I could take my clothes off.

Diana   I fear, beloved, that you have a very prosaic mind.

Faustino   Yes, I have. But it is interesting to consider, isn't it, that colour is a sort of clothing?

Diana   I wish you weren't always, always, always quite so calm . . . and matter of fact.

Faustino   Why?

Diana   It frightens me.

Faustino   That is in the nature of a paradox.

Diana   Worse and worse! Now you're being like Mr Turner.

Faustino   The Englishman. He's a very well-instructed fellow.

Diana   I know . . . I know! Let's leave the ship at the next port and go straight home.

Faustino   Do you really want to?

Diana   No, *I* don't want to. But you're not enjoying things.

Faustino I've just told you that I am.

Diana You're not. There's not a sight we've seen . . .! When we sat looking at the Acropolis by moonlight . . . I was in the seventh heaven . . . but I gave half a glance at you . . . and you weren't looking at the Acropolis or even at the moon . . . you were looking at me. And it was the same with the Sphinx.

Faustino Some women would be flattered.

Diana Some fools of women would be. You'll be far happier at home . . . taking a walk in the park on Sunday. Not even doing that! Sitting at home . . . and looking at me now and then over the edge of the newspaper.

Faustino But I shall only have to put down my newspaper to be back with the Acropolis . . . or the Sphinx . . . or here in the starlight . . . in thought. I've my own way of enjoying things. Now, you're a little apt, aren't you, to exhaust your pleasures at the moment? I store mine up. I . . . if you want me to go on talking about myself?

Diana Oh yes!

Faustino There never was a man yet who didn't enjoy that, at any rate. I prefer to be passively recipient. And in the stored memory of things may lie a juster appreciation of them, don't you think, than in the fever of the moment?

Diana Yes. You put things so convincingly.

Faustino I'm a lawyer . . . it's my business to. Then again . . . shall I go on?

Diana Oh, there's a shooting star! Did you see it?

Faustino No. Shall I go on?

Diana Yes, please, darling. Go right on . . . till you've finished.

Faustino There are surely few experiences in life . . . except toothaches and such-like . . . from which one cannot extract some enjoyment. And I'm told there is spiritual profit even in toothache. Thank heaven I've never had one.

Diana Never had a toothache?

Faustino Never!

Diana I rather wish you had once . . . just once . . . had a toothache.

Faustino What is more . . . I should be ashamed of myself if I couldn't enjoy sitting at home . . . with you, only with you, naturally . . . just as much as looking at the Acropolis by moonlight. In theory, that's to say.

Diana Yes, beloved . . . but in practice! You talk of your home as if it were . . .! Oh dear, oh dear! Why am I always being tactless about your home?

Faustino Nonsense! Say what you like about it. It's your home now . . . now that father and mother have given it to us and gone . . .

Diana So kind of them!

Faustino They've only had to move upstairs. And whatever I may feel for it I feel far more for you, I hope.

Diana Faustino . . . how you can have lived all your life in that drawing-room . . . and dining-room . . . with that wallpaper on the wall . . . and those curtains . . . and that carpet . . . .

Faustino Now tell me, Diana . . . in plain words . . . what precisely is wrong with them?

Diana Darling, how can I tell you if you do not know! Oh . . . do you think it would hurt their feelings dreadfully if when we got back we just sold whatever anyone would be fool enough to buy . . . and burnt the rest . . . and started fresh?

Faustino Yes, I'm sure it would.

Diana Yours, too! I am so sorry.

Faustino I should not allow my feelings to be hurt.

Diana And they don't much like me to begin with.

Faustino Diana . . . how can you say such a thing?

Diana They dislike me . . . and they distrust me. The whole household . . . except, perhaps, old Juliana!

Faustino I'm sure that my father . . .

Diana Oh, any pretty woman could get her way with him.

Faustino My dear!

Diana I'm none the less pretty because I'm his daughter-in-law, am I? Your mother prays to God every day that she may learn to do her duty by me . . . I see it in her eye.

Faustino And she will.

Diana Yes, won't she!

Faustino Margarita worships the very ground you tread on.

Diana Margarita's fourteen . . .

Faustino Fifteen.

Diana She must have some grown-up human being to idealise . . . and it doesn't matter for the moment what the sex is. She adores me just as this little Swedish girl on board . . . who might be twelve! . . . adores you.

Faustino Nothing of the sort!

Diana But for that matter, beloved, all the women on board adore you.

Faustino What perfect nonsense!

Diana But, of course, they adore you! Can't you see it?

Faustino   Diana, you are making me most uncomfortable. There is nothing that I do . . . there is nothing I've ever done . . .

Diana   Oh . . . it's no credit to you!

Faustino   It would be a great discredit to me if . . .

Diana   It's something you . . . just are. *I* don't feel it. I love you . . . that's different. I've no illusions left about you . . . or very few . . . and I still love you. And that is love! But all these women . . .

Faustino   Not the married ones. Now, come!

Diana   They're wilier . . . they begin by making up to me. Oh, I'm not jealous . . . and if I were I should pretend not to be. I really feel rather flattered, you know. To see women flinging themselves at your head . . . and you not turning it to look at one of them. While I wouldn't fling myself at the king's . . . and you took some trouble to win a few kind words from me, didn't you? Darling, don't you think we could at least change some of the furniture when we get back . . . and take that dreadful paper off the drawing-room wall? Yes . . . I know it'll come back into fashion if we only wait long enough . . . .

Faustino   Well, we'll see. But I do wish you wouldn't put these ideas into my head . . . .

Diana   About the wallpaper?

Faustino   No, about these wretched women!

Diana   Oh, never mind them. They won't hurt you. But my bedroom curtains I will change . . . .

A few moments back the dance music stopped. Now there arrive from the direction of it a body of six – or even eight young ladies, if the management can afford so many. **Sussy** *and* **Finna** *are among them, and the others should appear to be of varying nationalities.* **Mario** *shortly follows; then* **Mr Turner**, *who is soon joined by his sister. The talk rattles along.*

Finna   Here you both are!

Diana   Yes.

1st Young Lady   Flirting!

2nd Young Lady   With each other!

Sussy   Scandalous!

Diana   What are you all standing in a lump like that for?

Finna   We are a mutiny.

Faustino   Good heavens! Have you shot the Captain? Are the crew under hatches?

1st Young Lady   The officers have vanished . . . the three that were dancing. I don't know why.

Sussy   We are not that sort of mutiny.

4th Young Lady   But we mean to have no more nonsense!

Mr Turner   My dear young ladies, don't boast of being revolutionaries . . . no sensible revolutionary does that. Protest that you have come to bring order out of chaos.

1st Young Lady   Quite right.

Finna   Chaos . . . that's what it is.

Sussy   If something isn't done the dances will have to be stopped altogether.

Faustino   Well, on a night when the thermometer's at . . .

3rd Young Lady   No . . . we'll have no excuses.

2nd Young Lady   No more men sneaking off to the smoking-room.

Finna   Or to flirt with their wives.

4th Young Lady   There's to be discipline for the future . . .

3rd Young Lady   And no shirking . . .

2nd Young Lady   The men in this ship will do their duty . . .

Sussy   And dance every single dance with somebody . . .

3rd Young Lady   Or take the consequences.

Finna   We've drawn lots for them for the next to start with . . .

Sussy   And it's a tango . . . so you can't complain that it'll make you hotter.

Mr Turner   I came out of the hat first. No one congratulated my partner.

Faustino   Who have I fallen to?

Sussy   You're young . . .

Mr Turner   Don't, my dear young lady!

Sussy   . . . and you dance pretty well. So you've been split into three.

Faustino   Heavens! Two I might manage . . . one on each arm.

3rd Young Lady (*to* **Diana**)   We gave you a chance . . . though you didn't deserve it.

Sussy   Keeping a perfectly good dancer . . . and a whole one . . . to yourself!

2nd Young Lady   And not dancing with him either.

Diana   Well, if I drew a blank . . .

Sussy   Not a bit of it.

Mario   I have had the good fortune . . .

Diana   Oh!

She says it with marked coldness. For a minute or so the band has been playing the music for the tango.

4th Young Lady   Come along now, and round up the rest of the deserters.

Sussy   Quick march, Señor Faustino.

Faustino   But whose prey am I?

Finna   Mine!

1st Young Lady   And mine!

2nd Young Lady   And Astrid's. Where's Astrid?

Astrid   I'm here.

Faustino   Who has first bite?

1st Young Lady   We didn't settle that.

Finna   Shut your eyes. Turn round. Then take two paces forward and grab.

Faustino   Stop! Don't make me giddy.

When she has stopped twirling him he makes an unsteady pace forward.

Sussy   Keep your eyes shut.

3rd Young Lady   No cheating.

4th Young Lady   Now.

He puts his arm out and finds when he opens his eyes that it is encircling **Astrid**, *who looks at him fascinated but frightened. He carries off the situation coolly and easily.*

Faustino   Honoured!

Astrid   I . . . I think I won't dance, thank you.

Sussy   Nonsense.

Faustino   Not when I'm in such demand?

Astrid   Very well.

Finna   But no cheating now.

1st Young Lady   Four minutes by my watch.

Faustino   We'd better begin at once, then.

2nd Young Lady   Come along, the rest of you, to the smoking-room.

Faustino   I shall never be so competed for again.

Faustino *and* **Astrid** *are dancing off.*

Finna   If they lock the door we'll break it in.

3rd Young Lady   Where's the Third Officer, though? I drew the Third Officer.

4th Young Lady   I drew the Fourth . . . and he can't dance for cocktails.

Sussy   Tomorrow morning we start compulsory lessons.

The young ladies disappear.

Mr Turner   Women . . . saving your presence, dear lady . . . are terrifying creatures. We've been un-Wise Men of the West . . . to let them loose.

He is following towards the dancing when his eye catches **Mario**, *who is waiting near* **Diana**, *with a not very attractive expression on his face, though no doubt he thinks it is.* **Miss Turner**, *who has returned with the rest, to be a silently amused spectator of all this nonsense, has just seated herself on a deck-chair a little apart.*

Mario   May I now have the honour . . . ?

Diana   Thank you . . . I won't dance.

Mario   But I have fallen to your lot.

Diana   I'll be generous. I'll give my ticket away . . . to anyone you prefer.

Mario   Who could I prefer? You pay no compliment to my good taste.

Diana   If I pay one to your courtesy . . . will you deserve it? I don't want to dance, thank you.

Miss Turner (*helpfully*)   Sit and talk to me, won't you?

Diana   Yes . . . .

Mario   But this is to deprive me of my rights. I must report you to the authorities . . . to the young ladies who are now partitioning your husband.

Diana   They are quite welcome to him . . . for an hour or so . . . and . . . please don't make me say: to you.

Mr Turner *gives a loud exclamation of pain.*

Miss Turner   What's the matter, Henry?

Mr Turner   My rheumatics. How can I dance with these rheumatics? Signor Mario, since you're so anxious to be tangoing perhaps you'll take over my partner.

Mario   Thank you! Will you guarantee me a better reception . . . ?

Mr Turner   Oh yes . . . I'll guarantee you that.

Miss Turner   What a pretty dress! Paris?

Diana   No, Madrid.

Mr Turner   Clothes! There . . . that's a definite dismissal for both of us.

Mario   Very well. I will claim my rights later!

He abruptly departs.

Mr Turner   My leg's better. Perhaps I can dance a turn or two after all.

He gives them a smile and is departing too.

Miss Turner Nothing so good for it, Henry.

Diana I hope you'll never have another twinge . . . and thank you.

Mr Turner *departs.*

Diana Your brother's a dear. Why has he never married?

Miss Turner (*her eyebrows up*) Well . . . really . . .!

Diana Oh . . . oughtn't I to have asked? I forgot . . . we're only acquaintances . . . shipboard acquaintances too. And you're English. And if I'm to get on with you I must learn to be 'reserved', mustn't I?

Miss Turner There's no reason you shouldn't ask. But I fear I can't tell you . . . unless it's just because he is such a dear, and likes everyone so much that he could never come to love anyone . . . just that much more.

Diana But I wonder some woman hasn't insisted on marrying him.

Miss Turner (*with quite gentle irony*) Do ladies . . . you see how old-fashioned I am; I talk about 'ladies' . . . do they propose in Spain?

Diana Not . . . brutally.

Miss Turner They used not to in England when he and I were young.

Diana And, of course, he has you.

Miss Turner Thank you.

Diana Have you always been great friends?

Miss Turner Yes.

Diana And do you live together and always travel together?

Miss Turner Heavens, no! . . . or we shouldn't be great friends. I often don't see him for a year.

Diana I can't understand that.

Miss Turner A brother's not one's property, you know . . . as some women think a husband is.

Diana D'you mean that for me?

Miss Turner My dear . . . I trust I'm not quite so impertinent.

Diana I wonder if deep down I do feel that . . . if that's why I . . .! I don't want to feel it. Oh dear . . . I'm not showing reserve! And you're not interested. Why should you be?

Miss Turner But I am . . . and flattered you should want to talk to me . . . if you're sure you won't be sorry after.

Astrid *comes swiftly and quietly towards them like a little white ghost, and stands looking at them in silence for a moment.*

Diana You danced for a very short four minutes.

Astrid Yes, very short.

Diana Wasn't he dancing well?

Astrid Yes, very well. Beautifully. But I couldn't.

Miss Turner Too hot?

Astrid I never feel hot.

Miss Turner Come and sit here.

Astrid (*with no touch of discourtesy; aloof merely*) No, thank you . . . I think I won't.

She goes to the taffrail and stands looking out to sea.

Miss Turner Do you smell something burning?

Diana No.

Miss Turner They throw their cigarette ends anywhere.

Diana Oh, yes . . . here's one has been smouldering.

Miss Turner That's it, then.

Diana (*taking up their more intimate talk again*) No. I could say anything to you . . .! and I'd never be sorry. But all my life . . .! Why do you smile?

Miss Turner How old are you?

Diana Twenty-three.

Miss Turner Yes, that's when we talk about 'all our life'.

Diana I've been grown up for years.

Miss Turner Go on, my dear . . . it was a friend's smile.

Diana I've never yet been able quite to decide whether one ought to be what one is . . . brutally . . . or try to behave better.

Miss Turner What is there that's very brutal about you?

Diana Lots of things! Oh . . . quite unspeakable things!

Miss Turner Then perhaps you'd better try to behave better. Was that cigarette end alight when you looked at it?

Diana It's out now.

Miss Turner They do go on smelling, don't they?

Diana But in the long run . . . what profit is there in hypocrisy and pretence?

Miss Turner When you reach my age . . . how tiresome of me to say that! . . . you'll find it hasn't seemed such a very long run.

Diana What profit to other people even?

Miss Turner Yes . . . if we all followed our inclination it would be a most interesting and exciting world . . . and none of the dull things there are to do in it would get done at all . . . the things that make slaves of us. No one would build houses, or ships . . . or mind babies . . . or teach mathematics. I'm going below for a wrap.

Diana A wrap!

Miss Turner Well, no . . . not a wrap . . . a scarf for my shoulders . . . in case there's a breeze. You never know.

Diana But . . .

Miss Turner I'll come back.

She has talked herself out of sight, walking slowly and sedately. She made up her mind to go when she found that the cigarette end had not been alight for some time. **Diana** *stares after her.* **Astrid** *has at once noticed her departure; and she comes from the taffrail and stands again full in* **Diana***'s view.*

Diana Odd nation, the English! The more you think they like you the ruder they seem to get!

Astrid (*suddenly*) I heard you tell somebody yesterday that the other little wedding-ring you wear on your right hand was his.

Diana My husband's?

Astrid Yes . . . his.

Diana *is deliberately matter of fact.*

Diana It isn't a wedding-ring. It is one his mother gave him for a memento of his first communion.

Astrid He always wore it till he met you?

Diana Yes.

Astrid Did he love his mother very much?

Diana I hope so.

Astrid But he gave it to you for a sign how much more . . . how much more he loved you?

Diana No, he gave it me because it had grown too small for him.

Astrid You never take it off?

Diana Each time I wash my hands. Do you want to look at it? Catch.

Astrid No, no! (*She takes the ring.*) Is she dead?

Diana   His mother! Very, very far from it.

Astrid   Something's written inside.

Diana   Dolores . . . that's her name.

Astrid   It means sorrowful.

Diana   Yes . . . and she's the happiest of old ladies. And has the biggest appetite you ever saw! My dear child . . . you mustn't make too much of a fool of yourself about my husband, must you? It doesn't matter to me . . .

Astrid   No, of course not!

Diana   And it doesn't matter before me. And I like you . . . though it's very strange of you! . . . for being so frank with me about it. But if other people begin to notice . . .

Astrid   They won't. I keep away from him all I can. He has never noticed.

Diana   No, he hadn't . . . till I told him.

Astrid   Oh, you shouldn't have told him! Why did you? That was wrong. That was unkind.

Diana   There's my point of view too, you know . . . which you naturally won't understand. We had a good laugh about it. Well, you'd rather I laughed about it, wouldn't you . . . for you don't want it to hurt me? And I'd rather he did.

Astrid   Laughing at things doesn't make them ridiculous, does it?

Diana   No . . . that's true.

Astrid   I think it's you who don't understand. I love him . . . and I don't want him to come near me . . . or ever touch me. I couldn't bear dancing with him. And it isn't because he belongs to you. I'm thankful he belongs to you . . . and loves you. For if he didn't he might . . . oh, it's possible! . . . come to love me.

Diana   You were very ill a while ago, weren't you? That was why your aunt brought you this voyage.

Astrid   Yes . . . but I'm not ill any more. I'm going to die, though.

Diana   Nonsense. You mustn't let what that silly gipsy said run in your head.

Astrid   She wasn't so silly, I think. But I knew before she told me.

Diana   Well, we're none of us going to live for ever . . . though we all go on as if we were. And any of us may die at any moment. This ship might go down . . . now while we're talking.

Astrid   I shan't mind dying. It isn't . . . oh, please understand . . . that I've any grievance against the world. I could learn to live in it and become like everyone else . . . quite easily. But I don't want to. (*She throws her head towards the music and dancing.*) If all that's what pleasure is I should hate to find pleasure in it. If all this love-making in corners is what love's like . . . I don't want a lover. You and he are happy together . . . and I hope you always will be . . . if you're content with being happy. I couldn't be.

Diana You don't seem to want anything that's real.

Astrid No . . . that's it. Nothing that's real.

Diana May I have back my ring, please? One must not be afraid of realities.

Astrid I wonder if you'd let me wear it . . . just for five minutes?

Diana No, certainly not.

Astrid I'll walk up the deck and down again and bring it straight back to you. Things can never be as I imagine them, I know . . . or people. But he's . . . good, isn't he?

Diana You wouldn't believe me if I told you he wasn't. Yes . . . as men go, he's on the good side. He's good enough for me. Well, wear it for an hour or two if you like . . . if that's as near to robbing me of him as you want to come.

Astrid You'll never tell him I wore it, will you?

Diana I promise that . . . for my own sake.

Astrid Why?

Diana For fear we shouldn't laugh.

Astrid (*as she puts the ring on*) When I take it off again that will be the end. I shan't think any more of him after that.

Diana Which will be as well, perhaps.

Astrid Yes . . . I suppose so. I'll not be long.

She goes off. **Diana** *sits lost in thought, till she finds that* **Mario** *is standing by her. She feels that he has arrived with suspicious suddenness.*

Mario My dance . . . now.

Diana Have you been . . . eavesdropping?

Mario Certainly not.

Diana You have been. You've been lurking there listening to that child's secrets . . . and to me. You really are an unspeakable cad.

Mario May I have my dance?

Diana What . . . when I've just called you . . . ?

Mario You may call me what you like if you will dance with me. *I* am not afraid of realities . . .

Diana You see, you were listening . . .

Mario No . . . I overheard. But I am not afraid even of being a cad . . . if it gets me what I want.

Diana Will you go away, please?

Mario No, I will not.

Diana Then I must.

Mario *does not speak with a foreign accent; but his phrasing is meant just to suggest that he is using a language not his own.*

Mario No . . . you will not. You will stay here and let me make love to you a little. Please! I will be very respectful . . . to begin with. I will only tell you how beautiful you are . . .

Diana You insult me.

Mario Now . . . count one, two, three . . . and repeat that. You see . . . you cannot . . . because you did not mean it. It was only the proper thing to say. I am not so bad, you will find. But I have no use for silly phrases . . . and for schoolgirl nonsense . . . when one is not a schoolgirl. And you are not. Do not try, please, to dodge away. I have my scheme with you. Tonight I want my dance . . . I want to talk to you . . . I want to kiss your hand. Then tomorrow if I have made you like me a little . . .

Diana At what point in it do you have your ears boxed?

Mario Oh yes . . . you may do that if you please . . . for that will hasten matters nicely. I should answer that by kissing you at once. It is the correct answer. Not your hand . . . but right on your pretty mouth.

Diana Have you been drinking?

Mario No . . . I have had some cocktails. No, I have not been drinking. This is love.

Diana Let me pass.

Mario Oh dear! You must not use these literary phrases . . . you must not, Diana . . . .

Diana How dare you call me . . . ?

Mario There you go again! You really must not use them if you wish me to believe one word you say. May I have my dance? I will be good for this evening if I may have my dance . . . as good as that silly Astrid thinks your silly husband is. Yes . . . he is silly . . . and you know it . . . because you are not. Now you are thinking you will dodge me and run. Please do not. I know just how to catch you and hold you. I have studied it . . . I have had practice. It will be undignified for you to struggle. And I shall kiss you three times at least before you escape. No . . . do not look down the deck. They are all dancing. No one will come.

Diana There's nothing I can do, then?

Mario Except to be a little civil to me. It is not much to ask.

Diana And complain to my husband after . . . who will thrash you . . . and to the Captain . . . who'll have you put on shore at the next port?

Act One 175

Mario I do not think you would care to be the subject of such a scandal.

Diana I will give you while I count ten to stand aside and let me go. If you don't I'll have the whole ship about your ears. One . . . two . . . three . . .

Mario This is drama! I am curious to see how you'll do it.

Diana Four . . . five . . . six. You think I'm bluffing! Seven . . .

Mario I must risk it.

Diana Eight . . . nine . . . ten.

Mario Well?

Diana *calls at the top of her voice* . . .

Diana Fire! Fire! Fire!

There is a moment's pause. Instinctively they both look round to see what will happen next.

Mario That was fool's trick . . . if you'll allow me to say so. Nobody has heard you, luckily.

Diana Do you want me to call out again?

Mario No . . . for God's sake . . . get along!

The **Second Officer** *suddenly arrives.*

Second Officer Was that you called out fire, madam?

Diana Yes. I'm sorry . . . let me explain . . .

Second Officer Who let you know we had fire on board?

Diana No one. But . . . oh . . . have we?

Second Officer Yes . . . we've been fighting it since this morning. Everyone that knew has had orders to hold their tongues. It didn't look much till a couple of hours ago. But it's gaining on us. The smoke is the trouble. We're headed for land. The Captain has ordered the boats out.

Mario Good God!

Second Officer And your business, if you please, is to help stop panic . . . not add to it.

Diana But I'd no idea. It . . . it was a joke.

Second Officer (*grimly*) Really!

Mario Why weren't we told?

Second Officer Get some warm things from your cabin.

Mario Warm things!

Second Officer And your life-belts. Damn that band . . . it was told to go on playing till it dropped. And then get to your boat stations, please.

The music has suddenly ceased. He goes off swiftly and coolly. **Miss Turner** *has appeared with two life-belts.*

Miss Turner I've brought you this, my dear. I knew it couldn't be those cigarette ends. (*To* **Mario**.) Help her on with it.

Mario No, no . . . there's lots of time.

Miss Turner I'm none so sure. They ought to have let us know sooner.

Mario I can't go down. My cabin's on D deck. I must have a belt . . . .

Diana Where's Faustino? I don't know my boat station.

Miss Turner One never does.

Mr Turner *has now arrived. He is carrying a belt too.*

Diana I must find Faustino.

Miss Turner Help this child on with her belt, Henry.

Mr Turner Certainly.

To do so he puts his down. The ship's bell starts ringing.

Miss Turner I dislike a fire-bell . . . even more than a fog-horn . . . don't you?

Sussy *rushes on* . . . .

Sussy There's a fire . . . there's a fire!

Mr Turner We know, dear young lady.

Diana Faustino!

Mario I must have a belt . . .

His eye has fallen on **Mr Turner**'s *and his fingers go out to it. But* **Miss Turner**'s *eye is on him.*

Miss Turner Well . . . I shouldn't take Henry's. It's not done, you know.

Mario I . . . I didn't mean to.

Miss Turner No . . . but instinct is so strong.

The lights go out. **Sussy** *screams.*

Diana Don't scream. What's the use of that?

Mr Turner Never mind . . . I've tied the strings for you.

Two more young ladies are heard rushing on. One is calling . . . .

1st Young Lady's Voice Mr Turner . . . Mr Turner! . . .

2nd Young Lady's Voice My shoe has come off. I must find my shoe.

Miss Turner It's only the lights on this deck.

A man's figure is seen silhouetted against the sky as he walks past and his voice is heard . . .

Man's Voice   Stay where you are, please. We'll light up in a minute.

Diana   I must find Faustino.

Mr Turner   He'll be looking for you. Better stop quietly here. There's lots of time.

Finna's *voice is heard . . .*

Finna's Voice   Sussy! Sussy!

Sussy   Here I am.

1st Young Lady   Is there much danger, d'you think?

2st Young Lady   I wish I had my shoe.

Miss Turner   Well, the fire was aft . . . or we should all have smelt it. Now something else has happened.

Diana   They ought to have told us. They've no right to treat us like children . . .

Mr Turner   When it comes to this sort of thing I'm afraid we're not much more use.

Diana   I don't agree . . .

The lights go up.

Miss Turner   That's better!

A man's voice is heard calling 'Boat stations'.

Diana   I don't know my boat station.

2st Young Lady (*hopping around*)   I must find my shoe.

Diana   I must find Faustino.

1st Young Lady   But we've time to go to our cabins, haven't we?

Miss Turner   That man has taken your belt, Henry. I knew he would.

For in the darkness **Mario** *and the belt have disappeared.*

Mr Turner   There are lots about. Don't fuss.

Miss Turner   I am not fussing.

For, indeed, she is not. The voice again calls 'Boat stations'.

Curtain.

Act Two

The salon in **Faustino**'s *apartment in Madrid. One thing is immediately evident; that the changes* **Diana** *planned in its furnishing were never carried out. We shall soon know why. But she would have been wrong to meddle with it, perhaps; for its faded mid-nineteenth-century splendours have a charm of their own. The only thing in the room that conflicts with them is a portrait of* **Diana** *herself hanging in the place of honour, with some flowers standing before it, almost as if it were a shrine.*

There has been a family dinner party and the company have just come in to coffee and liqueurs. They did not – in Madrid – sit down to dinner till half-past nine, so it must now be nearly eleven. **Faustino** *is there; his father and mother,* **Don Francisco** *and* **Doña Dolores***; his sister* **Lorenza** *and her husband,* **Milano***;* **Margarita** (*or* **Margaritina** *as she is called*) *and* **Marcela***. The chief thing to say about* **Marcela** *is that she is as unlike* **Diana** *as it is possible to be. She is busy with the coffee. She is evidently the hostess.*

Marcela   Is the coffee . . .?

Doña Dolores   The coffee's perfect.

Marcela   Chartreuse, Papa? It's over there.

Don Francisco   I think I will . . . yes, I think I will.

Marcela (*to* **Margarita**)   Here's you coffee. Sugar . . . no?

Margarita   Yes.

Marcela   You'll have a *fine*, Milano?

Milano   Thank you.

Marcela (*to* **Faustino**)   And you won't, beloved. It's very bad for you. You'll have just as much *crème de menthe* as I give you . . . and no more.

Faustino   Not a drop, I promise.

Marcela (*to the other men generally*)   Your coffee's on the tray. (*Then . . .*) No high blood pressure for you!

. . . as she gives **Faustino** *a very small allowance of liqueur. He bows and kisses her hand.*

Milano (*with his coffee*)   There's a wife for you!

Lorenza   Small thanks I've ever had for trying to look after your health. And when did you last kiss my hand?

Milano   They've only been married a year.

Margarita   Cynic! Give me a cigarette.

Doña Dolores   Margaritina . . . how many cigarettes have you smoked today?

Margarita Not more than a hundred, Mamma . . . in fact rather less.

Doña Dolores I disapprove altogether of your smoking.

Margarita Milano, you've read your Bible. Is there a commandment: Thou shalt not smoke?

Milano No . . . but America hadn't been discovered when the good God spoke from Sinai.

Margarita A pity Mamma wasn't about . . . she could have made Moses slip one in.

Doña Dolores Margarita . . . don't say such things.

Marcela Another glass of Chartreuse, Papa?

Doña Dolores No, Francisco!

Don Francisco My dear . . . to drink their health.

Doña Dolores You did that at dinner . . . more than once.

Don Francisco Well, wait till next year . . . when we'll celebrate your second anniversary.

Doña Dolores If we're alive!

Don Francisco I have every intention of being alive.

Doña Dolores Francisco . . . do not tempt Providence.

Margarita (*sotto voce, to her neighbour*) Dear Mamma's always so morose after dinner. And the better the dinner . . . it was a good dinner, wasn't it? . . . the more morose she is. I wonder . . . oh, I wonder why!

Doña Dolores What's that you're saying, Margarita?

Margarita I was saying, dear Mamma, that *I* ate too much of that excellent strawberry ice. I'm afraid I'm a greedy little pig. It's hereditary failing. I get it from Papa!

Don Francisco What's that you get from me?

Margarita Your delicate digestion, dear Papa. But then I inherit your beautiful, meek, mild nature too . . . your patience under suffering. We let Mamma bully us all she pleases, don't we? . . . and we never say a word. Of course, I'm only her daughter. But you really might complain.

Don Francisco Young lady . . . there is one thing in my relation to you which I regret.

Margarita What's that?

Don Francisco That while you were still young enough to be smacked I didn't smack you oftener . . . and harder.

Lorenza Where you get your little devil's tongue from, I don't know!

Margarita   I'm sorry . . . dear Papa . . . I'm sorry. I'm an odious toad. But I'm very unhappy.

Lorenza   Nonsense!

Margarita   Now look here, Lorenza . . . I don't have to respect my sister at any rate. And . . .

Lorenza   What are you unhappy about, pray?

Margarita   Nothing that you would have the delicacy to appreciate.

Faustino   What is it, Margaritina?

Margarita   Nothing that matters apparently to anyone but me.

Milano   Out with it . . . silly!

Margarita   Well . . . here we are all drinking toasts and congratulating each other . . . and never a thought for . . . somebody I'm thinking about.

Lorenza   That's a tactful remark, I must say!

Marcela   Dear Lorenza, I don't mind. Why should I? But I do think about Diana, very often . . . as it happens. And we talk about her, don't we, beloved?

Faustino   Yes . . . quite often.

Marcela   I should hardly have her picture hanging there if I minded the thought of her, should I?

Doña Dolores   And considering that there was a mass said for her soul this very morning at St Pascual's . . . which you did not attend . . .

Margarita   No, I didn't! I hate masses for people's souls. And I hate to think Diana's dead.

Doña Dolores   Really!

Margarita   Well . . . we don't like anyone we were fond of to be dead, do we?

Marcela   Of course not. I quite understand, Margarita.

Margarita (*not too graciously*)   Thank you.

Doña Dolores (*to* **Marcela**)   My dear, we will say good night . . . before Margarita becomes more offensive than she has so far managed to be . . . if that is possible! Come along, Francisco.

Doña Dolores   I'm very comfortable.

Doña Dolores   You can be comfortable in your own chair upstairs. Besides, it's quite late. And Faustino has to be at the courts in the morning . . . and to work at his papers before he goes, I know.

Don Dolores   Do you?

Faustino   As a rule.

Don Dolores Good heavens, I never did!

Margarita But you were a genius, Papa!

Don Francisco Is that meant for satire?

Margarita No, I'm trying to be nice now. And nobody likes me any the better for it!

Senora Dolores *kisses* **Marcela** *affectionately*.

Doña Dolores A delightful evening, my dear. I hope you don't give Faustino such good dinners every day! (*She gazes at* **Diana***'s portrait.*) The ways of Providence are said to be inscrutable . . . but I could not wish for a better daughter-in-law than I have now.

Margarita Mamma!

Doña Dolores Have you any comment to make upon that remark, Margarita?

Margarita No, Mamma.

Doña Dolores I am glad. Good night, Lorenza.

Lorenza Good night, dear Mamma.

Doña Dolores Good night, Milano.

Milano Good night, Mamma.

Doña Dolores Lorenza could fatten you up a little . . . and no harm done.

Milano So I tell her.

Just as she is going she catches **Don Francisco** *making for that second glass of Chartreuse which is still untouched.*

Doña Dolores No, Francisco!

She departs. **Don Francisco** *heaves a deep sigh.*

Margarita Go on, Papa.

Lorenza It won't hurt you.

Margarita Don't you be bullied.

Don Francisco *takes up the glass again.*

Don Francisco I have so few pleasures left.

Margarita Quick . . . or she'll be back.

Don Francisco No . . . better not, perhaps! Good night, my dears. Good night, Milano

He goes out, **Faustino** *accompanying him.*

Lorenza Poor Papa!

Milano The thing is for a man to assert himself in time. Now we have been married five years and a bit . . .

Lorenza Yes . . . so it's just five years too late for you to begin. Good night, Marcela. You're a saint. *I* wouldn't have her hanging there.

Marcela But I like to have her hanging there.

Lorenza Well, I'm not sure you should. It's unnatural. Come along, Milano.

Milano One moment, Lorenza. Pray observe me.

He takes the glass of Chartreuse and swallows it.

Milano I didn't want it. I don't like Chartreuse. But no 'poor papas' for me!

Lorenza You're a goose.

They go out amid more 'good nights'.

Margarita I'm sorry if I was a beast. I love you. You know I do. But I loved her . . . differently.

Marcela She was different, I suppose.

Margarita Yes. But people can be different . . . and think differently . . . and behave differently . . . and all be very nice, can't they?

Marcela We must try to think so.

Margarita Good night, Marcela.

Marcela Good night, Margaritina.

Margarita *runs off.* **Marcela** *rings the bell, and, while waiting for it to be answered, puts the coffee cups on the tray. She pauses with one in her hand and gazes at* **Diana**'s *portrait.* **Juliana**, *an old family servant, comes in, takes the coffee tray and puts it on the waggon where the liqueurs are and is going to wheel it off when she misses the one cup.* **Marcela** *becomes conscious of her, and of this.*

Marcela Here it is!

Juliana, *coming for the cup, stands gazing at the picture too.*

Juliana The very image of her! Coming in of a morning sometimes I almost jump. It's so like her that it might be the young mistress.

Marcela (*a trifle sharply*) Juliana . . . why do you always call me the mistress . . . and speak of her as the young mistress.

Juliana I didn't know I did.

Marcela It should be the other way about if anything.

Juliana I'm sorry.

Marcela It doesn't matter.

Juliana I won't do it again.

Marcela You were very fond of her, I suppose.

Juliana Well . . . she was hardly married before they went off on that dreadful voyage . . .! But we were . . . most of us! And now, of course, we're very fond of you.

Marcela Thank you. Was she always laughing? You'd think so by the picture.

Juliana No . . . she didn't laugh much . . . but it was just the same as if she had. She kept the whole place gay. (*Then, as if in compensation.*) But I will say that it's much tidier now.

Juliana *wheels the tray-waggon out.*

Marcela (*to the picture*) Don't you laugh at me . . . don't you mock at me! Or I shall come to hate you . . . and God knows I don't want to.

Faustino *returns.*

Faustino Thank goodness that's over. These family gatherings are very trying.

Marcela That's a little ungracious . . . seeing that they all adore you.

Faustino Do they?

Marcela You know they do.

Faustino No well-constituted man likes being adored.

Marcela Not even by his wife?

Faustino 'No,' said he, spurning the flattery, 'not even by his wife!' I will even add that no well-constituted man is adored. Liked . . . loved . . . but not adored.

Marcela Well, I love you.

Faustino I am never tired of hearing it.

Marcela Shall we play our game of chess?

Faustino Aren't you too tired?

Marcela No . . . I take family parties more lightly than you.

She has been moving round, giving deft little touches to the disorganised room. Now she takes out the chessmen, and sitting opposite each other they set the board.

Faustino Yes, I was a spoiled child, I fear. But I try not to expect to be a spoiled husband.

Marcela Perhaps it would be good for you not to be loved quite so well . . . and for me!

Faustino Why for you?

Marcela It struck me the other day that it hadn't been at all good for my character . . . loving you.

Faustino (*amused*) I'm sorry!

Marcela No . . . before I came to love you I was fond of people and glad when they were happy and really sorry for them when things went wrong . . . and I did lots to help them. Now I don't give a dump whether anyone but you lives or dies. That can't be right. Which hand?

Faustino   The one with mother's ring on it.

Marcela   You begin.

He has risen to get himself a cigarette and light it; and, the board set, she has held out two pawns in closed fists.

Faustino   Pawn to king's fourth.

Marcela   You're not to stand over there and call out the moves. It frightens me.

He returns to the board.

And, with all my love . . . do I make you happy?

Faustino   I should be a most unreasonable man if . . .

Marcela   Well, say you are! What I want to know is: Are you happy?

Faustino   Quite.

Marcela   Not more than 'quite'? Then you're not really happy.

Faustino   The meaning of 'quite', if I may point it out to you . . .

Marcela   There's nothing I could be to you that I'm not?

Faustino   . . . is 'complete'. 'What more could you be or do? You're very pretty . . . you're as good as gold. And a perfect housekeeper.

Marcela   There's nothing you miss in me?

Faustino   Nothing! 'Quite' . . . oddly enough I had to look it up to remind myself only yesterday . . . comes first from the Latin *quiescere* . . . and it implies 'quiet satisfaction' . . .

Marcela   Nothing Diana once was to you that I can never be?

Faustino   Nothing you are not that I want you to be . . . for a single moment, my dear one.

Marcela   But she was . . . different . . . from anybody else.

Faustino   Yes . . . in a way she was. Aren't you going to move?

She advances a knight.

Knight! Oho! Rather rash, aren't you?

Marcela   I can do something different now and then . . . even if I can't be it. Faustino . . . promise to tell me if ever I begin to bore you.

Faustino (*moving a piece*)   Women have the oddest notions of what a man wants of his wife . . . of what he loves in his wife . . . of where his happiness lies. I loved Diana. But it was a bit of an adventure being married to her . . . far more of an adventure than the voyage round the world seemed likely to be . . . till they were both cut short at once. (*Suddenly the whole tragedy becomes vivid to him.*) Oh . . . my God!

Marcela It was terrible. What was the very last you saw of her? No, never mind! I know you hate to talk of it.

Faustino The ropes fouled as they were lowering our boat and we were all spilt into the sea. The sea was smooth enough . . . then. But, of course, it was quite dark. I swam about trying to find her. Then they called to me that she'd been picked up. But she wasn't in the boat that hauled me on board. They said everyone was safe . . . that it would be easy to keep in touch till the morning. I never saw her again . . . till I saw her . . .!

Marcela Poor Faustino.

Faustino Poor Diana! (*He turns his mind to the board.*) If you move your bishop there you'll lose it.

Marcela How?

Faustino Well . . . look!

Marcela Oh yes . . . I see. Then I won't.

Faustino But I feel no sense of adventure with you, beloved. I didn't think I should ever love anyone again. Everybody says that and I expect most people believe it. I don't think I could have loved anyone in the least like Diana. But with you there's a sense of perfect safety and peace . . . and that's very wonderful. We've been married a year and I only met you six months before . . . and that was hardly a year after . . . what had happened. But I feel as if I'd known you and loved you all my life.

Marcela You put things so beautifully.

Faustino (*in the very tone in which he said it to* **Diana**) My dear, I'm a lawyer. It's my business to. It's by putting things beautifully that I pay the rent . . . and we buy the dinner . . . and that very pretty dress you're wearing . . . and . . . check to your queen.

Marcela Oh, that's not fair! You make me talk . . . and then . . .! Now what am I to do? Tell me.

Faustino You can cover with the pawn . . . I shall take it with the knight . . .

Marcela But I don't want you to take my pawn.

Faustino Well? . . .

Marcela Oh, look at the time! I must step up and say good night to your mother.

Faustino Why . . . she has only just left us!

Marcela Never mind . . . she expects it . . . she's hurt if one of us doesn't go. Will you? She'd prefer it.

Faustino Certainly not.

Marcela Well, she won't love you the less. But *I* have a reputation as the best daughter-in-law in the world to keep up. It may have been a mistake to acquire it . . . but, having acquired it . . .! Don't cheat while I'm away . . . unless you like to improve my position a little.

Faustino Don't be long.

She vanishes. **Faustino** *lights another cigarette, leans back and closes his eyes in perfect comfort and content to wait for her. Perhaps he hums a tune. After a moment* **Juliana** *rushes in breathless and pale.*

Juliana Sir! . . . Sir . . . the young mistress . . .!

Faustino What's the matter . . . what's happened?

Juliana No . . . not the mistress . . . the young mistress. She's come back.

The words are not out of her mouth when **Diana** *rushes in like a whirlwind and flings herself into* **Faustino**'s *arms.*

Diana Yes . . . I'm here . . . I'm here . . . I'm here!

We hardly know her at first. She is as brown as a berry. Her hair has seen no coiffeur for many months. She is mainly dressed in one of those silk garments which rich Arabs near; bare legs, sandals on her feet. Round her neck is a string of uncut emeralds and diamonds. She has some sort of a hat in her hand but she flings it away anywhere. Altogether she is looking very lovely, is as strong and lithe as a panther, and, at the moment, radiant with happiness. **Faustino** *is almost speechless with astonishment and with something very like horror.*

Faustino Diana . . . you!

Diana Yes . . . and this is you . . . you . . . you . . . my darling . . . my own!

He has, almost mechanically, put his arms round her, since hers are ecstatically clasping him.

Hold me closer . . . closer.

Faustino I . . . I can't believe it.

Diana Can't you? (*She kisses him.*) Can't you! (*Another kiss.*) Can't you yet? Kiss me . . . then you will.

He searches for the correct spot – under the circumstances – upon which to print his kiss, saying . . .

Faustino I am . . . not quite myself for the moment . . .

. . . . and decides on her forehead.

Yes . . . it is certainly you . . . dear Diana! You . . . you . . . you!

He repeats her phrase, though the words hardly sound the same.

Juliana (*who has at last recovered her breath*)   Blessed Saint Lucia who has answered our prayers! Blessed be God who has brought us the dead to life again! Shall I pay the cab?

Faustino   Yes . . . pay the cab.

Juliana *departs, still praising God.*

Diana   My darling . . . my darling!

Faustino   Where have you come from?

Diana   From the station . . . and from Barcelona . . . and before that from . . . I'll tell you all about it . . . it's very wonderful. I ought to have telegraphed . . . poor darling, you're all upset . . . but I couldn't . . . it was too wonderful. I've been sitting with my eyes shut and holding my breath . . . I didn't want to open them or to speak till I found myself in your arms . . . hold me closer! . . . kiss me! . . . and home again. Oh . . . it's a beautiful room! I'll never say another word against it. Oh, darling! To be sitting down . . . on the sofa . . . with you . . . on the horrid old sofa . . . dear sofa. Oh, it's wonderful to be sitting here with you again. Beloved . . . how worn and ill you look. Grieving for me . . . grieving for me, I know! With nothing but that picture to keep you company! And it was never in the least like me. Now you say something.

Poor **Faustino**'s *mouth is dry.*

Faustino   Diana . . .! But where have you come from?

Diana   You'll never believe it. I've come from . . .! But that'll take so long to tell. I'll hear about you first. (*Her eyes fall on the chessboard.*) Poor lonely one . . . doing chess problems to pass the long evenings . . .

Faustino   No . . . no . . .!

Diana   Kiss me again. You don't seem to have kissed me at all yet. Dearest . . . are you very upset? Had you better have some brandy?

Faustino   No . . . no!

Marcela *has just come in. In a flash she realises what has happened. She is too horrified to move, but she gives an audible gasp which* **Diana** *overhears.*

Diana   No need for you to fuss, Juliana. Get the master some brandy. (*She turns and sees* **Marcela**.)

Diana   Who . . . who is this?

Faustino   This? This is . . .

Marcela   Are you . . . are you . . .? Faustino!

Faustino   Yes . . . she is.

Diana   Faustino!

Marcela (*clutching her heart*)   Oh, my God!

Diana   You've married again!

Faustino (*precise, if inarticulate*)   I have . . . I was . . .! I am . . .! I did!

Diana   Faustino!

Juliana *comes back. She is carrying an extraordinary object, a small alligator skin, which, with the head and paws still left, has been sewn up to make a bag. The claws form the handles, and the head still wears its grin.*

Juliana   Is this lizard all the luggage?

Diana (*fiercely*)   Yes.

Marcela   Luggage! Saints in heaven!

She faints into the nearest chair.

Juliana   She has fainted.

Faustino   Yes, of course she has. Get some water. Put that damned thing down. Get some brandy. Hurry . . . will you! Hurry!

Juliana *hurries out.*

Faustino   Here, Diana . . . do something. She has fainted. Do something to help.

Diana   Married again!

Faustino   I know . . . yes . . . I'll explain.

Diana   How could you!

Faustino   We'd better put her on the sofa.

Diana   How long since . . . you forgot me?

Faustino   I haven't . . . I didn't forget you.

Diana   How long?

Faustino (**Marcela** *inert in his arms*)   Oh, put those cushions straight . . . do!

Diana *puts the cushions straight with tragic gestures.*

Diana   How long have you been unfaithful to me?

Faustino   I haven't been unfaithful to you. How could I be unfaithful to you when I didn't know you were alive to be unfaithful to? Be reasonable.

Juliana *returns with the brandy.*

Diana   Reasonable!

Faustino (*to* **Juliana**)   That's right. Now you open her mouth and I'll pour the . . .! No, I'll open her mouth and you pour the . . .!

Diana   Don't be a fool, Faustino . . . you'll choke her. Damp her forehead and let her be. She'll come round soon enough.

Faustino Damp her forehead, Juliana. Where's my handkerchief?

Diana Reasonable! Here's a handkerchief.

Faustino This whole evening . . . I can't have had a handkerchief!

Diana Soon enough!

Faustino Thank you.

Marcela *gives a sigh and regains consciousness.*

Faustino That's better.

Diana (*eyeing the half-conscious offender as she might an unwelcome cat that had strayed in*) What's her name?

Faustino (*defensively*) Her name's Marcela.

Diana Pscha!

Marcela Faustino.

Faustino (*diminuendo*) Yes, my dearest . . . my dear . . . yes, Marcela.

Marcela Isn't she dead?

Diana (*violently*) No, I'm not dead. Why should I be dead?

Marcela You told me she was dead.

Faustino I was wrong . . . I'm sorry . . .

Diana Sorry!

Faustino Don't catch me up like that. Sorry I told her you were when you weren't. But glad . . . we must all be glad . . . that you're not . . . when you aren't. Don't glare at me, Diana. Won't you sit down?

Diana Thank you.

She sits, magnificent in wrath. **Marcela** *gives a sob.*

Faustino Don't cry, Marcela.

Marcela I'll try not to.

Faustino But . . . heaven help us all . . . what's to be done?

There is a vacant pause. Then **Juliana**, *whom they have forgotten, says . . .*

Juliana Shall I go upstairs and tell the old mistress?

Faustino No.

Diana No.

Marcela No.

They are at least certain about that.

Juliana Very well.

Faustino Not yet.

Juliana Shall I unpack the lizard?

Diana It's an alligator.

Faustino You can leave it . . . for the moment.

Juliana Would the young mistress like something to eat?

Diana Don't call me the young mistress.

Marcela Oh . . . !

Faustino Don't cry . . . dear Marcela.

Marcela I'm trying not to.

Juliana Would the mistress like . . . ?

Marcela Oh! . . .

Faustino Hold your tongue. Go away.

Juliana It's no use being angry with me, sir, because the good God has seen fit to make you a bigamite.

She departs with dignity.

Faustino (*with a flash of ecstatic agony*) Ah!

Marcela *now goes off into perfect floods of tears.*

Faustino But don't cry . . . don't cry! What good will that do?

Diana *suddenly begins to laugh, loudly, stridently.*

Faustino Don't laugh, Diana. It's indecent!

Diana Indecent! Be thankful I do laugh. Be thankful I don't kill you . . . both of you.

Marcela I wish you would . . . I wish you would!

Faustino And that's foolish.

Diana How dared you get married again?

Faustino I thought you were dead. I knew you were dead. I saw you.

Diana Saw me!

Faustino Well . . . some of you.

Marcela Don't . . . don't . . . it's too horrible.

Diana Will you be quiet, please? What's it to do with you? What do you mean, Faustino?

Faustino Nearly everyone was saved . . . but your boat had disappeared. I searched and searched . . . there was nothing I didn't do and have done . . . for weeks and weeks. Then one day I was sent for. They'd found you . . . they knew it must be you by your ring. I went . . . I should never have known . . . even I . . . no one could have known. But there on your finger was the ring.

Diana What ring?

Faustino My ring . . . my first communion ring that my mother gave me . . . that you always wore. So then I knew.

Diana Good heavens . . . I never thought of that. I gave it to Astrid to wear for an hour.

Faustino To Astrid!

Diana The little Swedish girl.

Faustino What little Swedish girl?

Diana Who thought she was in love with you. Poor Astrid! I'd forgotten about that ring.

Faustino Marcela's wearing it now.

Diana Is she indeed?

Marcela I don't want it. Take it back. Take it, Faustino.

Faustino No, no!

Diana Poor little Astrid! I suppose you'd have married her if the hand and the ring and the rest had really been me . . . or any other of the silly women that used to ogle you.

Faustino (*his self-respect wounded*) Diana . . . that's not fair . . .

Margarita *rushes in, whooping with joy, dashes at* **Diana** *and flings her arms round her.*

Margarita Darling . . . darling . . . I knew you weren't dead! I always told them so. It's marvellous . . . it's a miracle. But isn't it like you? To walk in one evening after dinner as calm as you please. How brown you are! Why are you so brown? Oh, we're so happy . . . all of us . . . all . . . ! (*She remembers* **Marcela***, and looks round to find her quietly crying on the sofa.*) I'm sorry . . . I forgot . . . I quite forgot!

Marcela It's . . . it's a little soon . . . to forget me.

Faustino So Mother knows?

Margarita Yes . . . Mamma knows. The porter came up . . .

Faustino Curse him! Is she coming down?

Margarita No. It was a dreadful shock to her.

Diana I'm sure it was!

Margarita She wants to telephone to Father Moreno to ask him what she's to do . . . but Papa says you simply can't get your confessor out of bed at this hour. So meanwhile she's praying herself.

Diana What for?

Margarita For guidance, of course.

Diana Why should she want guiding?

Faustino Is my father coming down?

Margarita Papa's longing to . . . but Mamma won't let him. She forbade me to . . . but here I am. Don't tell her.

Diana And why shouldn't you be, pray?

Margarita Mamma says you're all three living in sin.

Marcela Oh!

Diana I'm doing nothing of the kind. Why, I haven't been back five minutes!

Marcela I am . . . I am!

Diana If she's not very careful I shall go upstairs and tell your mother what I think of her.

Margarita But Diana . . . where have you been . . . where have you come from . . . how did you get here?

Diana What does it matter now?

Margarita But we're dying to hear. Where have you been?

Diana In Africa. And I wish I'd stayed there!

Faustino Margarita . . . run upstairs again now. You shall hear all about it in the morning.

Margarita All right. But, darling . . . you're not to worry. Everything can be arranged. I'm sure . . .! Oh . . . what's this?

She has almost stumbled over the alligator bag.

Diana Open it and see.

Margarita It's full of pebbles.

Diana They're jewels.

Margarita Real jewels?

Diana Sapphires and emeralds mostly. Help yourself

Margarita Oh no! But they're so big.

Diana Yes . . . they're pretty big.

Faustino   Margarita . . . will you run away?

Margarita   Don't let her worry, then. Darling . . . you're looking awfully well . . . and the brown suits you. Good night. Good night, Marcela. Poor Marcela! But you're not to worry either. We'll arrange it all quite nicely. (*She turns again to* **Diana**.) How did you get back from Africa?

Diana   I flew.

Margarita   Oh, fancy! How long did it take you?

Faustino   Margarita, will you . . .

Margarita   I'm going. Good night.

She departs. There is a pause, a silence broken only by the sound of **Marcela**'s *quiet sobbing.*

Faustino   Well . . . now we must think. Think! Good God . . . and half an hour ago . . . !

Diana   I wish you'd stop her crying, Faustino. I'm dead tired. I've been rattling in an aeroplane for three days. And it gets on my nerves. What's the use of crying?

Marcela (*plucking up a little spirit*)   Can't I cry if I like? Haven't I that right left me at least?

Faustino (*anchoring himself to sanity*)   We must think what's best to do.

Diana *rises and looks for her hat.*

Diana   The best thing *I* can do is to go to the nearest hotel.

Faustino   No . . . no.

Diana   Why not? I must sleep somewhere.

Faustino   You can't go to a hotel . . . looking like that . . .

Diana   Like what, pray?

Faustino   And at this time of night . . . alone.

Diana   You think I'm afraid of a hotel clerk after what I've been through?

Faustino (*the anchor dragging*)   And what have you been through? And how did you . . . ? But you'd rather tell us tomorrow.

Diana   There's nothing to tell. Good night.

She instinctively lifts the alligator bag.

Faustino   But you can't go to an hotel with no luggage except an alligator skin full of sapphires.

Diana   Why not?

Faustino   My mother will give you a bed.

Diana Do you think I'd ask her . . . or allow you to ask her . . .?

Faustino Well, Marcela can lend you some things . . .

Diana She! Lend me . . .! I'd go naked sooner!

Throughout this **Marcela** *has been making up her mind. Now she rises with quiet dignity.*

Marcela Faustino . . . dear Faustino . . . you forget. It is I who have no place here. It is I who must go.

Faustino No, no!

Marcela I can go to my mother's.

Faustino Good heavens, no! You'd have to tell her the whole thing. She'd have one of her heart attacks. It might kill her.

Marcela But I can't stay with you another minute. I'm not married to you. I've never been married to you.

Faustino You didn't know that.

Marcela But I know it now.

Faustino You can go to my mother's.

Marcela (*with dignity*) When she has just sent down a message to say that I'm living in sin! I won't stop here another second. Let me out.

Faustino But . . . but . . . if Diana's here too . . . to chaperon you . . . surely that makes it all right.

At this effort in tact the two women break out again, **Marcela** *into tears,* **Diana** *into sarcastic laughter.*

Faustino Don't cry, Marcela! Diana . . . don't laugh like that! Dash it all, then . . . I'll go!

This brings both tears and laughter to a sudden stop.

Diana No! No!

Marcela No! No! Don't leave me with her. She might kill me.

Diana And who'd blame me?

Faustino Very well, then . . . be sensible, both of you! And show a little consideration for me.

Diana For you, indeed!

Marcela For you, Faustino?

Faustino Yes. You're both all right. You've got your grievances. But who is going to pity me? I'm a bigamist. I shall find myself in the dock if I'm not careful.

Diana I dare say you will.

Faustino Oh, I've been a fool, no doubt. The proof you were dead wasn't good enough. But how could I think of searching Africa. Where exactly were you?

Diana Four point sixteen North by thirty-nine thirty-three East.

Faustino Where is that?

Diana That's what the aviator made it.

Faustino What aviator?

Diana The one who rescued us. He had a breakdown.

Faustino Us?

Diana There was Regina, too.

Faustino Who's Regina?

Diana The gipsy from the circus in the laundry on the ship. You remember her.

Faustino No I don't. Very well, then, I do. But don't let's complicate matters with Regina!

Diana She didn't want to be rescued. Her only fear is that her husband won't have married again sensible woman!

Faustino This will be a nine day's wonder. Why hasn't it been in the papers?

Diana There hasn't been time. He brought us so quick. But people did stare at us at Naples yesterday.

Faustino Wasn't there a crowd to see you land at Barcelona?

Diana Not a big one. I dodged the reporters.

Faustino You dodged the reporters! Well, you may get away from your tribe of what's-his-names . . . they're innocent, friendly people no doubt . . .

Diana Are they!

Faustino But you won't escape the reporters for long. No . . . there's a scandal in this.

Yet once more **Marcela** *bursts into tears.*

Marcela I shall be disgraced for ever. I shall be pointed at . . .

Faustino My dear . . . you've done nothing wrong.

Marcela What difference will that make? They'll put my picture in the papers!

Faustino Well, well . . . that happens to everybody sooner or later. Marcela . . . will you stop crying

Diana Don't bully her, Faustino. You've become a fearful bully. But I suppose she has been flattering you and giving in to you . . . .

Marcela (*protesting through her tears*) I haven't.

Faustino Never mind. I'm sorry. But I'm very upset. We're all upset. We must pull ourselves together we sit down and talk the whole thing over . . . calmly. Sit down. Sit down, Diana.

Diana I'm too tired to do much more talking.

Faustino Then you can listen.

Marcela I think I'm going to faint again.

Faustino No, you're not! Lie down. That's right. Now then.

Diana Give me a cigarette.

Faustino Excellent! Make yourself comfortable.

Marcela *reclines wearily on the sofa;* **Diana** *stretches herself in an armchair.* **Faustino** *sits alert between them.*

Faustino Now! We are facing . . . all three of us . . . and each from a different standpoint . . . a very serious . . . a very difficult situation . . . emotionally . . . intellectually . . . legally. Good! But there is no possible situation, is there . . . no difficulty, which man . . . and woman . . . cannot face and overcome by the exercise of reason . . . patience . . . and self-restraint?

Diana (*snapping at him*) Well?

Faustino Patience, Diana . . . patience! After all, we are rational beings.

A thousand years and more of Christian civilisation. The first thing we must do, then, is to call upon our . . . our ethical selves . . . and we shall certainly not call in vain. Shall we, my dear Diana? Shall we, dear Marcela?

Marcela (*wearily; her eyes closed*) You put things so well.

Faustino I am a lawyer, it is my business to. But I am not speaking as a lawyers. Let us . . . for the moment . . . leave that aspect of the case out of account. Let us also rule out the mere conventionalities of the situation. Let us . . . let us adumbrate, not what social convention and the law may expect us or permit us to feel and do . . . but what . . . faced with this tragic accident . . . we really, innermostly do feel . . . about it . . . and towards each other. In law, Diana . . . you were my chattel. I never thought of you so. Nor do you now return to claim me . . . as if I were a piece of property! God forbid, I hear you say . . . Go forbid! And you, Marcela . . . you . . .! I believe she's asleep.

Diana (*protesting against the accusation, which she has not caught – for excellent reasons – too exactly*) No, I'm not.

Faustino No . . . she's asleep.

Diana Well, let her sleep. All that crying has worn her out . . . poor wretch!

Faustino Yes . . . very well, then! Now . . . to look at the trouble from my own point of view . . . of necessity a far more psychologically complex one than yours or hers! Let me first of all be perfectly honest with myself. Nothing occurred while you were alive . . . while I thought you were alive . . . to shake my very deeply rooted love for you . . .

Here **Diana** *gives a deep somnolent sigh and makes a last struggle to keep awake herself.*

Faustino   . . . nor did your supposed death do so. Why should it? You may argue that it transmuted my love into a different category of feelings . . . leaving me free. . . as I supposed . . . to welcome . . . even to encourage the growth of a love . . . as true . . . for . . . for another. Not . . . let us be clear . . . an identical love. No! For there the personality of the person loved comes into the question. But now, what has happened? You have returned. Is my love for you . . . which I confess to without shame . . . love for your memory . . . or will it have been re-transmuted . . .?

He sees that **Diana** *is asleep too. He considers the situation, for a moment with some slight irritation, then with relief. Then he steals to the bell, rings it and waits near the door for it to be answered.* **Juliana** *comes in quietly enough, but not quietly enough for him.*

Faustino   Sh! . . . for heaven's sake! They're both asleep.

Juliana   Poor dears! What are we to do with them?

Faustino   Let them be. Get a rug or a blanket or something and cover up your mistress . . . .

Juliana   The young mistress . . . .

Faustino   Get two rugs and cover them both up.

Juliana   Are you going to bed?

Faustiio   Yes. No. Get me a rug and bring it to my study.

Juliana   Two such beautiful young ladies! And to think that you're married to them both!

Faustino   I know, I know! And not half an hour ago . . .! We must see what can be done about it tomorrow. But don't wake them now . . . whatever you do.

He turns off the greater part of the lights and steals away.

Act Three

The same room in daylight. At a table sit **Diana** *and* **Margarita** *and on it is a selection of the uncut jenels, which they are counting and sorting. The alligator bag is on the floor by them.*

Margarita   But go on . . . go on.

Diana   I'm weary of it . . . .

Margarita   I didn't mean go on counting. . . . I meant go on telling me things. I want to know everything that happened to you . . . every single little thing from the first moment to the last. I'll count while you talk.

Diana   I'm so weary of talking about it. I haven't been here forty-eight hours . . . and I'm sure I've told everything there is to tell forty-eight times over at least. What was there in it after all?

Margarita   Heavens! To be shipwrecked . . . and to drift all those days . . . and to have the boat wrecked . . . and for only you two to be saved . . . and to be carried off!

Diana   No . . . it was the slave-traders carried us off.

Margarita   And they sold you.

Diana   We think so. We were too ill to know . . . or care.

Margarita   I wonder they didn't murder you.

Diana   Why should they murder us when they could make money out of us?

Margarita   But I wonder the savages *others* didn't murder you.

Diana   When they'd just paid for us!

Margarita   And they ended by worshipping you.

Diana   Well, yes . . . it was a kind of worship. We entertained them. They used to stand outside our hut for hours . . . and when we came out, they'd stare and stare . . . and follow us round. The sort of thing people do here to cinema stars.

Margarita   It must have felt strange! But they'd never let you go?

Diana   No . . . we were entertaining.

Margarita   *Did they cheer you?*

Diana   Sometimes.

Margarita   I should have loved that!

Diana   No, you wouldn't. Not for long. There's nothing more boring than just being entertaining. But I'll tell you what is stranger . . . stranger than anything which happened with those poor, well-meaning people . . . and that is to come back here and find one's husband married to someone else!

Margarita   I suppose so.

Diana   And to find him loving her just as he used to love me. And I love him still. And what's stranger yet is that I'm sure he still loves me. Well . . . why shouldn't he? And strangest of all . . .! Here the three of us have been living together in these half-dozen rooms for two nights and a day, and I've not taken the carving-knife to cut the woman's throat . . .!

Margarita   Oh . . . you don't want to do that?

Diana   Well . . . do I or don't I? When I was married to him . . .

Margarita   But you are married to him.

Diana   I mean when I was just ordinarily married to him . . . not in this complicated way! . . . and women used to run after him . . . then I used to be so afraid I'd feel savage about it that I'd laugh and pretend I didn't care at all. And the first night here . . . when we both fell asleep in this room . . . and he went off and locked himself in his study . . .

Margarita   Locked himself . . .!

Diana   I woke up about daybreak . . . and there she was fast asleep still on the sofa . . . and I could have cut her throat. I got up and I said to myself: there'll be a carving-knife in the kitchen . . . I hate her . . . we, if I hate her I ought to cut her throat. Then I went over and looked at her . . .

Margarita (*all sentiment and admiration*)   And you felt you couldn't hate her anymore.

Diana   Not at all. I hated her worse than ever. But she seemed very chilly . . . and the rug had fallen off her. So I tucked her up again and went back to sleep. That's no way to hate people, is it?

Margarita   Was it very difficult all yesterday? I kept telling Mamma it would ease matters if she'd let me come down. Because I can be tactful . . . and I did so want to know what was going on.

Diana   Oh, no . . . we dodged each other. She took a long nap in the afternoon . . . she was quite done up still. And I had to have a dressmaker and send out for a lot of clothes and things. I couldn't go out because of all the newspaper men hanging round. The day went pretty quickly. Faustino had to go to the courts . . . so he said. He was thankful to get away, of course. It is awkward for him. But he came back to lunch . . . and we managed to talk a little . . . about the weather . . . and things like that. Oh . . .!

Margarita   What is it?

Diana (*rubbing her leg*)   These stockings. Stupid things! I haven't worn stockings for two years. And at dinner he told us a long, long story . . . an endless story . . . about some silly case of his. I believe that got on our nerves more than anything. I tried to say something horrid to her once or twice . . . but it always turned into: Pass the salt, please. I'll get used to stockings and shoes again, I suppose . . . but suspenders and corsets . . . curse them! . . . I will not war. And I'm going to take them off now.

Margarita What did you do about clothes out there? You didn't have to go . . . naked?

Diana No, but it might have been better to. It would have been far less conspicuous.

Margarita You used to dress so beautifully.

Diana Did I? No doubt! And the time it took . . . and the trouble it was . . . buying your clothes . . . and being fitted for your clothes . . . and changing your clothes . . .

Margarita But one must look nice . . . and attractive. Not to men, particularly . . . but just attractive.

Diana Then the sensible thing would be to wear lots of jewels and ornaments and feathers . . . and no clothes at all!

Margarita Oh, Diana! I wish Mamma could hear you!

Diana How is 'Mamma'?

Margarita She went to confession yesterday . . .

Diana Sh! Here she is.

Margarita Mamma?

Diana No. My . . .! Faustino's . . .! Well, what does one call her? The other one.

Margarita Marcela!

Diana Come along. Come and help me change. I don't want to see her. I never know if I shall manage to be civil to her or not. This can't go on much longer.

Margarita No, of course not!

Diana *and* **Margarita** *go out . . . and, from the other door,* **Marcela** *and* **Lorenza** *come in.*

Marcela She ran away from me.

Lorenza So should I in her place, I must say.

Marcela She's not afraid of me. I wish she were. She's a wonderful creature!

Lorenza She has coarsened very much. She's really no better than a savage.

Marcela But that's what's so wonderful! When her eyes flash . . .! And you should hear her growl . . . yes, growl!

Lorenza Nice women don't growl.

Marcela It is an amazing story, isn't it?

Lorenza Very!

Marcela Almost unbelievable.

Lorenza Except that no one would think of inventing it . . . quite!

Marcela They say men's second wives are always like their first. But I'm not . . . like her.

Lorenza I should hope not.

Marcela I wish I were!

Lorenza Nonsense!

Marcela I'm just pretty. She has character! Don't keep on comforting me, Lorenza. It only makes me feel worse. Did I tell you Mamma sent me a message . . . not my mamma . . . your mamma . . . his mamma?

Lorenza Why doesn't she see you?

Marcela But suppose she has to . . . to keep Diana for a daughter-in-law?

Lorenza That won't happen. I'm sure it won't. It would be monstrous.

Marcela I feel it can't . . . I feel it mustn't.

Lorenza What was the message?

Marcela Just that Father Moreno says I've nothing to be ashamed of . . .

Lorenza I could have told him that!

Marcela . . . and that I'm to go on praying. But he didn't say what for! I don't wish her any harm . . . at least I ought not to. But there are times when I'm afraid I do.

Lorenza How have you managed here . . . all three? How has there been room for you?

Marcela The first night we both . . . she and I . . . fell asleep in here. I was on the sofa . . . because I'd been feeling faint. And she had the big chair. At least she hadn't . . . for when I woke once . . . there she was curled up on a cushion on the floor . . . like a dog.

Lorenza Disgusting!

Marcela But last night . . .! I couldn't sleep in my room . . . because she feels that's her room. She wouldn't go in the guest-room. And I couldn't take the guest-room, could I? . . . for that would have been as good as owning I'd no right here at all. So we slept in here again.

Lorenza She could have had the dining-room floor.

Marcela I said I'd take the dining-room. Then I made out I felt a draught and came back. I'm afraid I . . . I wanted to keep my eye on her. In case she . . . in case he . . .! Oh, isn't it degrading?

Lorenza It's outrageous her being here at all.

Marcela No, no . . . degrading to feel as I do . . . jealous and wicked! I watch every look they give each other. I listen outside the doors! I do!

Lorenza So should I!

Marcela But I'm not like that really . . . at least I never thought I was. And I loved and admired her so when she was dead? I used to pray to be given all them good qualities . . . so that Faustino wouldn't miss them . . . and to have all my own improved too. Now I sit hoping she'll swear . . . or get drunk or something . . . just to show him the sort of woman she is. But if I found he liked that I'd swear . . . and get drunk too . . . yes and drunker. Something must be settled . . . or I shall turn into a perfect fiend. Here she is again. Come along. We can go in the dining-room. No, we'll go in his study.

Lorenza You must keep calm, you know. That's what we all learned to love in you . . . your gentleness . . . and repose.

Marcela I know. But I'm beginning to think it doesn't pay . . .

They go out. After a moment **Faustino** *appears, hat and coat on, latch-key in hand; he has just let himself in. Finding the room empty he gives a sigh of relief.*

Faustino Thank God!

Juliana *comes in. He jumps; then recovers himself.*

Faustino Oh, it's you.

Juliana Only me, sir.

Faustino Where's your . . .? Where's my . . .? Where are . . . they?

Juliana Well, sir . . . they're about. But where . . . why, from one minute to another you never know. Dodging each other round the flat like a couple of . . . not in any disrespectful sense, sir . . . cats!

Faustino I came back for some papers. My head's like a beehive. Go into my study . . . they're in a long envelope with a black seal on the left of the writing-table . . . and if you don't find me here . . . I'll be outside the front door.

Juliana Yes, sir. I hope something will be settled soon. This sort of thing, sir . . . it's very bad for my cooking.

She goes off for the papers. **Faustino** *stands on tiptoe by the door ready to fly. But with no warning at all,* **Diana** *dashes in and he is transfixed.*

Diana (*in great surprise*) You're back!

Faustino Only for a minute.

Marcela *appears . . . as suddenly; but she hardly shows such surprise.*

Marcela You're here!

Faustino I'm just off again.

Marcela I didn't hear you come in.

Faustino (*somewhat tetchily*) I've not been here two seconds.

Marcela (*darting a look at* **Diana**) They've not been wasted.

Juliana *comes back with the envelope.*

Juliana Are these them?

Faustino Those . . . thank you, Juliana . . . are they. Well . . . goodbye!

Marcela Back to lunch?

Faustino I . . . I doubt . . . .

Diana Don't stay away, please, because of me. Juliana could bring me a tray in here.

Marcela Why don't you lunch at the courts . . . in peace? I might go home with Lorenza.

Faustino Well . . . we'll see . . . .

He is off.

Diana Where's your muffler? There's a bitter wind.

Marcela He never wears one now. And he never has sore throats.

Diana Really!

A slight pause.

Juliana How many for lunch?

Marcela Three.

Juliana Eggs or fish to begin with?

Marcela (*to* **Diana**) Eggs or fish?

Diana Why ask me?

Marcela As a guest!

Diana If I order the lunch it will not be as a guest.

Marcela Fish!

Diana Eggs!

Marcela The doctor has forbidden me eggs.

Diana Wednesday was never a good day for buying fish.

Juliana I'll make a risotto.

She goes out.

Marcela For just a few hours longer . . . we can perhaps succeed in being reasonably civil to each other.

Diana I have been, I think, almost unnecessarily civil up to now.

Marcela A tropical climate, I suppose, is trying to the temper.

Diana Not so trying as this stifling hole is!

Marcela If that's how you feel . . .

Diana It's a pity I didn't stay there?

Marcela No! You'll have more air to breathe . . . I was about to say . . . very soon . . . when I'm gone.

Diana Why should you go, pray?

Marcela The law is on your side.

Diana I have said twenty times at least . . . and I say it again . . . I am not going to stay here because the law gives me the right to. He either loves me or he doesn't. He either doesn't love you or he does.

Marcela He may learn to forget me if you give him a little time.

Diana Thank you. I've no intention of living with a man while he's learning to forget my rival.

Marcela *I* had to.

Diana That was no fault of mine. And if you hadn't been a horrid little hypocrite you'd have got rid of that picture and everything that reminded him of me . . . and never let him speak of me again.

Marcela Yes . . . Mother advised that. But I said it would only make him think about you the more.

Diana I dare say he's not still in love with me. Why should he be? He's a man . . . and he'd learned all about me there was to learn. You're a novelty.

Marcela What a brutal . . . what a vulgar thing to say! But if it comes to that you're the novelty. They all think you've utterly changed.

Diana I haven't. I was always what I am now. I've learned not to be ashamed of it . . . that's all.

Marcela Then I don't see how he ever fell in love with you . . . if he's the man I think he is. I don't! (*With a sudden wail.*) Oh, why can't we be ladylike and polite?

Diana You hate me far more than I hate you. Why not be honest about it?

Marcela I don't hate you at all. I wish I did! It's so confusing. I believe I'd like you very much if it wasn't for . . . all this.

Diana I don't want you to like me. But I'm sorry for you. If I was a nuisance to you dead I shall be far more of a nuisance to you living. I fear I can't offer to commit suicide. But if he doesn't love me I am willing to go.

Marcela I'm willing to . . . whether he loves me or not . . . and I mean to.

Diana We might both go . . . of course.

Marcela That would be the most self-respecting thing to do.

Diana   But rather silly.

Marcela   And hard on him . . . in a sense.

Diana   Yes . . . when a man has had the enterprise to marry two wives he might be allowed to keep at least one of them.

Marcela   I suppose . . . in that tribe of yours . . . We'd neither of us be needing to go away.

Diana   No.

Marcela   Horrid people!

Diana   Oh, there he could have half a dozen more.

Marcela   Is it quite respectable?

Diana   It's particularly distinguished.

Marcela   And do they all get on together . . . the . . . the wives?

Diana   Well . . . the first bullies the second . . .

Marcela   Oh!

Diana   But the second can bully the third . . . and so on. It works out well enough.

Marcela   Doesn't the husband interfere?

Diana   Not if he has any sense. Sometimes he hasn't and does. Then he wishes he'd never seen any of them.

Marcela   I don't think men . . . just as men . . . are very nice.

Diana   Are women . . . when they needn't be?

Marcela   Oh . . . aren't we? I should hate to believe that. But you're right, Diana . . . it's our duty to consider his happiness. We'd better agree perhaps to do nothing . . . either of us . . . .

Diana   Do nothing?

Marcela   I mean . . . to influence his decision . . .

Diana   (*a shade of suspicion in her voice*)   Oh . . .!

Into this atmosphere of rather ominous peace comes **Don Francisco**. *He is carrying a parcel which he starts to undo.*

Don Francisco   Good morning.

Diana   Good morning.

Marcela   Good morning, Papa. I mean: Good morning.

Don Francisco   Slept well? No, of course not. Tactless of me! But . . . snatched a little rest, did you?

Diana   I slept perfectly well, thank you.

Marcela   I slept.

Don Francisco   Good! Your poor dear . . . my poor dear wife never closed her eyes. Nor let me! I'm not intruding?

At this question each looks politely at the other as much as to say: Will you answer? Then . . .

Diana   No!

Marcela   Oh, no!

Don Francisco   Now . . . where can I put the brown paper?

Diana *begins to show some signs of irritation.*

Diana   I don't know.

Marcela   Give it me.

Don Francisco   Thank you.

The parcel being undone, it appears he has been out to buy a fair-sized steel box, with a business-like lock and key to it.

Diana   What on earth is that?

Don Francisco   That is a box.

Diana   Thank you. I've not become such a savage that I don't know a box when I see one. What is it for?

Don Francisco   To lock the jewels in.

Diana   Why?

Don Francisco   Because you can't leave jewels lying about.

Diana   Why not?

Don Francisco   My dear Diana! Because they may be stolen.

Diana   Let them be stolen! Who cares?

Don Francisco   No, no. We have a duty to our property. The stones must first be sorted . . . and counted . . .! Ah, I see you've been sorting them.

Diana   That was Margaritina. She started counting and sorting . . . she couldn't stop counting and sorting . . .!

Don Francisco   A sound instinct. Then a list must be made . . . in triplicate. You must keep one copy . . . another copy must . . .

Diana   But why . . . why . . . why?

Marcela   Papa . . . they're not our jewels.

Don Francisco   My dear Marcela . . . that question . . . if it is a question . . . can be settled later.

Marcela What question about it can there be?

Don Francisco Well . . . the return of our . . . our dear friend here has raised most important and interesting questions . . . legal as well as moral . . . of which this question must be a part. But, without arguing that, there is, I say, our duty to property as property. And this . . . though I am no expert . . . is probably very valuable property. So come along both of you and help me sort.

He is busy already; they neither of them respond.

How, my dear Diana, did you accumulate such a quantity?

Diana It was a tribute.

Don Francisco (*gallantly*) To your beauty?

Diana Certainly not. To my position . . . to my goodness.

Marcela You forget. She was a goddess. The people worshipped her.

Don Francisco I don't wonder! Do come and help, Marcela.

Marcela I'd much rather not, thank you.

Diana It was no fault of mine. Regina worked the whole thing. She did conjuring tricks every Wednesday and Sunday morning from eight to ten.

Don Francisco (*with jovial tact*) Fetching rabbits out of hats?

Diana There were no rabbits and we hadn't a hat between us.

Marcela (*with a touch of sarcasm*) What did you hand round afterwards, then?

Diana She used to finish by producing sixteen snakes from my hair.

Don Francisco How very unpleasant!

Diana Not at all. They were quite harmless . . . and it made a great sensation. I don't want to talk anymore . . . about Africa . . . or Regina . . . or the wretched stones . . . or anything.

Don Francisco You'd find it'd calm your nerves wonderfully to come here and help count them.

Diana I wish I'd dropped them in the sea!

Don Francisco Now, now . . . !

Diana And tied them round my own neck first.

She goes out, banging the door.

Don Francisco Tut, tut! We must forgive these little outbreaks. But always, when in trouble . . . when your brain is in a whirl . . . concentrate, as I am now doing, upon some simple, useful task. Nothing more soothing! If unable to muster resolution to do so in solitude . . . seek genial companionship . . .

Marcela, *who feels that if she stays another minute she will assassinate him, steals unobserved from the room.*

... and concentrate, in particular ... as I am doing ... upon the details of the task. Bring an inquiring mind to bear. Why, now, are some jewels more highly esteemed than others? Is it for their rarity ... or for their intrinsic beauty? Why, indeed, are jewels ... apart from the artistic achievement of their setting ... considered beautiful at all?

As quietly as **Marcela** *stole out,* **Faustino** (*apprehensively too*) *has now stolen in. He is relieved to find his father alone, but quite alarmed when he realises that the old gentleman is talking to himself.*

Don Francisco   But that will carry us into regions of vague and profitless speculation. Let us be practical. This counting is a mere preliminary. There will be the value to estimate ... and that is, first of all, a matter of carats. Now what, exactly, is a carat?

Faustino   Father!

Don Francisco   Hullo. When did you come in?

Faustino   Just this minute.

Don Francisco   Where's Marcela?

Faustino   I don't know. What's the matter?

Don Francisco   Nothing. Don't stare at me like that.

Faustino   But what are you doing here all alone ... asking what a carrot ... ? Oh, that sort of carat!

Don Francisco   What other sort of ... ? Don't be a fool, Faustino. Sit down and pull yourself together. You're losing your mind.

Faustino   I dare say. I thought you were. I wonder we all don't.

Don Francisco   Come and help me count. You'll find it very calming. Never mind the size. Put each sort in tens.

He thrusts an unsorted heap across the table and moves the alligator bag nearer to the opposite chair. **Faustino** *almost mechanically sits; and, for a while, manages to do some counting as he talks.*

Faustino   Marcela was here with you?

Don Francisco   Yes. Then ... for no reason at all ... she dashed out and banged the door. No, I'm wrong, that was Diana.

Faustino   She was here too?

Don Francisco   Obviously.

Faustino   They were quarrelling?

Don Francisco   No ... the best of friends apparently ... when I came in.

Faustino   Good God! I'd rather they'd quarrel. I'd really rather they'd quarrel.

Don Francisco   That's not a very kind thing to say. I thought you'd to go off to an important case?

Act Three   209

Faustino   I had. But I found another man to do it. I came back for the papers . . . I'd forgotten them. No . . . I've been reading up my own case . . . all the authorities.

Don Francisco   Well?

Faustino   I haven't nearly finished. But . . . there's a lot to be said upon both sides. If no bad faith can be proved . . . or if bad faith in any of the parties can be prove . . . it all depends. There are various solutions.

Don Francisco   Good!

Faustino   It's not good. I want to be told quite definitely what I have to do. I must go back and read more. But I can't keep my mind on it. I must have advice. I'm in a horrid state. I can't stay in the house . . . for I'm terrified of meeting them . . . either of them. But the moment I'm away I want to be back again . . . I am drawn irresistibly back again. Someone must tell me what it is I have to do.

Don Francisco   Hadn't you better first make up your own mind what it is you want to do? . . .

Faustino   Yes. No. That's just it! I can't.

Don Francisco   . . . which of them it is that you love.

Faustino   I love them both.

Don Francisco   My dear boy . . . you cannot, any longer, love them both.

Faustino   I do. Why the devil shouldn't I? I never stopped loving Diana. She died. That wasn't her fault. Why should I stop loving her because of it? Now she's alive again. That's not her fault either, is it? Why should I love her the less because of that?

Don Francisco   True. (*He has sorted the jewels on his side of the table.*) Give me some of those if you don't mean to count them all. But there's Marcela, you know.

Faustino   Of course there's Marcela! And what has she done, pray, that I should cease to love her?

Don Francisco   Nothing. You're quite right. Put it this way then. Which of them do you want to be married to?

Faustino   I want to be married to them both.

Don Francisco (*protesting vigorously*)   No, no! No, no!

Faustino   Quite so. I know I can't be. I don't mean to try to be. But you didn't ask me that. You asked me what I wanted.

Don Francisco   But these are most immoral sentiments. Thank heaven your dear mother doesn't hear you.

Faustino   They are not immoral sentiments. On the contrary. You know perfectly well, Father, that I have never been an impulsive, passionate sort of man. I didn't run wild when I was young. No great credit to me! Rakish women always disgusted me. I detest that sort of thing in women. No . . . with me, quite naturally and happily, love and duty have always gone together. And they do now . . . or they would if they could. I love Diana . . . as a husband should whose wife has by the mercy of God been restored to him. And in all this year we have been married I have never felt more tenderly and deeply attached to Marcela. Poor darling!

Don Francisco   Well . . . if those are your feelings you'll have to get over half of them. And you'd better make up your mind pretty quickly which half.

Faustino   Yes. It would be easier to do, my dear Father, if I were not so . . . so estimable a character.

Don Francisco   How's that?

Faustino   If my passions were more unruly . . . if this sense of moral responsibility did not weigh upon me . . . if I could be carried off my feet by one of them . . .

Don Francisco   But which one?

Faustino   Never mind . . . for the sake of argument . . . which one. If I could compromise myself again with either one . . . why, then I should have to behave badly to the other. I should regret that . . . I should be consumed with remorse. But really, I'd rather be consumed with a little straightforward remorse than be in the muddle I am now. This can't go on . . . it can't go on another day . . . it can't . . .! What's the matter?

Juliana *has come in.*

Juliana   The dressmaker has brought some things for . . . the young mistress.

Faustino   Well . . . tell her. I don't know where she is.

Juliana   Yes, sir.

She crosses the room and goes to find **Diana**.

Don Francisco   I'm no judge of jewels, of course . . . but I should say there is a fortune here. Enough for you to live on in luxury for the rest of your days.

Faustino   They are no concern of mine.

Don Francisco   She's still your wife, you know.

Faustino   Not . . . for the time being, at any rate . . . in that sense.

Don Francisco   It's a factor in the situation.

Diana *comes in.*

Diana   Back again?

Faustino   Just for a moment.

Diana   You seem to be running in and out a great deal.

Faustino   Do I?

Diana   My dressmaker has actually kept her word. I can go to the hotel tonight now. Shall we meet again?

Faustino Diana!

Diana Better, no doubt, that we should never meet again. But I only meant – before I go. If not . . . thank you for your hospitality.

Faustino But my dear . . . my dearest . . . I can't bear the thought . . . we should both hate to feel that we were turning you out . . .

Diana We?

Faustino (*guiltily covering the slip*) My father and I.

Diana My dear Faustino . . . I cannot go on sleeping on the floor. Even in Africa I had a hammock.

She goes out. **Faustino** *is indignant.*

Faustino Now what have I done that she should behave like that to me? She has no right to. It hurts me.

Don Francisco Why the devil has she been sleeping on the floor?

Faustino I don't know. I don't know where either of them slept. I didn't want to know. I locked myself in my study. I locked the key of the door in my safe, and I put the key of the safe in a bucket of cold water.

Don Francisco Good heavens . . . what for?

Faustino So that I might be sure that I was wide awake and in my sober senses before I let myself out . . . or anyone else in! I am a well-conducted man, I hope . . . but I am not a fish.

A slight pause.

Don Francisco Diana's a handsome creature.

Faustino Not more so than she ever was.

Don Francisco Considerably more so, *I* think. The jungle . . . and the goddess business . . . have done a lot for her. Such a colour . . . such eyes! And such supple strength! She reminds me of a passionate young panther leaping through the grass.

Faustino My dear Father . . . we have never seen a passionate young panther leaping through the grass.

Don Francisco Well, as it happens, in that big-game-shooting cinema last week there was a panther leaping through the grass . . . and Diana reminds me very strongly of it.

Faustino Please do not indulge in those romantic fancies. Diana . . . thank heaven! . . . is well in health . . . except for a little indigestion, brought on, she says, by the tinned food they gave her in the aeroplane. She is a little sun-tanned, naturally. But . . . for the rest . . . as modest . . . and ladylike . . . at heart . . . as ever! I do assure you.

Don Francisco For two pins . . . if you ask me . . . she'd tuck you under her arm and be off with you . . . back to Africa.

Faustino No, no . . . you misunderstand her . . .

Don Francisco And if I were in your shoes . . . I should be tempted to let her do it. Look here . . . why don't you have a little quiet talk to her alone?

Faustino Father . . . I am surprised at you! You are suggesting that I should submit myself to . . . to a vulgar form of temptation . . . that I should forget the respect . . . and the duty . . . that I still owe . . . to Marcela!

Don Francisco Well . . . if the wind blows that way . . . have a quiet talk to her . . . .

Faustino I am taking particular care to see neither of them alone.

Don Francisco But, my boy, you must get the matter settled somehow . . . and quickly.

Faustino I know! I know!

Don Francisco Here's Father Moreno coming to call upon your mother. That's one reason I came down to tidy up these jewels . . . and small thanks I get for it . . . *I* don't want to meet him! If he hears that you're all three still down here together . . . he'll have you excommunicated, or something. There is the religious aspect.

Faustino I recognise it.

Don Francisco And now Marcela's mother has been told. I sent Milano to her. Well . . . let him do his share! She is probably in such screaming hysterics that if you opened the window you could hear her . . . she's only a mile away. She'll telephone to her brother at Segovia. He'll be here in an hour or so. He's a colonel in a crack regiment. He has his reputation to consider. What can he do but challenge you and shoot you? There's the social aspect of the matter.

Faustino I fully recognise it.

Don Francisco And if Diana goes to a hotel the reporters will get hold of her . . . there are twenty of them clustered round the front door now . . . if it wasn't for the way out into the next street by the cellars we'd be prisoners here . . . and then the scandal will break! You'll never be able to go into a court of law again . . . except into the dock.

Faustino I know it.

Don Francisco Then don't stand there being conscientious. Do something, my good fellow.

Faustino But what . . . what?

Don Francisco It doesn't much matter what . . .

Faustino I feel as if I were being torn in two.

Don Francisco I wish to heaven you could be. That'd settle everything.

Marcela *comes in. She is dressed to go out; but we remark that she has changed and put on a very alluring – though dove-like – costume indeed.*

Marcela Papa, dear . . . they have sent down to say that Father Moreno would very much like to see you if you'd please go upstairs.

Don Francisco Oh! Well . . . don't let anyone disturb these while I'm gone.

Faustino No . . . no! Better stop and finish now. He can wait.

Marcela Oh, yes. Don't hurry, Papa. He can wait, I'm sure.

She sits down, very plainly saying by this: So can I. There ensues a pantomime between **Faustino** *and his father: 'Don't leave us together.' 'No use, she'll sit there till I do,' etc., etc. Finally . . .*

Don Francisco He won't keep me more than a very few moments.

Marcela I think the message said . . . I'm not quite sure . . . that he'd only keep you a very few moments.

Don Francisco That's all right, then . . . that's all right.

He departs, leaving **Faustino** *most uncomfortable,* **Marcela** *sweetly serene. After a pause; anything to break the silence . . .*

Faustino Well, my dear?

Marcela Well . . . Faustino?

Faustino Where . . . where's Diana?

Marcela Trying on some dresses, I believe.

Faustino Yes . . . so she said.

Marcela You've seen her?

Faustino No . . . yes . . . she just came through . . . flashed through you know . . . while I was busy with my father.

Marcela They'll be charming dresses, I'm sure. She always dressed delightfully . . . didn't she?

Faustino No doubt. People used to say so. I . . . I never noticed particularly. That's a charming dress, now, that you're wearing.

Marcela This! Oh, the first thing that came to hand.

The little hypocrite!

Faustino But that's just it. With you, my dear . . . whatever comes to hand . . . !

Marcella Don't say things like that to me . . . they hurt. They used to make me so happy. But now . . . they hurt!

Faustino Diana . . . speaks of leaving us.

Marcela Yes . . . she has sent Juliana for a cab.

Faustino Already!

Marcela Oh, don't be afraid! *I* shall take the cab. I am going . . . to my mother. She has been told.

Faustino (*shocked*) No, no! No, no!

Marcela I must . . . sooner or later. So the sooner the better.

Faustino But not like this . . . not . . . not in a cab!

Marcela (*putting her own interpretation on this quite meaningless exclamation*) It shan't look conspicuous, I promise you. I'll only take a dressing-bag . . . a very small one. You can send the luggage tomorrow. But keep nothing belonging to me, please . . . nothing that could remind you I ever existed. You must forget me utterly . . . if you can.

Faustino How can I?

Marcela Well . . . you must try.

Faustino I may not be able even to try . . . I may not want to try.

Marcela Hush . . . hush! Don't make things harder for me. Let our parting be as serene and beautiful as our life together has been. It has been, hasn't it?

Faustino The most beautiful thing in the world.

Marcela Come and sit by me for a moment. You need not be afraid to do that.

Faustino I have every right, I hope . . . to sit by you.

He does so.

Marcela But not too close.

Faustino I shall sit as close to you as I . . . as I . . . well, as I think fit.

He does not sit so very close, but close enough to take her hand.

Marcela Do you think you ought to hold my hand?

Faustino Certainly! If a husband . . .

Marcela Faustino!

Faustino I beg your pardon.

Marcela Be careful what you say. Be careful what you do. I have much to bear. I am not made of stone.

Faustino Well, if your late husband cannot . . . !

Marcela *bursts into tears.*

Faustino There, there, my dearest . . . never mind. It's a nasty word . . . a nasty, horrid, coarse word. We won't use it at all. Don't cry, sweetheart . . . don't cry.

Marcela *lets him dry her eyes.*

Marcela Let us try and think, dearest, if we can . . . while we say goodbye . . . here . . . on this dear sofa . . . where I've sat so often in your arms . . . slept in your arms

... with no one to say us nay ... think of ourselves ... since we must part ... as two disembodied beings ... freed from all earthly ... from all fleshly passions! (*She blushes.*) Let us say farewell, Faustino ... as the angels do.

Faustino But they don't! Now there's the point ... they don't. They don't have to. And it has yet to be made clear to me that we need utterly and irrevocably say goodbye. All sorts of things may happen yet. If you feel that you should go today ... I am not saying you should, but if you feel so ... then, when I come and ... and see you at your mother's ... nothing wrong in that! ... tomorrow ...

Marcela Darling ... let us be frank. We can be ... we have known each other so well. If we meet again after today ... why, yes ... all sorts of things may happen ... and they will. We are not angels.

Faustino (*encouragingly*) Not yet, perhaps. We've had no chance. But wait till we try. It only needs practice.

Marcela But, my darling, shall we want to try?

Faustino Why ... here we sit like brother and sister! How simple ... and how satisfying!

Marcela (*a little disappointed with him*) Is it?

Faustino Don't you find it so?

Marcela (*with modest abandonment*) No.

Faustino (*a little shocked at her*) My dear Marcela ... really!

Marcela I am a wicked woman. I am consumed. With an illicit love for you. And it isn't fair! Till just two days ago I was as good as gold ... everyone said so. And it's the same love.

Faustino I know ... I know. Very confusing! We must keep calm.

Marcela No ... I'm telling lies. It isn't the same. If you could only see inside me. Do I look the same outside?

Faustino You look adorable.

Marcela Inside me ... I am a seething flame of passion ... I am steeped in sin. And I like it! That's the worst! It makes me feel wonderful ... as if I could catch you up in my arms and carry you out of her reach ... carry you off to ... to ... to my mother's. Goodbye, Faustino. There, that's how I feel!

She flings herself into his arms and kisses him passionately; at which most unlucky moment **Diana** *appears. She has been trying on a dress which, though it is simple enough of its sort, makes her look even more splendidly barbaric than before.*

Diana So! The moment my back is turned ... the moment you think me safe in the hands of the dressmaker! Can't you wait ten minutes longer before returning to your ... your amorous transports? As soon as my cab comes I shall be gone ... and I can't go any quicker.

Marcela *I* shall take the cab.

Diana You will do nothing of the sort. If you want a cab you can call one of your own. But you'll call no cab! Take your hat off. Hypocrite.

Faustino Now don't be abusive, Diana . . . and don't be unfair.

Diana Faustino . . . I may have lost your love . . . but at least I make no shameless efforts to recover it.

Marcela Serpent!

Faustino Marcela . . . keep your temper, please.

Diana So while I remain in your house show me at least respect that is due to me . . . as your wife.

Marcela Self-righteous serpent!

Diana Marcela . . . I shall tell you very plainly what I think of you in half a minute.

Marcela Dressed up like that!

Diana This is a perfectly simple dress . . . the skirt is nothing like right yet and there's something terribly queer about this shoulder. But if I look well in it . . . and I trust I do . . . that is no fault of mine.

Marcela Did you come in here to exhibit yourself to him in that dress . . . or did you not?

Diana You have a vulgar and suspicious mind. And if I did?

Marcela There, Faustino . . . what do you think of that?

Diana Yes, Faustino . . . what do you think of it . . . and me? Speak the truth.

Faustino It's . . . it's a very pretty dress.

Diana And am I attractive? Am I . . . or am I not?

Faustino Yes . . . yes! Oh . . . anybody would think so.

Diana (*to* **Marcela**) You little fool! D'you think . . . if I wanted to lure him back to me . . . I shouldn't know how?

Marcela Don't let her call me names, Faustino.

Faustino Now, my dear Diana . . . my dear Marcela . . . this is not the way . . . is it . . . to solve our complicated and distressing problem? Let us rather consider calmly and like the rational beings that we are . . .

Diana Faustino . . . it isn't one in the morning now. It's no use trying to talk me to sleep . . .

Marcela No, don't, Faustino, please! You do it beautifully . . . but it gives me such a headache.

Faustino (*his temper rising*) Very well then . . . very well! If you'd sooner fight it out . . .!

Diana Faustino . . . do you love me . . . or don't you?

Faustino Diana . . . you are . . . or were . . . or are my wife . . . .

Diana Never mind that. Say I've no more claims upon you than Marcela has . . .

Marcela Oh . . . but I've lots . . . still!

Diana Less then . . . none at all. Do you love me?

Marcela He doesn't . . . he doesn't! He's afraid of you. He has been running away from you ever since you came back.

Faustino Nothing of the sort. I am not afraid of any woman. Least of all my . . . my legal wife.

Marcela You locked yourself in your room because you were afraid she'd come in and make shameless love to you.

Diana Yes . . . and who sat in the passage half the night to see that I didn't?

Marcela And how did you know I sat in the passage if you didn't come out and try?

Faustino I will not have this undignified squabbling.

Diana Did you lock yourself in because you were afraid of me?

Faustino Certainly not. I locked myself in . . . and put the door key in the safe and the safe key in a can of cold water . . . for fear I might suddenly find myself breaking out and making love to . . .

Diana Aha! Aha! I knew it!

Faustino . . . to . . . to either of you!

Marcela To either of us! Oh, that's not very nice.

Faustino Yes . . . to either of you . . . whichever happened to be awake. Or to both!

Diana Faustino . . . you forget yourself!

Faustino Now don't try propriety with me, Marcela . . . and don't turn whatever I say, Diana, into something it suits you to be shocked at. I love you. you're a damned attractive woman . . . what's more, you're my wife. I love you as much as ever I did. What else do you expect?

Marcela Let me die . . . let me die!

Diana How can you be so cruel as to say that in front of her?

Faustino But, Marcela . . . my darling . . . I have loved you from the first moment I saw you . . . Haven't ceased to love you. How could I?

Marcela Go away! I won't be fondled. I detest you. I loathe you. You're a horrid man.

Faustino Do you detest me . . . do you loathe me, Diana?

Diana No . . . I'm head over ears in love with you. But I'll knock you down if you come near me. And I know how. Regina taught me.

Faustino You little devil . . . you beautiful little devil . . . will you please to remember that I am your husband? Be careful now . . . you'll tear that pretty new dress.

By some slight trick he takes her unawares, and seizes her wrists.

Diana Don't you dare to kiss me! Marcela . . . run for help. No, no . . . don't leave me alone with him. Scream!

With one accord they scream.

Faustino (*the lord and master*)   Now . . . I won't have any of this nonsense from either of you!

They scream again; and, one after the other from various quarters of the flat, arrive to their assistance **Margarita**, **Lorenza**, **Don Francisco**, **Doña Dolores** *and finally* **Milano**. *They all gabble together* . . .

Margarita What's the matter? Have they been fighting? I knew it would come to that. I'll hold Marcela.

Diana Don't be a goose. Let me go, Faustino.

Lorenza What on earth has happened?

Marcela Oh . . . it's too dreadful.

Diana Papa . . . I appeal to you . . .

Don Francisco What is it . . . what's it all about?

Diana Am I to be insulted?

Don Francisco There . . . there . . . I'm sure she didn't mean it.

Marcela (*rushing to* **Doña Dolores**)   Mamma . . . protect me!

Doña Dolores My dear!

Lorenza Don't be afraid.

Doña Dolores She shan't touch you . . . the savage creature.

Diana No . . . no . . . by him!

Marcela No . . . it's not Diana . . . poor Diana! It's Faustino . . . he's going mad.

Lorenza Milano!

Faustino Am I? I almost hope I am!

Lorenza Get your walking-stick . . .

Margarita Nonsense . . . he can't hurt us.

Don Francisco   But what has he said . . . what has he done?

Marcela   He has insulted us.

Diana   He says he loves us both.

At this, in varying tones of outraged propriety, they exclaim one after the other.

Marcela   Both!

Lorenza   Both!

Don Francisco   Both!

Doña Dolores   Both!

Margarita   Both!

Milano   Both!

Marcela   And he's making the most shocking proposals to us.

Don Francisco   Good God!

Doña Dolores   Margarita . . . leave the room.

Margarita   Why?

Faustino (*distracted and indignant*)   I am not. I'm proposing nothing.

Diana   He offered me violence. You saw it.

Margarita   Yes, *I* saw it.

Diana   He can't deny it.

Marcela   Before me too!

Don Francisco   And you said that you loved them both?

Faustino   Yes, Father.

Doña Dolores   Faustino!

Faustino   Yes, Mamma?

Don Francisco   But, man alive, how tactless!

Doña Dolores   I have given birth to a monster.

Faustino   I said it . . . and I say it . . . for it's true. I was happy with Diana . . . she's all that a wife should be. Marcela's an angel. We've been married for a year . . .

Diana   No!

Marcela   No.

Faustino   Yes! And never one angry word. I give thanks to them both. And I love them both . . . as a good husband should.

They shout at him in chorus . . .

Everybody But you can't!

Faustino But I can . . . and I do.

Don Francisco You can't be married to them both.

Faustino I ought to be. I feel I am. If I can't be . . . then as a man of principle and a man of honour . . . I'll be married to neither.

A moment's comparative calm.

Don Francisco That is one way out.

Margarita Will that suit you, Diana, dear?

Doña Dolores (*to* **Marcela**) That may be the best way. You'll be our daughter still.

Diana (*in level tones*) I am legally his wife. Nothing alters that.

Doña Dolores Father Moreno thinks that under certain circumstances the church may . . .

Milano (*to* **Marcela**) I've just come from your mother, you know. She sent for a lawyer at once. And, all else apart, he says there's the question of damages . . . very Serious damages . . .

Faustino Oh, the law will make us all miserable . . . that's its business. I'm a lawyer . . . I know that. How are we going to behave to each other? That's the question.

Diana (*quietly and collectedly*) I may have forfeited your love, Faustino . . .

Faustino You haven't!

Diana . . . but I shall always be ready to do my duty by you.

Marcela (*as collectedly and quietly*) I have been your wife in the sight of God, Faustino . . . and I shall never cease to love you.

Faustino (*distraction rending him again*) There you are . . . there you are! Then there's no way out . . . except the one way which . . .

Lorenza Faustino!

Doña Dolores Wretched boy! Margarita.

Margarita I'm not shocked, Mamma!

Don Francisco But come, come, you know . . . we ought to be able to discuss this . . . calmly . . . as reasonable beings . . .

Lorenza No, for heaven's sake, Papa . . .

Doña Dolores Francisco, this is not a subject for argument . . . .

Diana I cannot discuss the matter now . . .

Milano I was particularly to tell you not to commit yourself . . .

Marcela Oh, it's too dreadfully painful!

Faustino No use, Father . . . I've tried that. It either shocks them or sends them to sleep.

Juliana *appears.*

Juliana The cab's at the door . . . and a nice time I've had finding one.

Doña Dolores What cab?

Marcela My cab.

Diana My cab!

Faustino Ah . . . that's an idea!

He goes to the table where the jewels are and begins to fill his pockets.

Margarita Faustino . . . what are you?

Don Francisco Let those be . . . just when I've been sorting them!

Faustino A husband has still some rights left in this country . . . to his wife's property, at any rate.

Milano But the damages may have to come out of . . .

Lorenza Are you going away?

Faustino Yes.

Don Francisco Where to?

Faustino If I knew I wouldn't tell you.

Don Francisco But you can't . . . you can't bolt!

Faustino We'll see!

Doña Dolores Oh, how shameful!

Don Francisco Be a man, sir, be a man. Face your responsibilities.

Faustino I like that! I was facing them! I have faced them! And you tell me I am a monster! You can settle it between you. I've done!

He vanishes.

Don Francisco Good heavens!

Doña Dolores He is mad!

Lorenza Somebody ought to follow him.

Margarita I don't see why.

Marcela He'll come back.

Milano I doubt it.

Diana (*with practical good sense*) Perhaps . . . on the whole . . . I had better keep him in sight. Milano, come and find me another cab.

Diana *vanishes too.* **Milano** *is following her.*

Doña Dolores   Well . . . I don't approve of her. But, after all, it is her duty. Now come upstairs with me, little Marcela. Father Moreno has some very comforting things to say to you . . .

By this time the curtain has fallen. Then, in front of it, appears **Faustino** *in hat and overcoat and carrying a travelling-bag.*

Faustino   But wherever I go they'll track me! What with aeroplanes and wireless there isn't a spot left on this globe where a man can be safe. I suppose the law won't fetch me back . . . but my confounded conscience will. There was my mistake. Treat women badly . . . as badly as the law will let you. That's not very badly . . . the law's on their side nowadays. But don't be conscientious . . . don't be honourable. That's fatal. They've no conscience . . . they've no honour where you're concerned. You're just their property. They'll love you . . . they'll look after you . . . as they do their children and their dogs. But treat you like a fellow-creature . . . oh dear, no!

A faint voice is heard calling 'Faustino!'

I knew it! Which of them is it? Which do I want it to be? Marcela? Diana? Ah . . . there we go again! What's the use? There is no way out.

The voice is heard nearer.

I wonder whether . . .! Well, that's an idea too! Perhaps, then, I couldn't get back. I'll try it.

He steps over the footlights and seats himself in stage box. **Diana** *appears before the curtain.*

Diana   Faustino! Where . . .? Oh, there you are!

Faustino *nods.*

Diana   How did you get there?

Faustino *makes a more or less expressive gesture.*

Diana   Can't you speak?

Faustino   Sitting here? No, by rights I shouldn't. But perhaps . . . for once . . .

Diana   I don't call this fair. Come back. Come back immediately.

Faustino   I'd really rather not.

Diana   But how's the play to finish?

Faustino   It is finished.

Diana   Not properly.

Faustino   Well . . . it's only a farce.

Diana   I shall come over to you.

Faustino I'm not sure you can. I'm not sure you're life-like enough.

Diana Nonsense. I'm every bit as life-like as you were.

Faustino I shouldn't risk it. I'm feeling very evanescent myself.

The footlights go out.

Good lord . . . they've turned the lights out!

Diana Oh . . . what a horrid feeling!

Faustino Get back . . . quick! You're beginning to fade.

Diana But, Faustino . . . dear . . . dear Faustino . . . what's to happen to you when they open the doors and . . .? They have opened them . . . they're calling cabs. What a draught!

Faustino Oh, I shall just melt into the crowd, you know . . . with all the other nonentities. Don't worry. We'll meet again tomorrow. At least I hope so. I'll go now . . . to avoid the crush.

Diana Dear . . . dear Faustino!

He leaves the box. She disappears behind the curtain.

3 The Granville-Barkers

Postscript

HELEN AND HARLEY: TRANSLATING TOGETHER

The translations and their success

Helen and Harley Granville-Barker collaborated on fourteen published translations of Spanish plays.[1] It is also likely that they collaborated on another three translations of plays from the French, for which Helen does not receive credit in the published texts. Seventeen play translations is a large body of published work, but these translations weren't made only for publication; they found their way, or in some instances were commissioned for, major theatre productions in London's West End and New York's Broadway. A number were also broadcast on radio and filmed for television.

Many of Martínez Sierra's plays centre on a female character or characters and richly portray a world though a woman's or women's eyes. The Martínez Sierra plays the Barkers translated attracted such leading actresses of the English and American stage as Eva Le Gallienne, Gertrude Lawrence, Peggy Ashcroft, Jane Cowl, Joyce Carey and Ethel Barrymore.

Harley Granville Barker

When Harley Granville Barker married Helen, he was a renowned actor, an innovative and challenging playwright, and the leading director in the English-speaking theatre. Plays from other languages, especially those by Ibsen, had been central to the campaign for a new theatre of which he had been a key figure, and he had performed in and directed several, from Maeterlinck and Brieux to Euripides, Hauptmann and Heijermans. Barker had collaborated on translating Schnitzler with his friend Charles Wheeler, and had wrestled with the issues thrown up by translating in debate with William Archer and Gilbert Murray, champions respectively of Ibsen and Euripides, whose versions Barker had directed.

Returning to the subject at around the same time as the introduction to the Martínez Sierra plays, Barker in his essay 'On Translating Plays' argues that 'the written text is not a play's final and complete manifestation. This it will owe to its actors and their interpreting ... If we nowadays forget to think of its text as something in the nature of an orchestral score, it is only because the notation is so familiar ... The reader,' he says, 'has to imagine both sight and sound – the action of the scene as well as the spoken word.'[2]

For Barker, this insight also explained the deep connection between theatre and nationality, which underpinned his interest in plays from other cultures. 'Drama in presentation is the most national of the arts,' he wrote. 'Not only are the actors speaking a vernacular, they are re-inforcing it by gesture, behaviour and personality in general, by an allied language even more native to them and to their audience – as any translator will find when his [sic] work comes to be staged and the mere words take their proportionate place in the body of the living play.'[3]

In their collaboration, it was Helen who brought a nuanced understanding of the original language (Spanish or French) and Harley who brought a nuanced understanding of the theatre.

Helen and her family of authors

Helen Granville-Barker was the niece of the railroad baron Collis Huntington, one of the wealthiest men in America during the late nineteenth century. Helen's father, initially a minister, became Collis's right-hand-man or 'confidence man' and ran the railroad business out of a New York office. Helen's mother was a noted poet and 'hymn writer' who was once singled out for praise by President Abraham Lincoln. Helen would marry her uncle's adopted (and biological) son, Archer, who himself would become a well-known scholar of Spanish literature and art, and the founder and benefactor of the still existent Hispanic Society of America in New York City, where he formed one of the world's great collections of Hispanic art and literature. Archer wrote scholarly books as well as poetry. Helen's daughter, Mildred, by her first marriage to a Mr Criss, was the author of a series of successful children's books, including *Isabella, Young Queen of Spain, Pocahontas, Young American* and *Mary Stuart, Young Queen of the Scots.* Throughout her twenty-three-year marriage to Archer, Helen travelled extensively throughout Europe, often accompanied by her mother-in-law, Belle, an avid art collector mentored by the art historian Bernard Berenson. Fluent in Spanish, German and French, Helen travelled with Archer and Belle in the most rarefied circles of great wealth. She was an ardent visitor to art museums, historic sites – and to the theatre.

Helen was an author herself. Eventually she would publish ten novels, a book of short stories, six books of poetry, an anthology and two books of poetry translations from the Spanish, often to critical, though never commercial, acclaim.

About her late novels *Living Mirrors* (1928), *Moon in Scorpio* (1932), *Come Julia* (1931) and *Traitor Angel* (1935):

> There is much in Mrs Granville-Barker's method which recalls the early Henry James . . .
>
> (*The Observer,* 8 May 1928)

> Her unerring sense of character and scene, her steady sympathy and her quiet distinction of manner make *Moon in Scorpio* as notable a book as [her] *Come, Julia.*
>
> (*The Spectator*, 4 November 1932)

> For me, *Come Julia* is a perfect tale, told perfectly, but of so intimate and personal appeal . . . for all her acclimatized response to the heart of English country life, still proclaims this author's share of Henry James' birthright, that extra sharpness of perception that the true-born American brings with him to his love and understanding of foreign land.
>
> (*The Time and Tide*, 1931)

Traitor Angel is 'extremely well written, subtle and interesting . . . remarkable subtlety and strength.

The Times, London (25 October 1935)

Helen and Harley: A relationship in words

In 1914, Harley, at the invitation of the Stage Society of America, was brought to New York to create a series of stage productions. It was at this time, when both Harley and Helen were married to others, that they supposedly first met. Three and a half years later, after difficult divorces, they married in 1918.

Although there is no mention in any of their existing letters of having met earlier, Harley's first biographer suggests they may have, and there is a great deal of circumstantial evidence to back this up.[4] It suggests that they met many years before, perhaps as early as 1906, when Helen, thirty-seven, and the twenty-seven-year-old Harley found themselves staying in Tyrol, Austria, or perhaps nearby in northern Italy. He was there writing his play *Waste* and Helen was on her annual excursion to Europe. At this time, one can speculate that they developed a keen intellectual friendship, though not an affair – she was ten years older and, given her life and travels, much more experienced than the young actor/playwright.

Helen seems to have written about this time in an unfinished novel, later published anonymously after her death. Eventually this book would be credited to her friend, Gladys Huntington, the wife of a distant relative of Helen's, and the beneficiary in Helen's will of all of Helen's papers and manuscripts. This book would become the international bestseller *Madame Solario*. Today, Helen is still not recognized as its author.

Evidence of Harley and Helen having met earlier than 1914, and of the beginnings of their at first thwarted love affair, can be found within their own writings of this period. Harley first visited America in April 1908 at the invitation of a group of wealthy Americans who were hoping to build a new theatre and were looking for its director. Helen's husband, Archer, was one of these wealthy men. Perhaps this invitation to Harley had something to do with Helen's initiative; in any event, Harley arrived in New York and announced a three-week visit, only to suddenly cut that short and sail back to England two weeks earlier than planned. Something seems to have happened on this trip, which contributed to this sudden departure.

Harley returned home and that summer fell desperately ill. Over the next months, Helen would write her first novel, *The Sovereign Good*, which was published in November 1908. Immediately upon its publication (in America and England) Harley, now recovered, would write and publish his first short story, 'Georgiana', in *The English Review*. These two works have amazingly similar stories, with a few interesting differences.

The Sovereign Good tells the story of a wealthy woman who meets a much younger wannabe playwright from England; they immediately form an intellectual friendship; she encourages him with the play he is writing and introduces him to influential people in the theatre in New York. The play is produced and becomes a critical, though not commercial, success. Coming home from the opening night of the play, the young man suddenly kisses the woman, thus changing the entire nature of their relationship. She panics, fearing the age difference between them is too great, and escapes to Europe. Eventually, they meet again. By now she has decided that they do have a romantic future together, but it is too late, as the young man has found a young woman to marry. We learn that the future life of this young man is unfortunate, and that his young wife turns out to be very boring.

'The Sovereign Good' is another name for love, and the woman character is called Fidelia, or the faithful one.

'Georgiana', Harley's story, concerns a married young man, and a somewhat older woman. They develop a platonic and intellectual friendship, until one night *she kisses him*, thus – again – changing the entire nature of their relationship. In Harley's story they then become lovers, and instead of their age differences being the problem, it is the young man's marriage, especially given that his wife has recently lost their child. (Harley's wife at this time, the actor and manager Lillah McCarthy, lost their child a year before.) The young man decides he can't leave his wife, and the affair sputters out. The older woman marries someone else. We learn that the future life of this older woman is also unfortunate, and that her new husband turns out to be very boring.

This back and forth, seemingly private/public conversation, in their published or produced works continued with Harley's next play, *The Madras House*, and Helen's next novel, *An Apprentice to Truth*.

Begun on his voyage back from Harley's first visit to America in 1908, and so just after the 'event' which caused his sudden departure, *The Madras House* appears to be full of private references to his relationship with Helen. These range from the serious to the questioning.

In Act Four, the Harley and Helen-like couple, Philip and Jessica, discuss how to live on a very reduced income:

Philip We must learn to live on a thousand a year . . .

Harley and Helen would have assumed that they too would find themselves impoverished should they leave their partners; Helen did not at this time have money of her own.

Philip . . . put Mildred to a sensible school.

Mildred is the name of Helen's daughter, and she was at this time in an expensive Swiss boarding school. This part of the play would be cut from the revised 1925 version.

In Act Three, there is a long digression about a new hat style from France – which is called *La Belle Helene*. This seems to be a teasing reference of Harley's to Helen's hats. In every surviving photo of Helen from this time, she is wearing a gigantic hat. Probably this was the style of the time, but also an easy source for kidding.

In Helen's novel *An Apprentice to Truth*, a young woman lives in the clutches of her wealthy, social climbing female cousin, who destroys her chance of marrying an exciting young man. Harley could easily have read this as Helen's painful description of life under the weight of her powerful and oppressive, social-climbing, mother-in-law, Belle.

Helen seems to chronicle throughout her writing life her and Harley's lives.

And the two seem to also inspire each other.

During their divorces, Helen wrote her novel *Eastern Red*, in which a woman, in a loveless marriage to a wealthy philanderer, meets a young man in Italy, who has been living in England. He tries to kiss her; he wants her to get a divorce; she panics, afraid of scandal, and ends the relationship and stays with her husband.

While at this same time, Harley began his play *The Secret Life*, in which a Harley/Helen-like couple meet years after having ended their affair. Now it is too late for them to come together, that time having passed them by. In a way, this play can be seen as almost a continuation of Helen's novel, now years later. In Helen's novel there is even this line:

> For so many weeks now her thoughts had been going around and around the same old circle, her secret life had been so entirely disunited from the life which people knew . . .

There seems to be evidence that from the likely beginning of their relationship, Helen and Harley shared a very personal partnership with, and in, their books and writing. Given the initial great distance between them (Helen in New York, Harley in London) they found a way to speak to each other, not through letters (which would have been difficult, given their marriages), but through their own published writings.

Eventually this bond would be codified with an insignia – two 'H's bound together within another 'H', which would appear, beginning in 1922, on the frontispiece of every book they would they would publish, either separately, or together.

Helen and Harley working together

In Paris, in February 1918, while waiting out her divorce, Helen, as was her wont, went to the theatre. Playing this night was Sacha Guitry's *Deburau* at the Théâtre du Vaudeville. She wrote to Harley, who was in London, about the show: 'the whole play has real quality – what you/and I like.'[5] She offered to get him a copy of this play. By April she was writing to him:

> Darling – would you like to have me do the dog's work on translating 'Deburau' for you? I think I could. Then you could go over it afterward yourself – and with Sacha Guitry. I thought it might save some time for you.

Deburau opened at Broadway's Belasco Theatre on 27 December 1920, directed by David Belasco; a year later it was at the Ambassadors Theatre in London. The translation was published in 1921 by G. P. Putnam's Sons, the publisher of most of Helen's (and her mother's) books. There is a note by 'HGB' about the translation. HGB could fit Harley or Helen, so which one?

So, their collaboration, their writing together, began even before their marriage, though with Helen uncredited in this first effort. Their next work together, however, would more than correct this.

Helen's first published work, in 1900, was a translation from the Spanish, *Folk Songs from the Spanish*, which came about after her many trips to Spain with her husband, Archer. Helen developed deep and numerous ties to Spain (she was once honoured with an award by Spain's queen), and, given her avid theatre-going, it is likely she immersed herself in her passion, during what had become and is now considered Spanish theatre's 'Silver Age'.[6]

The Romantic Young Lady, the first play translation credited to both Helen and Harley, opened in its original form at the Teatro Eslava in Madrid in 1918 a few months after her marriage to Harley and it was published that year. She must have read the play, and she most certainly would have known the plays of G. Martínez Sierra, perhaps the foremost playwright (along with Jacinto Benavente) and director in Spain at the time, and the artistic director of Teatro Eslava, its most important theatre. She may have seen other Martínez Sierra plays: *The Two Shepherds* in Madrid in 1913, *Wife to a Famous Man* in Madrid in 1914, or *The Kingdom of God* in Barcelona in 1915. Eventually, she and Harley would translate all of these plays, as well as *The Romantic Young Lady*, *Lily Among Thorns*, *Fortunato* and *Take Two from One*. The latter play especially would influence Helen's writing, and her short story collection (1927) *Wives and Celebrities*.

The Romantic Young Lady was completed during 1919 within a year of marriage, and on 27 September 1920, it opened in London's West End at the Royalty Theatre, in a production, according to the programme, 'overseen by *both* Helen and Harley Granville Barker. Here was the most noted director of the English stage sharing directing credit with his novice wife. It is almost as if Harley needed to make up for the slight with *Deburau*.

Or perhaps it was just an acknowledgement of her insights and knowledge of theatre, and of the Spanish theatre in particular, especially as the Spanish theatre was virtually unknown in the British theatre at this time. In letters written around the time of their divorces and marriage, Helen shared her theatre opinions with Harley, and he solicited them from her, asking her about his work and his writings.[7] She responded honestly and sometimes critically, though at times she found this exchange hard to imagine, aware of Harley's stature as director/playwright/producer:

> Beloved – I have to stop or laugh at myself for writing about theatres to H. Granville Barker. Tomorrow I shall pass a few words on military strategy to General Haigh.[8]

Women wronged

At this point, it is interesting to ask when the Granville-Barkers first came across the work attributed to Gregorio Martínez Sierra. The Martínez Sierra libretto for the ballet composed by Manuel de Falla, *The Three-Cornered Hat,* premiered in London at the Alhambra Theatre on 22 July 1919, produced by Diaghilev, by which time Helen and Harley were married and living in England – and Harley would certainly have known of Gregorio's Teatro Eslava in Madrid, it often being compared in its ambitions to his for the English theatre. One can speculate that it was now that the Barkers acquired the translation rights to Martínez Sierra's *The Romantic Young Lady*. According to María's memoir, she met the Barkers at the London opening of this play in 1920, attending a rehearsal and having a dinner with the translators.[9] Gregorio was not present, though he and the Barkers did correspond from at least 1919, and in the late 1920s to early 1930s letters between María and Harley mention separate correspondence between Harley and Gregorio.[10] In 1923, Helen writes to Maria, thanking her for help in translating *The Kingdom of God*, specifically the passages relating to the bullfighter Juan de Dios.

The first four plays of Martínez Sierra's that Helen and Harley translated were initially published in a collection in 1922; they constituted the second of a two-volume set of Martínez Sierra's plays, the first volume containing translations by John Garrett Underhill. This volume includes an appreciation of the plays by 'H Granville-Barker'. Whenever this introduction is referenced by scholars or critics, it is always attributed to Harley. This attribution, of course, as with the *Deburau* introduction, also fits Helen; and Helen was the more knowledgeable partner about Spanish and Spanish theatre.

This volume also carries a foreword by Underhill that mentions María at the end as a valued collaborator. By 1931, Underhill's foreword has changed; María is no longer at the end but up front: 'Gregorio Martinez Sierra is not only a name but a pen-name, and the works which have appeared under it are the result of a collaboration that began even before marriage and has continued through all their books and plays ever since.'[11] The Barkers must have been aware of this shift, but there is no rewrite of their appreciation of Martínez Sierra when republished in 1929.

A letter in November 1927 from Harley to María, however, implies that the matter of joint credit had been raised. He writes that he has seen in an American paper 'both your names were attached to a play' but it 'will not be possible to make the alteration here upon any publication' as the books are already in print. 'I gather it has for you more of a legal importance than any other,' he adds, and says in 'future editions I could doubtless arrange it'.[12] When the Barkers translated *Triángulo* as *Take Two from One*, the play shared a joint credit of Gregorio and María. During Gregorio's lifetime, only two of the plays were accredited as a *collaboration* with his wife – the first in the programme of the Broadway production of *The Cradle Song*, and the second with *Take Two from One*, the last play (in 1931) translated by Helen and Harley. In both the programme and the published text of this play, 'Gregorio and María Martínez Sierra' are listed as the authors.

Although it has recently been widely accepted in Spain that 'Gregorio's plays' were written by María – and not as collaborations – it also seems she did not insist on this, so it is likely that Helen and Harley Granville-Barker never learned that she was the sole author of the plays they translated.

Given the extensive production history of these plays in Europe, England, Ireland, South America and the United States, María would have then been the most produced and successful female playwright, in any language, of the first half of the twentieth century. At the time this was of course unknown, her authorship being uncredited, or in a few instances given as co-writer. Fortunately, María's day of recognition has come in Spain; over just the past few years she has been rightly feted for her achievements and successes as a playwright; books have been written about her, she appears as characters in plays, and conferences celebrating her work have been organized and held. Helen's fate is very different.

From almost the moment she and Harley married in 1918, Helen was slandered for 'stealing' Harley away from the English theatre, and was even called a witch by Shaw. Harley Granville Barker gained the infamous moniker of 'Lost Leader', and Helen has never shaken off this blame.

> Helen Huntington had formed an attachment to him . . . She was a poetess in a small way . . . the novels were no more than women's magazine affairs. . . . No doubt she disappointed Barker because of her intellectual abilities . . .[13]
> (C. B. Purdom, Harley's first biographer)

> She disliked the theatre, distrusted actors, and detested Shaw.[14]
>
> (Dennis Kennedy)

> He was completely dominated by her ... she made him do translations of Spanish plays, or put his name to her translations; she cut him off from all commerce with the theatre, she tried to turn him into a country gentleman ... [15]
>
> (Hesketh Pearson)

> Her poems are almost wholly imitative – full of tired locutions and jaded images ... her novels are a little better ... [16]
>
> (Eric Salmon)

> Shaw thought that Barker had buried himself alive on account of his new wife, who had little time for the theatre and none for Shaw.[17]
>
> (Richard Eyre)

In 1950, three and a half years after Harley's death, Helen died in Paris. She is buried, alongside her husband, in the Cimetière du Père Lachaise. Constant Huntington, a long-time London resident and publisher, and Helen's distant relative, helped sort out Helen's estate. (As mentioned above, in her will Helen gave money and 'all of her personal papers, letters, MSS, etc.' to Constant's wife, Gladys.) From Constant's own narrative, 'notes on domicile' (unpublished), written for the tax authorities, we get a clear picture of how she was seen: Helen 'found herself the object of bitter criticism in England dramatic and literary circles ... She was a very proud and sensitive nature, and she found her position in London untenable.' At 'a dinner party in my London house ... Helen sat next to Sir John Squire. He taxed her with ruining Harley's career and she burst into tears.'[18]

Constant's defence of his distant cousin only went so far. Tasked with organizing her funeral, he would have been responsible for the words now engraved on her tombstone:

Helen Huntington Gates

It's the wrong name. This was never Helen's name. 'Helen Manchester Gates' was her maiden name. When she first married a Mr Criss, she became 'Helen Gates Criss'. When she married Archer Huntington, she became 'Helen Gates Huntington'. When she married Harley she was 'Helen Gates Granville-Barker'.

She lies buried and so remembered under a name she never had.

Richard Nelson with Colin Chambers

Notes

1. The Barkers introduced Martínez Sierra to English-speaking audiences (the 1920 production of *The Romantic Young Lady* was the first Martínez Sierra staged in English), as well the Spanish playwrights the Quintero Brothers. Martínez Sierra's *The Cradle Song*, in John Garrett Underhill's translation, was first staged in the UK in 1924 (Oxford Playhouse) and in London in 1926.
2. 'On Translating Plays', in *Granville Barker on Theatre: Selected Essays*, ed. Colin Chambers and Richard Nelson (London: Bloomsbury, 2017), 75.

3   Harley Granville-Barker, *On Dramatic Method* (London: Sidgwick & Jackson 1931), 187.
4   C. B. Purdom, *Harley Granville Barker* (London: Rockliff Publishing, 1955), 170.
5   Letters held in the British Library, Add MS 71902. See Simon Shepherd, *The Unknown Granville Barker: Letters to Helen and Other Texts, 1915–1918* (London: Society of Theatre Research, 2021), which also refers to Helen's helping Harley with his staging ideas for a production of Maeterlinck's *The Betrothal* (1921).
6   Besides her collaborations with her husband, Helen wrote, with sole credit, the essay 'The Art of the Quintero Brothers: Dramatists of the Gaiety of Common Life', *T.P.'s Weekly* (4 February 1928).
7   See British Library, 71897-71920.
8   British Library, 71908.
9   *María Martínez Sierra, Gregori y yo*, ed. Alda Blanco (Valencia: Pre-Textos, 2000), 148–56.
10 Correspondence to María Martínez Sierra from both Harley and Helen Granville-Barker is held in the Archivo María Lejárraga.
11 John Garrett Underhill in G. Martinez Sierra, *The Cradle Song and Other Plays* (New York: E. P. Dutton & Co., 1931), vii.
12 Letter in Archivo María Lejárraga.
13 Purdom, *Harley Granville Barker*, 172.
14 Dennis Kennedy, *Granville Barker and the Dream of Theatre* (Cambridge: Cambridge University Press, 1985), 198.
15 Hesketh Pearson, *George Bernard Shaw: His Life and Personality* (New York: Atheneum, 1963), 461.
16 Eric Salmon, *Granville Barker: A Secret Life* (Rutherford, NJ: Fairleigh Dickinson University Press, 1983), 249–50.
17 Richard Eyre, programme for the National Theatre production of *Waste* (2015).
18 Constant Huntington's papers, which were generously made available when held privately, are now kept in the Amherst College Archives and Special Collections.

Translations of Helen and Harley Granville-Barker[1]

The Romantic Young Lady by María Martínez Sierra (credited to Gregorio)
Premieres: London: 16 Sept. 1920, Royalty Theatre; New York: 4 May 1926, Neighborhood Playhouse; Radio: BBC, 8 June 1928; TV: BBC, 12 Sept. 1938. Published: *Plays of G. Martinez Sierra*, Volume Two, New York: E. P. Dutton & Co., 1923.

Deburau by Sacha Guitry [Helen Granville-Barker uncredited]
Premieres: New York: 27 Dec. 1920, Belasco Theatre; London: 2 Nov. 1921, Ambassadors Theatre; Radio: BBC, 20 Jan. 1952. Published: New York & London: G. P. Putnam's Sons, 1921.

Wife to a Famous Man by María Martínez Sierra (credited to Gregorio)
Premieres: London: 25 May 1924, Play Actors Company; New York: 1925–6 season, Vagabond Players; Radio: BBC, 19 Oct. 1928. Published: *Plays of G. Martinez Sierra*, Volume Two, New York: E. P. Dutton & Co., 1923.

The Kingdom of God by María Martínez Sierra (credited to Gregorio)
Premieres: Dublin: 3 Nov. 1924, Abbey Theatre; London: 26 Oct. 1927, Strand; New York: 20 Dec. 1928, Barrymore Theatre; TV: 13 Apr. 1947. Published: *Plays of G. Martinez Sierra*, Volume Two, New York: E. P. Dutton & Co., 1923.

Doctor Knock by Jules Romains [Helen Granville-Barker uncredited]
Premieres: London: 27 Apr. 1926, Royalty Theatre; New York: 27 Feb. 1928, American Laboratory Theatre; Radio: BBC, 6 Dec. 1932; TV: BBC, 17 Jan. 1938. Published: London: Ernest Benn, 1925.

The Lady from Alfaqueque by Serafín and Joaquín Álvarez Quintero
Premieres: London: 22 Oct. 1928, Court Theatre; New York: 14 Jan. 1929, Civic Repertory Theatre; Radio: BBC, 26 July 1953. Published: *Four Plays* (with introduction by translators) and on its own, London: Sidgwick & Jackson, 1927.

Fortunato by Serafín and Joaquín Álvarez Quintero
Premieres: London: 22 Oct. 1928, Court Theatre; New York: 14 Jan. 1929, Civic Repertory Theatre; Radio: BBC, 13 Feb. 1944; TV: BBC, 7 Apr. 1947. Published: as above.

The Women Have Their Way by Serafín and Joaquín Álvarez Quintero
Premieres: Dublin, 12 Nov. 1928, Abbey Theatre; New York: 27 Jan. 1930, Civic Repertory Theatre; London: 1 June 1933, Everyman; Radio: BBC, 8 June 1952. Published: as above.

A Hundred Years Old by Serafín and Joaquín Álvarez Quintero
Premieres: London: 21 Nov. 1928, Lyric Hammersmith; New York: 1 Oct. 1929, Lyceum; Radio: BBC, 25 May 1932; TV: BBC, 19 June 1938. Published: as above.

Take Two from One by María Martínez Sierra (credited to Gregorio)
Premiere: London, 16 Sept. 1931, Haymarket. Published: London: Sidgwick & Jackson, 1931.

Doña Clarines by Serafín and Joaquín Álvarez Quintero
Premieres: UK: 21 Sept. 1932, Liverpool Playhouse; Radio: BBC, 2 May 1943; TV: BBC, 26 Nov. 1957. Published: London: Sidgwick & Jackson, 1932.

Peace and Quiet by Serafín and Joaquín Álvarez Quintero
Premiere: New York: 9 Apr. 1933, Neighborhood Playhouse; TV: BBC, 19 Mar. 1957. Published: London: Sidgwick & Jackson, 1932.

The Two Shepherds by María Martínez Sierra (credited to Gregorio)
Premiere: London: 11 Feb. 1935, Old Vic. Published: *Plays of G. Martinez Sierra*, Volume Two, New York: E. P. Dutton & Co., 1923.

Six Gentlemen in a Row by Jules Romains [Helen Granville-Barker uncredited]
Premiere: TV: BBC, 25 Jan. 1939. Published: London: Sidgwick & Jackson, 1927.

Don Abel Wrote a Tragedy by Serafín and Joaquín Álvarez Quintero
Premieres: London: 13 Jan. 1944, Arts Theatre; Radio: BBC, 7 Apr. 1945. Published: London: Sidgwick & Jackson, 1932.

Love Passes By by Serafín and Joaquín Álvarez Quintero
Premiere: London: 23 Feb. (?) 1950, Gateway Theatre Company; Radio: BBC, 6 Sept. 1940. Published: London: Sidgwick & Jackson, 1932.

They also translated María Martínez Sierra's *Lily Among Thorns*, which was published in the US in 1930 but has no record of production.

Note

1 On their own, Harley co-translated Arthur Schnitzler's *Anatol: A Sequence of Dialogues* (1911) and *Das Märchen* (1912), and Helen translated *Folk Songs from the Spanish* (1900) and *Some Greguerias* by Ramon Gomex de la Serna (1944).

www.ingramcontent.com/pod-product-compliance
Lightning Source LLC
Chambersburg PA
CBHW070311230426
43663CB00011B/2080